J. B. (John Beauchamp) Jones

Life and Adventures of a Country Merchant

J. B. (John Beauchamp) Jones

Life and Adventures of a Country Merchant

ISBN/EAN: 9783337054687

Printed in Europe, USA, Canada, Australia, Japan

Cover: Foto ©ninafisch / pixelio.de

More available books at **www.hansebooks.com**

LIFE AND ADVENTURES

OF

A COUNTRY MERCHANT.

A Narrative

OF HIS EXPLOITS AT HOME, DURING HIS TRAVELS, AND
IN THE CITIES.

DESIGNED TO AMUSE AND INSTRUCT.

By J. B. JONES,

AUTHOR OF "WILD WESTERN SCENES," "THE WAR PATH," ETC.

PHILADELPHIA:
J. B. LIPPINCOTT & CO.
1875.

Entered according to Act of Congress, in the year 1854, by

J. B. JONES,

in the Clerk's Office of the District Court of the United States for the Eastern District of Pennsylvania.

TO

JOHN GRIGG, Esq.,

SO GENERALLY KNOWN — SO HIGHLY ESTEEMED
BY THE
SOUTHERN AND WESTERN MERCHANTS OF THE UNITED STATES,

𝔗𝔥𝔦𝔰 𝔙𝔬𝔩𝔲𝔪𝔢

IS RESPECTFULLY INSCRIBED, BY HIS FRIEND,

THE AUTHOR.

PREFACE

TO THE SECOND EDITION

THE similarity of title might lead some of the author's friends to suppose that this work is merely a revised edition of the "WESTERN MERCHANT." But such an impression will be removed upon an inspection of its contents. Yet it must be owned that it was the success of that work, and of the "WILD WESTERN SCENES,"* which emboldened the author to undertake the preparation of a new volume,—one of greater magnitude, based upon broader foundations, and embodying characters and occurrences of a later date. And this he submits as a substitute for the "Western Merchant," believing it will afford a greater amount of entertainment, and quite as many useful lessons of experience.

THE AUTHOR.

BURLINGTON, NEW JERSEY,
1854.

---

* Five editions of the "Wild Western Scenes" were sold last year. The large edition of the "Western Merchant" is entirely exhausted.

THE PUBLISHERS.

LIFE AND ADVENTURES

OF A

COUNTRY MERCHANT.

CHAPTER I.

On the banks of the "Mad Missouri"—Nap and Jack watching for a boat—A brief retrospection—New goods—Ambitious longings.

It was upon the right bank of that gigantic river, the "Mad Missouri," and surrounded on every hand by wild scenery. Two young men stood near the edge of the water gazing far down the stream, in momentary expectation of seeing a steamboat come in view.

"Jack, I think I hear something!" said the shortest, but not the least of the young men.

"So do I, Nap," replied the other, "but it is not the boat. She is not yet in sight; and as we can see several miles down the river, it is not probable we shall hear her before we see her."

"But, Jack, don't you hear a puffing sound? I think it must be the boat. They say, on a calm, clear morning like this, the boats may be heard before they come in sight."

"I hear the puffing, Nap; but I'm very certain it comes from Mr. Black's great Newfoundland dog, lying yonder under the wild gooseberry-bush."

"I believe it does!" responded Nap, looking and listening. "But the boat is coming, I'm sure; for now I hear the wheels."

"The wheels of Mr. Black's wagon, Nap; and yonder it is. Don't you see the oxen winding down the hill? I engaged it to haul up the goods; but it comes too soon."

Nap turned, and perceived the wagon lazily descending the road from the storehouse on the summit of the hill.

Nap Wax and Jack Handy were nearly of the same age, and both were young adventurers from Kentucky. Jack was a slender youth of fair complexion, whose teeming imagination had preceded him to Missouri, and which was apt to picture scenes in a seemingly fresher and brighter world than the one he had hitherto inhabited; and hence he had determined to abandon the old one.

Generally without patrimony, and hence with no means of acquiring professions, and always too proud to learn any of the mechanic arts, it is surprising to contemplate the vast number of youthful adventurers from Kentucky, Tennessee, and Virginia, who annually go to the new States in quest of fortune. And it is no less astonishing to behold the large proportion of them that succeed in achieving their object.

Jack Handy had been preceded several years in his emigration to Missouri by his brother Joseph, who was his senior. Joseph had risen from an humble clerkship to become a partner in a branch concern; then he had bought out the interest of his partners, and found himself possessed of sufficient capital to commence business at a new point of his own selection. The place pitched upon was that where our young Kentuckians are introduced to the reader. A town had been laid off on the hill, by commissioners appointed for the purpose, and who bestowed upon it the inappropriate name of Tyre.

Jack Handy was now to be his brother's clerk, and was to receive a salary of one hundred and twenty dollars per annum besides his board, for which Mr. Black, whose house was within a hundred and fifty yards of the store, (and there were no other dwellings in the town,) was to be paid fifty dollars in merchandise.

and hove in view. And by the time there were upon the ground a sufficient number of wagons with their long ox-teams to convey the packages up the hill, the boat had landed, and Joseph Handy leaped ashore and grasped the extended hands of the young novices who were to be his only assistants in the store.

Then followed the boxes, bales, barrels, &c., which were piled up on the river-bank under the spreading forest trees where Daniel Boone had once killed the buffalo and chased the roving savage. Such a novel spectacle made the natives stare. It was the first assortment of goods direct from the eastern cities that had ever been landed in the new town, and they looked upon the elder Handy as another John Jacob Astor.

It had been rumored by a store-keeper located some twenty miles distant, and who had bought his own stock of wares in Boonville, that Handy's goods would be nothing more than remnants picked up in St. Louis. A single glance at the cases was sufficient to detect the calumny. They bore the names of jobbers of the highest standing in New York and Philadelphia; and the Rockhills, Chittendens, Copes, Woods, Bowen & McNamee; the Stuarts, Conrads, Drapers, Siter, Price & Co.; the Moultons, Sowerses, Wards, Lippincott, Grambo & Co.; the Schaffers, Carpenters, Robertses, Hendersons, &c. &c. &c., were deliberately spelled and distinctly pronounced by many an honest pioneer, who believed that henceforth he would be enabled to purchase his merchandise on reasonable terms, and without having to go out of the county for them.

And Nap and Jack, who had been upon the ground several days, stimulating the carpenters to have the house in readiness for the reception of the goods, had received many flattering attentions from the neighbours interested in the growth of the place and in the probability of an increase in the value of their property, situated in the vicinity of a well-established store. They had not failed to perceive and appreciate the importance attached to their persons, and they really began to feel as if they were the undisputed lions of those bushes where the town had been staked off. Being looked upon as oracles and benefactors, it was natural that they should take advantage of such an opportunity to exert their newborn influence in behalf of their employer. Hence they promised much, and boasted a great deal, as young merchants have been known to do occasionally. And if the expectations thus raised were not to be realized to the letter, they created at all events a very favourable impression at the beginning.

It must be remarked, however, in passing, that the distinguished attentions which Nap received had begun to have the usual deleterious effect upon his susceptible nature; and Jack became somewhat fearful that his companion might, in a moment of lofty aspiration, suddenly relinquish the idea of becoming a merchant. There were decided indications in his self-complacency, and in the expression of his conviction that the Missourians had chosen less eligible men than himself to represent them in Congress, to afford reasonable grounds for an apprehension that he might sacrifice his fortune and character and sink into a mere politician. But when at eve they were left to themselves, it was no difficult matter to chase away the absurd notion. Then Jack would fill his friend's head with romantic fancies, and make him believe that life in the wilderness, without disputation, and beyond the reach of the caprices of a more fastidious society, was the happiest condition in which one could be placed. He cited the contented lives of Boone and other pioneers, who had not only enjoyed supreme happiness amid those beautiful scenes of nature, fresh from the hand of the Creator, but had likewise been loudly heralded to the world by the trumpet of fame, and whose names were more likely to go down to posterity than those of ordinary members of Congress. In short, he procured for Nap a copy of the "Wild Western Scenes," which most effectually banished his ambitious longings.

CHAPTER II.

Opening and marking the goods—Curiosity of the crowd—Snakes about—Sleeping and snoring—Nap dreams—The footing of it.

JOSEPH HANDY'S first day as a merchant at Tyre was a busy one, both for himself and his inexperienced clerks. The opening and marking of goods, and arranging them in order on the shelves, occupied the whole of the day, retarded and obstructed as they were continually by the careless remarks and curious inquiries of the eager crowd around them. Every piece of goods taken from the boxes was subjected to the inspection of the bystanders; and those that were wrapped in papers, such as Irish linens, the contents of which could not be readily seen, were *pinched* by the ingenious youths from the country, to ascertain, if possible, the nature of the "plunder," as they called it, hidden within. Some *smelt* the parcels whose contents they could not ascertain either by gazing or pinching. And it might have been impolitic to repulse such an interference. All of them were very honest and well-meaning people; and it was the policy of the merchant to keep them in a good humour. Yet some were not destined to escape with impunity. Nap had wrenched off the top of a box from the drug-store of the Messrs. Harris & Co.; and the force of example being as usual irresistible with him, he regaled his nostrils frequently with the highly perfumed soaps, essences, &c. But happening to apply a parcel of *gum fœtid* to his nose, he started back and suffered it to fall upon the floor. The pack of juveniles, supposing its fall to have been accidental, and having hitherto enjoyed all the sweet odours of the parcels as they were lifted from the box, pounced upon it like hungry wolves, and were instantly set to howling by the disagreeable smell.

Toward night all the inquisitive people departed for their homes, many of them promising to bring their wives and daughters the next day, or in a few days, when the young gentlemen would be prepared to wait upon them. Nap, observing the condescension of his principal, and the tact he employed to create the impression that great bargains were to be undoubtedly had at his establishment, giving way to the enthusiasm he felt, launched out in a strain of superlative extravagance. He not only assured the gaping and staring portion of the crowd that Handy's goods were to be offered at lower prices than usual in that section of the country, but that they were absolutely superior in quality to any others ever imported.

After night, and deep in the night, their labours were continued. The practised merchant will need no special assurance to believe it was no slight undertaking for them to open, mark, and properly arrange, ready for business, some six thousand dollars' worth of goods in one day and evening. At length the work was completed, and they sat down on the log steps before the door to rest, and to arrange their plans for the next day. But they were completely exhausted, and mused long in silence. The loneliness of the scene made a deep impression on Jack. The moon was midway in the heavens, casting down a flood of light, which caused the smallest objects to be distinctly visible. The river, so turbid by day, resembled a sheet of liquid silver by night. The trees that fringed its margin, and those around the rude house, were perfectly motionless, not the slightest breath of air disturbing the repose of their half-grown leaves. The only sound they heard was the plaintive note of a solitary whippoorwill. The stillness which brooded over the scene threw but a momentary shade of melancholy over the face of Joseph, as he was less susceptible of poetical influences than his brother. His mind was more inclined to dive into the chances of the future than to dwell upon the past; and so Jack found all his romantic meditations suddenly put to flight by the following inquiry:

"Jack, what amount do you say we will sell to-morrow?"

"I suppose," said Jack, after some little bewilderment and hesitation, "about seventy-five dollars' worth."

"I say a thousand, at least!" said Nap, slapping his hands together violently.

"Nonsense, Nap," continued Joseph. "If we sell that amount in a month, at the prices marked, it will not be a bad business. But, Jack, how much of your seventy-five dollars will be in cash?"

"I think about half."

"And I say about a quarter," said Nap; "for they don't look as if they had much money."

"You must not judge people by their clothes in Missouri, Nap. You believe about half, Jack?" continued Joseph, smiling. "Now I will venture a prediction. I say we will sell about one hundred dollars' worth, and seventy-five dollars of it will be in ready money. The first day's sales in a new establishment exhibit a larger proportion of cash than subsequent ones."

Though almost exhausted with fatigue, Jack listened attentively to the many other words of wisdom and experience which his brother uttered for his edification. But Nap was soon quite oblivious of every thing that had been said after he ceased to participate in the conversation. His head was thrown back, his mouth wide open, his eyes closed, and, as usual when asleep, he began to snore most astoundingly. Indeed, at the conclusion of Joseph's lecture, he gave vent to so startling a snort as to awaken himself.

"What's this? What's the matter?" cried he, springing up.

"Oh, nothing, Nap," said Jack, "only you were sleeping too fast, and I suppose you got off the track in your dream."

"Well! I really dreamt there was an earthquake!"

Soon after, all three of them entered the store and prepared to take the rest so necessary after the incessant exercises of the day. They had no beds; but it is a part of the country merchant's discipline to do without one. So it was not long before the rubbish was swept from the floor, and three pallets, consisting of coarse cotton cloth and saddle-blankets, with three pieces of flannel covered with muslin for pillows, were in readiness for the repose of their weary limbs.

Nap was the first to sleep, as was ascertained from the unmistakable signal of his nasal trumpet. Joseph soon followed, notwithstanding the annoyance of the disagreeable sound in his immediate neighbourhood. But it was in vain that Jack sought repose. His overwrought body and mind seemed to repel the approaches of slumber, and it was long before he ceased to turn uneasily from side to side. And when some degree of bodily composure was attained, the perturbation of his mind continued. In his snatches of dreams he beheld only venomous snakes, and heard the startling rattle of the fatal reptile. Once he sprang up and awakened Joseph. He could not be sure he had not heard the rattle in reality instead of merely dreaming it. And so he and his brother placed their pallets on the counter, and called to Nap to follow their example. Nap ceased to snore, and growled some unintelligible mutterings, but could not be so easily awakened.

"Awake!" cried Jack, going to him and shaking him violently.

"Oh yes, very well, then," responded Nap.

"But why not get up?"

"Very well—all right, I say," said Nap, closing his eyes again.

"Nap, there are snakes about! Up, before you are bitten!"

"Snakes!" cried Nap, his eyes now wide open.

"Rattlesnakes," said Joseph.

"Wake snakes and come to taw!" yelled Nap, springing

at one bound, heavy as he was, into a chair, at another on the counter near the window, and was then in the act of leaping out upon the ground, when Joseph, laughing heartily, seized him by the leg.

"Let me go!" cried Nap, with a cold perspiration on his forehead. "Dod blast the snakes! Where are they?"

"I doubt, Nap," said Joseph, "if there is one within a mile of us. It was merely one of Jack's dreams. His imagination is so strong that the creatures flitting in his dreams are remembered as realities. His dream of snakes awoke him, and then he believed it was no dream."

"Was that all?"

"Or perhaps it was only to frighten you, and stop your snoring until he could get asleep. He is sleeping now: I am certain of it, from his deep breathing."

"I wonder if it *was* a trick of that sort? But do I snore, sure enough?"

"Does the escape-pipe of the old steamer Boreas make a noise?"

"Don't it!"

"Then taking into consideration the difference in your dimensions, I must say you can beat old Boreas. If you were as large as the boat, you could be heard all the way down to St. Louis."

"Well, now, I wasn't aware of that! But don't you think there *might* be a rattlesnake under the house? Since snakes have been mentioned, I'm afraid there *is* some danger. I'll lie here between you, my head to your feet, and my feet to Jack's head."

Nap adjusted his couch accordingly, and continued to talk long after Joseph ceased to make any answers, for the latter endeavoured to take advantage of the cessation of sound from Nap's escape-pipe, to sink into a recreating slumber. Nap finally composed his limbs as well as he was able on the narrow counter, and fell into an unquiet doze, being encompassed by rattlesnakes in his dreams.

Again Jack became restless in his sleep. The light had

not been long extinguished, and Nap's organ had just run its discordant diapason, when Jack, making a sudden lurch, tumbled from the counter, but luckily alighted on his feet.

"What's the matter now, Jack?" inquired Joseph, who had failed in the attempt to slumber before Nap's organ sounded its alarming tones.

"Oh, nothing at all," said Jack. "I merely rolled off the counter."

"You must learn to lie better than that: the counter is nearly thirty inches wide," said Joseph.

Neither the fall nor the colloquy that ensued seemed to have any effect on Nap, who, although he seemed to turn and writhe as if tormented by unpleasant visions, still blew off his steam as loudly as ever. Indeed, sometimes it would come in such startling explosions, as nearly to arouse himself, and which Joseph declared was almost sufficient to awaken the dead, if there could be any virtue in braying trumpets. However, the imperious demands of nature had to be answered, and all of them finally succumbed to the approaches of oblivious slumber.

Yet the brothers were destined to be startled once more by the provoking Nap. It was just about the dawn of the morning, and at the still and solemn hour when the whippoorwill utters his last plaintive note, that Nap, from dreaming he was the victim of hissing and rattling serpents, awoke with a conviction that his peril was real, and not the mere "fabric of a baseless vision," which was to "leave no trace behind." Within, an impenetrable darkness still reigned. But in the silence, rendered more profound by the cessation of his own inharmonious snoring, his quick ear was conscious of a low sound in his immediate vicinity, while a slight gliding motion could be distinguished near his head. With eyes dilated, trembling limbs, and a violently beating heart, poor Nap remained horror-stricken, and for many moments knew not what to do. If he moved, he might be bitten; whereas he had heard it said, or had read somewhere, that a snake, and particularly a magnanimous rattlesnake, would never strike its fangs into an inanimate object. Such thoughts as these ran through his brain with the rapidity of lightning, during which time he continued perfectly motionless. Again the rustling was heard, and the movement continued, even touching his hair, which stood straight out from his head. At last he could no longer bear the loathsome proximity of the venomous **reptile**. **By a** desperate effort he succeeded in **springing to** his knees, and seizing his pillow (a piece of flannel) **as he** faced about, began to belabour the deadly foe most **furiously,** striking rapidly to the right and left, for the purpose of dashing it to the floor. It may be supposed the poor fellow's surprise was great, and relief profound, when Joseph exclaimed—

"Nap, what are you beating my feet **for** ?"

"I thought they were snakes!" said **Nap**, panting. "I **was** dreaming! I beg your pardon!" Saying this, he embraced the feet most affectionately.

"Let my feet alone!" **cried** Joseph, vexed at being so often disturbed by his brace of novitiate clerks.

CHAPTER III.

The first day's business—A "bogus" dollar—A word and a blow—Polly Hopkins—Nap's hair-breadth escape from matrimony.

Soon after **Nap's** last adventure, and long before the sun was up, the pallets were cleared away, the floor brushed nicely, and the goods properly arranged and displayed to the best advantage, for a busy day was anticipated.

When the horn was sounded for breakfast over at Mr. Black's, and the young men stepped out upon the green and proceeded along the winding path through hazel-bushes, and under towering oaks, they were in ecstasies with the magnificence of the scene, and yielded unconsciously to the inspiration of the moment.

The sun was rising in unclouded brilliance over the distant hills to the eastward and beyond the river, and bathing in a sea of gold the intervening forest. Dewdrops stood upon the motionless green foliage, and the fragrant wild rose and honeysuckle cast their perfumes upon the air. The mocking-bird, the thrush, and the lark strained their throats in emulous rivalry; and the gentle humming-birds flitted by in such near proximity as to fan perceptibly the young men's faces.

After a hearty breakfast—and there is something in the climate of Missouri which seems to create a voracious appetite, particularly if one will take sufficient exercise, as our young men had done the day before—the merchants were at their posts in readiness for action.. And they were not to be disappointed; for parties of men and women followed each other into town until there were not houses enough to hold them. They were really in each other's way at the store, and the crowd greatly confused Nap and Jack, who were making their first attempts in the capacity of salesmen.

Among those present during the day were the families of Mr. Townly and Colonel Hopkins. Whole families go in a body to the country stores. In the families named there were two young ladies of very different temperaments, but who, nevertheless, seemed to fascinate, in some degree, both of the young gentlemen. The first, Mary Townly, was a delicate, modest prairie-flower; the other, Polly Hopkins, was a tall, handsome, eccentric girl, who thought boldly on all subjects that occupied her mind, and never hesitated to express her thoughts. Many ludicrous blunders that our young gentlemen fell into might have been traced to the mischief-making Polly. She bantered and bullied them in divers ways, laughing at their embarrassment, and enjoying the bright scarlet of poor Mary's blushes. She said she had heard of a young Western merchant, named Luke Shortfield, who had some years before, in another county, not only "thrown in his thumbs" when measuring the goods, but had made it a practice to offer his hand to all the young ladies who dealt with him. Then she demanded to know if our young gentlemen had not promised to be quite as liberal in every respect as any of their competitors or predecessors. Of course both Nap and Jack answered in the affirmative. She then declared her intention to test the matter some day. They said she would find them quite ready to accommodate her.

But before the close of that busy day there was to transpire an unpleasant occurrence. One of the Mulroonys, a well-digger, from the "old country," taking advantage of the absence of Joseph Handy, who had gone to dinner, passed upon Nap a dollar of "bogus money," which Jack discovered to be spurious by the application of a drop of acid, and then demanded another in its place.

Mulroony denied that he had passed the counterfeit money, but intimated that some of the ladies might have done so. And as if to prove that he was innocent, he put down on the counter several genuine Spanish milled dollars.

"Be the powers," said he, "I kape good money, and a plenty of it!"

"But this counterfeit came from you, and I would swear to it," said Jack, throwing down the false coin and taking up a good one which he placed in the drawer.

"Then be St. Patrick ye'd swear to a lie!" was Mulroony's reply.

Jack could not stand this. His Kentucky blood revolted at it. So, having nothing else in reach of him at the moment which he could use with effect, he snatched up the Irishman's bottle of whisky that stood upon the counter, and broke it over its owner's forehead.

Paddy was staggered and blinded. He ran out for his club, which had been left in the bushes where his old horse was tied, and soon returned with fury in his eyes and vengeance in his heart. But before he could approach near enough to deal a blow, Nap had dodged under the counter, and Jack presented a formidable-looking pistol. Mulroony lowered his club and gazed steadfastly in the young man's face. He saw indications of danger, and begged Jack not to kill him. Jack said he would not fire, unless it was in self-defence. Mulroony then gathered up the dollars he had left on the counter. He said he would take the bogus coin and make Handy a present of the good one. He could afford to do it. He was not so poor as to mind the loss of a dollar.

But Mulroony was a dangerous man, and Jack was warned by the witnesses of the occurrence to be on his guard against him. Nap, who had risen from his hiding-place unperceived, declared that Mulroony had better be on his guard against Jack and himself, for they both had guns, and intended to practise firing at a target.

This affair, however, was soon forgotten. A constant succession of new customers did not permit the thoughts of the young men to dwell upon it; and the old inhabitants of the county were accustomed to seeing the Irishman, particularly on occasions when many people were drawn together, get up some sort of a quarrel. In the present instance, however, Mulroony had been disposed of and driven from the ground in a more summary manner than usual.

When the sun had declined low in the west, and the last of the company had departed, our merchants gladly availed themselves of the opportunity to sit down and rest their weary limbs. They sat in split-bottomed chairs, leaning back against the counter, and mused on the events of the day. The Handys were in high spirits, although much exhausted in body, for the result, when summed up, exceeded the calculations of Joseph.

"How do you like the business, Nap?" asked Joseph. No reply being made, he turned his eyes toward his clerk and found him nodding.

"He's off," said Jack. "Listen; that's his first snore." It was true. But the second one being accompanied by a convulsive start, caused by a flitting vision of Mulroony with his club, the legs of the chair in which Nap was sitting slipped along the floor, and he lay prostrated on his back.

"Where is he? He struck me!" he cried, leaping up and preparing to run away. "Hold him—he's got a club!" he continued. But the laughter that saluted his ears relieved him. He was soon wide awake. And then, in something like vexation at being the subject of merriment, he confessed, in reply to Joseph's repeated question, that although he was well enough pleased with the vocation of the merchant, he was utterly disappointed at the small amount of business done that day. But Nap was a novice, and was yet to learn a great deal; and particularly that a country store may be filled with customers from morning until night, and yet the sales amount to less than they had done on that occasion.

Days and weeks followed, and still there was no material diminution of the business; but the proportion of goods sold on credit increased. Nap and Jack soon became sufficiently familiar with their duties to dispense for days together with the presence of their principal, who was frequently absent at the town of ———, where he was paying his addresses to a Miss C———.

It was during one of these absences that the young men were visited again by Miss Polly Hopkins. After making her purchases, she remarked that she intended to take one of the young men home with her. This was characteristic of Polly; but it made Nap and Jack stare.

"I'm quite in earnest," said she. "I have bought your goods, supposing all the time that one of the salesmen would be 'thrown in' afterward."

"But—but," stammered Nap, half in merriment and half in confusion at such a singular and unexpected announcement.

"No buts—but come to the point," said she, while the half-dozen people in the store evinced some curiosity to see the end of her assault on the gallantry of the clerks.

But I'm—almost engaged to another!" said Nap. "Yet not exactly, either. Hang me, if I know what to say, Miss Polly! But it is true that I am half disposed of to another"——

"Who!" she demanded so imperiously, that Nap blurted out his secret before he was aware of what he was saying.

"To Molly Brook."

"Moll Brook? That sounds like the name of a tune one of our negroes plays on the fiddle, and I like it very much. How long have you known her? How much do you love her? Does she love you?"

"No matter—never mind," said Nap, recovering his composure, and seeing Jack smile. "She is not my wife, and I am free to have you. But you are merely joking. I know you wouldn't have me."

"How do you know? I think I would, provided you are not the one that snores so outrageously. Our old Tom says, when he came here the other night for some ague and fever medicine, one of you was snoring so loudly that it scared his horse, and he came near having a fall."

This produced some laughter, in which Nap heartily joined, and secretly rejoiced for the first time that he did snore. But before he had time to own he was guilty of the abominable practice, Jack, foreseeing what might be the consequence if Polly should direct her battery against him, interposed the following mendacious speech:

"Oh no, Miss Polly; I can clear Nap of that. With shame and sorrow I must confess that I am the guilty one."

"What? what's that you say, Jack? You, *you* snore? Why, haven't you declared a hundred times that my snoring disturbed your rest?"

"Very true. But I was jesting."

"I never heard *you* snore."

"That proves nothing," said Polly. "Perhaps you get asleep first. Did you ever hear yourself snore?"

"No, I never did," said Nap, ingenuously.

"That proves you don't snore. Therefore I'll take you."

"Well, suppose you do! I doubt if Molly will have me before I make a fortune, and that may be too long for me to wait. Durned if I'm afraid! I'll try your mettle, Miss!" said Nap, determined to stand his ground bravely, not doubting that the indomitable Polly would soon take the alarm and beat a retreat.

"Ready, sir! Try me!" said she.

"I'll try you! Will any one present marry us?" asked Nap, turning toward several countrymen who were the amused witnesses of the scene.

"I will accommodate you," said one of them, who was a stranger, stepping forward very gravely.

Nap now supposed the girl would "hang fire;" but she seemed to be "as true as steel." She grasped his proffered hand with animation, and with a determined expression of features.

"Go on, stranger," said she.

"I pronounce you man and"——

"One moment!" said Jack, quickly, and at the same time placing his hand on the stranger's mouth.

"What have you got to say?" asked Polly, turning to Jack.

"Nap's innocent"——

"Innocent? You don't suppose marrying a man is hanging him, do you? Or that the uttering of a marriage ceremony is a sentence of death? Do you think I would have him if he had been guilty"——

"But he *is* guilty. That's what I meant to say."

"Guilty of what?"

"Snoring. He snores like a porpoise. I did him great injustice."

"Is that all? And if *you* can bear to be near him in his sleep, why not I?"

"I keep him awake by scratching and kicking, until I'm asleep myself."

"Why can't I do the same thing? It is too late now. Go on, stranger!"

"Dinged if it is too late, though!" said Nap, breaking away, and leaping over the counter. Jack had heard some one say the stranger was a magistrate, and he contrived to whisper the information in Nap's ear, who instantly began to tremble.

Polly, apparently vexed at the interruption, next assailed Jack.

"Then, sir," said she, "since you own that you are not the snoring gentleman, suppose I take *you*. I must have one of you."

"Oh, take your choice!" said Jack, so composedly that the wild girl desisted from her folly, and soon after departed, but not without uttering threats of what she would do if ever she caught either of the young men from home. She told them to beware of her, as well as of Mulroony, for they would find her quite as dangerous a subject to deal with.

CHAPTER IV.

Taking an account of stock—Venice preserved on speculation—Fruits and moonlight—The buck and bear—Nap goes into poetics—Hot and cold—Ague and fever *versus* love.

AT length our merchants were in the midst of the dull season. Seasons in business fluctuate periodically like other seasons. Joseph Handy had suddenly resolved to take an account of the stock on hand, and make an estimate, while he had nothing else to do, of the amount of profits he had realized.

Jack, of course, did not relish the job, and perhaps no

clerk ever did. So he combated the project as long as he could, but all in vain. His brother was inexorable.

One day, when not a single customer was in the store, the senior Handy announced to Jack that they would begin the inventory at once; and he told him to awaken Nap, who was lying on his back upon the counter, fast asleep and snoring very loudly. He wanted him to weigh the heavy articles in the wareroom.

Jack, finding his opposition unavailing, made a virtue of necessity, and assumed a cheerful air. Having called Nap once or twice without receiving an answer, or even causing a suspension of his snoring, he walked softly to where he lay, and yelled loudly in his ear these startling words:

"I pronounce you man and wife!"

"Hello! stop! stop!" cried Nap, bouncing up, and then tumbling down on the floor. "I won't have her! I don't consent!" he continued, as he scrambled toward the door, where the hot rays of the bright sun were pouring in, unintercepted by the presence of any object.

"What's the matter with you?" asked Jack.

"The matter! Haven't they married us, in spite of all I could do to prevent it?"

"Have they? Where's the bride? Where's the magistrate?"

"Sure enough, where are they?" exclaimed Nap, glancing round. "I'm sure I heard some one pronounce the fatal words, and I thought I had Polly by the hand."

"Nonsense, Nap; it was the counter-brush, and it is still in your hand. You were dreaming. But now that you are awake, you must know we are going to commence taking an inventory forthwith, and Joseph wishes you to weigh the iron, the castings, and the sugar and coffee in the other room."

"Very well. I'd rather do that or any thing else than have such terrible dreams. But still I don't know, Jack, why I should be so much frightened at the idea of marrying

Polly Hopkins. She's not ugly. Yet, you know, even when one has been ill-treated by his first love, he can't love any other girl for a long time."

"I know that very well," was Jack's assenting reply, while his thoughts reverted to the one he had left behind him.

The young men worked slowly. There was no necessity for being in a hurry. At the end of a few days the operation was completed, and Joseph declared himself satisfied with the result. He then made another visit to his lady-love and married her.

During the days of solitude that now often occurred, for whole days often passed away without more than one or two customers being in town, Nap employed his idle time in a correspondence with Molly Brook. In reply to his voluminous letters, he received a brief note, equivocal and unsatisfactory in its expressions. This treatment roused the lion's spirit which had so long lain dormant within his capacious breast. He resolved to make a *large* fortune. Hitherto he had supposed he might be contented with what was merely termed a fortune. But now it should be a large one. And it was his intention to constrain Molly to manifest a more obliging disposition. As yet he had not supposed it possible, under any circumstances, for him to make overtures to any other damsel. In pursuance of his ambitious determination, he gave fifty dollars for some forty acres of land situated on the river bottom about twenty miles above Tyre. And upon this alluvial tract, densely covered with immense forest-trees, workmen were soon after employed in the erection of a rough wooden storehouse, and in clearing away the vines and bushes where it was designed to lay out the streets. Nap, although his purchase of the land was much laughed at in the country, considered himself a rich man the moment the deed was executed. And after some reading, and no little cogitation, he bestowed a ridiculous name upon his town. It was VENICE, and he was to be a merchant prince, if not doge. Late in the fall it was his intention to begin business on his own account.

When no customers were "in town" to occupy the attention of the young men, they sometimes amused themselves firing at a target, or catching huge catfish down at the steamboat landing. And they partook of other enjoyments. Fruits and melons grew in great abundance in the vicinity, and were most delicious. No country produces them in greater perfection. Of course they were brought to the store every day and presented to the young merchants. The merchant in a new country is always an influential character, and every thing good and desirable is laid at his feet. Our young men did not spare these luxuries of the season, during the prolonged absence of Joseph. They were, however, ultimately to pay dearly for them.

But that which afforded them the most exquisite delight was their moonlight rambles, and interchange of romantic cogitations. The sky seemed to be of a deeper blue and the moonlight of a greater brilliance in Missouri than elsewhere. And they enjoyed themselves. They traversed the roads, and became familiar with all the deer-paths in the vicinity. Sometimes they conversed upon the incidents of the past, in their still beloved Kentucky, and formed gigantic projects for the future. But always, when their fortunes were made, they concurred entirely in the purpose of returning to the cherished homes of their childhood, and after first making their mistresses undergo the penance of some mortification and delay, then to marry them.

It was during such rambles and confidential intercommunication of thoughts as these, the young men had observed that several fine deer were in the nightly habit of meeting them near the centre of a grove of oak saplings, through which one of the narrow paths they traversed wound its serpentine way. For several evenings in succession, at the same hour, and near the same locality, they were confronted by this promenading company of browsing bucks. The deer would suffer the young men to approach within sixty feet of them, and then leap aside into the bushes, showing the white portion of their tails and snorting loudly.

When this had been repeated several times, Jack conceived the idea of adding some fine venison to the luxuries he was in the daily habit of enjoying. So he and Nap formed a plan which they thought must result in the death of a buck. At that season, the flesh of the buck is peculiarly tender and deliciously flavoured. Their horns are soft, and their broad fat backs are covered with short red hair. So one day they informed Mrs. Black of their intention to provide her with a royal haunch of venison some time during the ensuing evening. The incredulous lady merely smiled, and said she would be much indebted to them if they succeeded in performing their promise.

At early twilight, the young men, one armed with a rifle, and the other with an old musket charged with buckshot, set out on their bloody mission. When they reached the vicinity of the grove, which was not more than two hundred yards in length, and much less in width, they separated, Jack making a detour for the purpose of entering the wood by the narrow path at the farther extremity, while Nap was to penetrate it at the opposite point. Thus they were to guard both ends of the path which traversed the grove. When arrived at the point agreed upon, they were to conceal themselves and await the approach of the deer.

Nap had penetrated the grove some thirty paces, when he halted behind a tree of somewhat larger dimensions than the rest in the vicinity, and awaited the event. Jack did the same at the other end of the grove.

For more than an hour the young men awaited the coming of the deer in their silent coverts. No sounds were heard but the cries of the whippoorwill, the hooting of an owl, and the occasional howling of a wolf in the distance. Still, for a long time they did not doubt that the party of bucks would as usual cross their path.

In the mean time, however, the sky became slightly overcast by light, dappled clouds, and it was difficult for the eye to penetrate more than a few paces along the crooked path. Besides, it was in many places obscured by overhanging hazel-bushes and the spreading branches of the trees.

"If they were to come now, I couldn't see well enough to shoot them," soliloquized Nap. "I will get up in the tree. That is the best position."

He did so. The tree forked some seven feet from the ground, and there he sat, with his musket across his knees, striving to trace the windings of the path dimly seen beneath. But the intervening vines and foliage of the bushes, together with the deepening obscurity above, rendered his vision quite as indistinct as it had been when he stood upon the ground. Yet he determined to remain where he was, thinking several times he distinguished the approach of the deer, and knowing that if they did not leave the path they usually traversed, they must pass within reach of the muzzle of his gun.

Jack had hitherto met with no better success, and even despaired before Nap did of seeing the game. He recollected that upon mentioning their project to an old hunter during the day, he had been informed that the deer could discover a man by the smell as easily as they could distinguish him by the eye or the ear; and as the wind had changed from the point it had been recently blowing, it was probable the bucks would walk that night in some other direction. Hence, after waiting until the arrival of the time when they were in the habit of confronting the deer, and finding no indications of their presence in the vicinity, he placed his rifle on his shoulder, and strolled along the path in the direction of Nap.

It was the approach of Jack which had been detected by the ear of Nap, and which he felt more and more convinced must be the deer! He cocked his gun, and pointing the muzzle in the direction of the sound of Jack's feet now heard quite distinctly, prepared to fire upon the first movement his eye might detect.

Jack, not supposing Nap had penetrated so far into the grove, was altogether ignorant of his dangerous proximity. Nevertheless the clicking sound attending the cocking of the gun up in the fork of the tree had not escaped his ear, and it caused him to pause abruptly. Upon casting his eyes upward, he beheld the indistinct outlines of his friends form; but instead of recognising him, partly hidden as he was by the pendent leaves that hung between, it flashed upon his mind that he stood in the presence of a BEAR! And after the first tremor of excitement subsided a little, he prepared to take a steady aim at his victim.

Thus the two frinds were unconsciously taking deliberate aim at each other, and both with their fingers on the fatal triggers! But as they were now motionless, each awaiting some movement which might reveal the other more distinctly, there was a long pause. Finally, being impatient to fire, and mutually convinced from the proximity of the objects they were aiming at, that there was no probability of missing the marks, it occurred to them both at the same instant that, still holding their guns to their shoulders, they would venture to cough slightly, and see what effect it would produce. Upon the slightest movement they intended to fire.

They did so. Their astonishment may be imagined.

"Why, you ain't a buck!" exclaimed Nap.

"Nor you a bear!" replied Jack, uncocking his gun, and lowering the muzzle as he stepped forth in full view.

"No! don't shoot—for mercy's sake!" cried Nap, sliding down to the ground as quickly and as heavily as even a bear might have done.

"I was very near shooting you, Nap: I had a bead on you, and my finger on the trigger. If you had moved hand or foot instead of coughing, I should have killed you."

Nap had sunk down beside the path, and did not hear

the conclusion of the speech. He had fainted. For a long time Jack's efforts to produce animation were unsuccessful. At length, some water brought from a brook in his hat restored his friend to consciousness.

That was their first hunting adventure. As they returned side by side to the store, scarcely a word was exchanged between them. They were occupied with their own fearful thoughts. Both of them, if they had fired at the same moment, might have been slain, and then in all probability another "fatal duel" would have been chronicled. They might have grown angry at each other as they walked silently homeward, for presuming to point the murderous tubes as they did; but then the thought that both had offended in the same manner, constantly recurred to them, and each had to acquit his friend on the same plea that vindicated himself. Yet it was one of those unpremeditated affairs such as they mutually hoped might never again occur.

Their taciturnity continued after their arrival at the store. Nap made his pallet in one room, and Jack in the other. The rays of moonlight streaming through the unshuttered windows, rendered the igniting of a candle unnecessary.

"Now, Nap," said Jack, when they had thrown themselves down on their couches, the partition door between them being always open, "I think your infernal snoring won't disturb me. If I am not mistaken, you will not be able to sleep much before morning."

"You still insist upon it that I snore; but I have sometimes doubted it," said Nap. "I have often thought of getting Tom Black to come over and sit up beside my bed, and give me his candid opinion. I know he never jests No matter; sleep on; I'll not annoy you to-night."

"Thank you. I thought not. But what will you do? What will you think about?"

"Molly Brook! O, Jack, just to think! Here we are, tender young men, a thousand miles from home, lying on our backs, and the solemn moon playing through the crannies and streaming its light on our pale faces. The great 'mad Missouri,' like a muddy eel, a mile broad and a continent in length, crawling for ever past our feet! The whippoorwill wailing down in the dark valley, through which Mr. Black's spring-branch is running; and ever and anon the wolf is heard howling in the river bottom. The katydid"——

"Why, Nap!" exclaimed Jack, starting up on his elbow, "you are growing romantic and poetical."

"I know it. How can I help it? I'm homesick."

"Homesick! Is there any romance in that?"

"Lots of it; and love too."

"Love! Oh, you said you would think of Molly. But to your figure. The katydid"——

"That's a typification of Molly—only Molly didn't do what Katy did. Her cousin Kate married Oliver Hodge, because his father had a fine farm—and I, poor me! am driven a wild wanderer into solitary exile."

"Not solitary, Nap. I am with you, as well as the moon, the continental eel, the whippoorwill, the wolves, and the katydid. Is there no comfort in that?"

"Oh yes,—but it's all dashed down again, and made a torment, when I think how near I was losing you to-night. My gracious! Suppose my gun had gone off! What would I have done then?"

"I'll tell you. You would probably have lain a corpse at the foot of the tree, with a bullet through your brain. I had a fine aim at the centre of your head, for I was certain it could be nothing else than a bear's head."

"True, Jack. Don't think of it. Let us promise never to mention the occurrence; never even to think of it again."

"Very well. I'm sure it would frighten my mother to hear of it a year hence."

"To be sure it would, and Kate Frost too. Your Katy that didn't, as well as my Molly. I wonder what Molly would say, and how she would look, if she were to hear of it? Jack, you must let me write an account of the transaction to my mother. I will get her to read it to Kate and Molly, and then write me how they bear it. What do you say?"

Jack said nothing. He was asleep. If he did not snore, he breathed heavily, and occasionally uttered a groan in his fitful slumber.

Nap did not disturb him; but finding it impossible to sleep himself, continued the indulgence of his own teeming thoughts and half-coherent images. Thus he lay and tossed from one side to the other of his couch until late in the night.

The wolf ventured to approach within a few paces of the door, and there uttered his discordant howl. The whippoorwill alighted on the roof of the house, and mocked him with its monotonous note. The moon sank down sadly, throwing her horizontal streams of fading light athwart the recumbent young men. The one troubled by unpleasant visions in his slumber, and the other startled by the fancies of his waking dreams.

But all within was still, and silent as the grave, save the chirp of the cricket, and the tick of the beetle, known as the death-watch.

It was at such a moment, when Nap, who had for some time been lying without any resemblance of animation, sprang up suddenly and ran to the corner of the room in which the guns had been placed. He seized them, one after the other, and hastily examining the locks, burst forth into a hearty fit of laughter. He drew forth the ramrods and plunged them down the barrels, and the result produced a more boisterous cachinnatory explosion than ever. He then replaced them, and danced a hearty jig upon the floor. The whippoorwill flew away, and the wolf vanished mutely in the dark bushes. Even the cricket and the beetle were heard no more.

"Nap! Nap! What in the world is the matter with you? Are you crazy?"

"No, Jack, but a little wild."

"Wild? What made you so?"

"Joy."

"Joy?"

"Yes. Don't you recollect we intended to wash out our guns before supper, that we might go on the hunt as soon as we got back from Mr. Black's, and that I got the tow and the water?"

"Yes. And didn't you wash them out while I was selling the cloth to Colonel Miller?"

"No, indeed. For when you were waiting on the colonel, didn't Burton Lawless buy a bushel of salt and a long-handled skillet of me in the wareroom? Didn't you see me charge them in the blotter?"

"Yes. Then the guns were not cleaned?"

"No,—neither were they loaded. Ha! ha! ha!"

"And so a brace of fools went out to kill game with empty guns!"

"Good! Oh, I'm rejoiced to the heart. I'm not homesick, now; and I'll sleep as calmly as an infant. We were in no danger, after all. And yet we were frightened as much as if we had made a narrow escape."

And Nap did sleep. And he snored tremendously, while Jack, vexed and suffering with aching limbs, for he had not been quite well for several days, fruitlessly strove to regain his lost repose. Near the dawn of day he was seized with a slight ague. He called to Nap to throw more blankets on him. But if Nap's sonorous organ, now in full blast, did not disturb his own slumber, it was absurd in Handy to suppose his cries might awake him. So he ceased the attempt in despair, and, ill as he was, and as had been predicted by Mr. Black when he saw the young men eating immoderate quantities of fruit, and indulging in romantic moonlight walks through the woods, he had to help himself in the best manner he could. The whole stock in trade of woollens was brought in requisition; and although he was almost smothered under the weight, yet the desired circulation in the extremities of his limbs could not be produced. He shivered and groaned for many minutes, and then he was assailed by a scorching fever. The mountain of wool was overturned and tumbled down; even the sheet was cast aside; the front-door was flung wide open; the pitcher was emptied of its contents; and a large fan snatched from the shelf was industriously used,—but the heat remained unassuaged, and the pain in his head knew no diminution.

When Nap awoke in the morning, the slanting rays of the sun were pouring though the door and reaching midway across the room. He looked in astonishment at the blankets and other goods tumbled about in confusion.

"Jack!" cried he, "get up, and see what a deuce of a scatterment has been made by somebody. Who opened the door? We've been robbed, by jingo! Burglars have been about. No!" he continued, finding the money had not been taken from the desk, "the cash is safe. Do you think it could have been a wolf, Jack?"

"I *know* it was a wolf," said Jack, half deliriously, referring to the howling that had annoyed him in the night.

"But how did he get the door open? I put the bar of steel across it as usual."

"I opened it myself."

"You were very accommodating, truly! How did you know he wouldn't eat a slice of your ham?"

"Deuce take the wolf! Nap, please to get a pitcher of fresh water. Water, water, blessed water!"

"Water? I'll bring some as usual when we come from breakfast."

"Breakfast! Pah! Don't mention it, Nap."

"Why, what's the matter, Jack! Your face is as red as flannel. Are you not sick?"

"I believe I am."

"You *believe* you are? I *know* it," continued Nap,

placing his hand on his friend's forehead. "It is the confounded fever and ague, the disease of the country they warned us against."

"Warned *us*. Why not warn *it*. What good does it do, warning a man against the air he breathes? For heaven's sake get me a pitcher of water!"

"I'll get Mr. Black to come over. He says he can cure the ague as well as Dr. Sappington."

Nap went over alone to the boarding-house; but, while sitting at the breakfast-table, was taken ill himself. He hastened back to the store. Mr. Brown promised to follow him as soon as he could get ready his medicines. Nap found Jack sitting up, with his shirt torn from his neck, waiting impatiently for the refreshing water.

"Where's the pitcher, Nap?"

"Mr. Black will fetch it," replied Nap, between his chattering teeth. His nose was cold and tallow-hued, his fingers purple, and his step unsteady. Without pausing, he gathered up the scattered blankets, and piling them on his own couch, in the room he had occupied during the night, burrowed under them in a shivering spasm.

Jack sat still, and watched the motions of his comrade in silence, save the occasional utterance of a groan, which was replied to by a sighing yawn.

"Oh, I'm burning up!" at length he exclaimed, regarding the pile of blankets heaped upon Nap, which he could discern through the partition door.

"And durned if *I* ain't freezing!" replied Nap.

"I say it's infernal hot! Nobody can freeze in such weather!"

"I swear it is bitter cold!"

"Come here, in this room, and you'll find it warm enough without blankets."

"Come in this, and you'll not require water to cool you.

"Water, water, water!" cried Jack.

"Fire, fire, fire!" cried Nap.

"You are saying it is cold, to annoy me, Nap."

"You are saying it is warm, to vex me, Jack."

"Come, come, boys—no quarrelling, now!" said Mr. Black, who entered just then, with an ill-suppressed smile on his face. "You are both ill; but I'll cure you."

"The water, Mr. Black, if you please!" cried Jack.

"But I don't please—that is, you shall not have more than a mouthful. It will make the fever worse. Here; drink just a spoonful."

"Make a fire! Give me an armful of hot bricks, if you please!" cried Nap.

"It don't please me," said Mr. Black; "it would do you harm. I would rather give you your sweetheart."

"Sweetheart! Don't talk to me of sweethearts," said Nap. "I wouldn't give a fig for Molly, now. They say love is incurable. It's a lie. This Missouri ague can do the business."

"Nonsense; your love will return like your appetite," said Mr. Black, pouring out his medicine in a couple of spoons. "Here, drink this, both of you; and after it has been swallowed two hours, each of you must take a dose of calomel. Measure it on the point of my knife. I will lend it to you to-day. You'll both be in the bushes this evening. Those chills are nothing to men who are used to them. I've known many a man have an ague in the morning, and kill a deer in the afternoon."

They swallowed the liquid he held to their lips, Jack stipulating for another sip of the water, and Nap begging Mr. Black to hold his shoulder-blades in their places. He declared they would flap together like a pigeon's wings if not forcibly held apart. But soon a moisture began to spread over the temples of Handy, and the fever followed Nap's chill. Nap then owned that his room was quite warm enough, and that the blankets were equally as superfluous to his comfort as Molly would have been.

Mr. Black remained with them until the emetic had produced the desired effect. The boys were dreadfully ill.

under its operation, ignorantly supposing all the time that their new sufferings were occasioned by the disease, and not the remedy. Mr. Black did not undeceive them, because he had more than once heard Jack say no consideration would induce him knowingly to swallow an emetic; and that he would punish any physician who should venture to administer it to him.

But it was indispensable, in Mr. Black's estimation, and doubtless it contributed much in arresting the progress of the disease.

Fortunately there were not many customers in town that day. The few that came had to be waited on alternately by the debilitated salesmen; but toward evening both were much better, and the next day they had voracious appetites, and their affection for their absent sweethearts returned as glowingly as ever. Yet they had several returns of the chills, each less violent than the last, on alternate days; and, as Mr. Black had predicted, they soon ceased to terrify them.

CHAPTER V.

Adventure with Mulroony—Polly in the prairie—Model Missouri farm—A pig's tail and a tomcat.—N. B. The dumb-waiter—A monkey cruelly murdered.

At the beginning of autumn there was a great camp-meeting to be held in the vicinity of Tyre, and it was decided by Joseph, who had returned in high spirits with his bride, that both Jack and Nap should go thither on an electioneering and collecting mission. As the people were to be gathered together from the four quarters of the county, and from several of the counties adjacent, it was no novel thing in the merchant to seize upon such occasions to participate in the ceremonies with an eye to business.

But Joseph scorned to dissemble. Once a zealous participant in such scenes, his pride of consistency, if not the force of conviction, would have held him fast in the faith. His day of salvation had not yet dawned. And so the boys were permitted to ride out to the encampment, having permission to remain on the ground as long as they might be disposed to tarry there.

Nap's impatience to be at a Missouri camp-meeting could brook no delay. He could not wait until the morning fixed upon for going thither; and it was arranged that he should depart in the evening alone, to be followed by Jack the next day. Jack had to post the books, which might keep him at the desk until late in the night.

Nap set out alone, humming a hymn. He was a famous singer, and could be easily heard a mile in the woods. And it was the knowledge of this fact, perhaps, which had caused brothers Steele, Weighton, and Nave to press him so flatteringly to be present on the camp-ground. But he had not been gone more than twenty minutes, before he was seen returning at full speed, lashing and spurring his fleet horse at every leap.

The clatter of hoofs attracted the attention of the Handys.

"That's Nap's brown horse," said Jack.

"And that is Nap on him," replied Joseph, looking up the road, with a hand over his eyes.

"Something has frightened his horse, surely."

"I think it more likely that the rider has been frightened."

When Nap arrived in front of the store, he sprang to the earth and ran into the house precipitately, and panted excessively.

"What's the matter, Nap?" exclaimed Joseph, following him into the farther room.

"Has any thing happened to you?" asked Jack.

"Yes. I saw him—I met him"——

"Who? Who?"

"The wild"——

"A bear? a panther?" demanded Jack, quickly, and taking up his gun.

"No—'twas the desperate wild Irishman, Mulroony, whose face you split open with the bottle. He wanted to kill me"——

"How do you know?" asked Joseph.

"I saw it in his devilish smile. And when I turned my horse, he whipped after me. But there is no animal on this side of the river that can overtake mine. See what it is to be a judge of a horse—he saved my life."

"Jack, get on your horse and go with him—I will post the books," said Joseph, perceiving his brother's anxiety to be in the prairie.

As Jack and Nap rode away, Nap denied that he had been scared. He declared that he had only hastened back to get some weapon with which to defend himself.

Jack, as usual, had his rifle with him. Perhaps fifty men who attended the camp-meeting—which was to last a week—carried their rifles along. It is the custom in the far-western States. While some are singing and praying, others are procuring venison. Besides, as Jack and Nap had a number of accounts along with them to collect, if possible, and an unlimited leave of absence, they might, in their long rides, after departing from the camp-ground, have some use for the gun.

After emerging into the glorious prairie, and riding some minutes along the smooth, dry road, the young men entered one of those solitary groves scattered at pleasant intervals over the fertile plains. The road was just wide enough for carriages to pass. On either side a dense growth of hazel, plum, and persimmon bushes, entangled with grape-vines, rendered any attempt at penetration for man or beast seemingly impracticable.

It was just where the road made a slight angle, that Nap, always looking ahead since his late unexpected meeting with the Irishman, perceived that desperate worthy again, not fifty paces ahead, seated quietly on his horse, which stood drinking in the centre of a large transparent rivulet that ran sparkling across the road.

Jack perceived him, and instantly recognised his enemy. Resolving not to remove his eyes from Mulroony, he did not turn his head toward Nap, who was several paces in the rear, upon hearing a plunging noise behind. He supposed it was a deer leaping through the bushes.

The Irishman had his rifle on his shoulder, and a cold chill was experienced by Jack when his foe raised his head and gazed steadfastly at him from beneath his dark brow. They were now not exceeding twenty paces asunder. It would not do to flee away, as Nap had done; yet he was conscious of the sensation of fear. Jack knew, however, that if it must come to the arbitrament of arms, he was deservedly a famous shot. Having made up his mind that there was no other alternative but to meet his deadly foe in that narrow road, his subsequent conduct was the result of an unerring instinct which had more than once extricated him in moments of sudden peril. He checked his horse and dismounted, and pretended to adjust the girth. But he so arranged the animal—(apparently by accident, though in reality altogether by design)—that while there should be ample room for his adversary to pass, his horse's body would at the same time be interposed between them. He kept his eye fixed on the Irishman, and his rifle at rest on his left arm, while he held the breech and lock in his right hand. His foe did not seem to have any inclination to turn and fly. But he *hesitated*, when his horse was done drinking. He had once received a blow from Jack's hand which had wellnigh sufficed him. Perhaps he was speculating about the chances of receiving further injury, rather than meditating vengeance. This idea occurred to Jack, and caused him to act with more decision. He would have been justified had he killed him, for it was notorious that he still threatened to take his life. But Jack had no such intention. His purpose was only to escape with an unperforated skin. Assuming as much fierceness as possible, he compressed his lips, and still kept his eye fixed upon the Irishman. At length the latter touched his horse with the spur, and advanced very slowly. His gun was still on his shoulder, but his hand was on the lock and guard. When he was within about five paces of Handy, his ear distinguished the clicking of the young man's trigger, for he was setting it preparatory for action. The Irishman paused an instant. His gaze became unsteady, and his head drooped slightly, so that his wide-brimmed straw hat almost obscured his eyes. Jack saw that he was pale, and that the hand which held the reins was trembling. Although it was palpable he was a coward, yet he was undoubtedly a dangerous man, and would, if an opportunity offered, shoot an enemy in the back. And another chill ran up Jack's spine, when he perceived, for the first time, that Hap had vanished.

"What are you going to do?" asked the Irishman, in a tremulous tone. Jack had been unable to utter a word himself. He felt that he could not speak without betraying great agitation and alarm. So he merely responded by a motion of the head for him to pass.

"Do you intend to shoot me?" continued the subdued foe.

Again Jack motioned for him to pass, and this time with greater energy and impatience. The bully now looked imploringly in the face of the young man, which was plainly understood to be a petition for mercy. Treacherous himself, he feared he could not safely rely upon the honour and forbearance of others. So he rode on very slowly, his face still turned toward Jack, who had the advantage of position. As he rubbed past, Jack turned slowly, keeping his eyes upon him, knowing that the first to fire, if shots were to be exchanged, would be the victor. But his enemy passed on, and as he got farther away, his gait was increased. Presently he put spurs to his horse, and hastily disappeared.

"Nap!" cried Jack, "where are you?"

"Here I am," replied Nap, not more than two rods off, in the vines and bushes.

"Nap, you always were a despicable coward, and always will be."

This was followed by a tremendous struggle in the bushes, and the next moment Nap succeeded in urging his horse back into the road, bleeding from the many scratches he had received. Nap himself soon followed, holding by the tail of his steed.

"That was a very unkind remark, a very harsh observation of yours, Jack," said he, "after what I have just been doing for you."

"What have you been doing for me, but hiding from me!"

"I saved your life!"

"Pray tell me how."

"I will. When the fellow saw us, I perceived he had his gun"——

"No doubt, no doubt!"

"But listen. Being behind you, he could not see that *I* had none. He merely got an imperfect glimpse of me. Then I plunged into an ambush. Don't you understand?"

"Oh yes, perfectly!"

"No, you don't! I see you don't. But you must learn that an experienced woodsman never follows a rattlesnake into the grass. When he loses sight of him, the man is careful to get away from the ground as quickly as possible. Well, the fellow having seen me, and knowing I was in concealment, but within shooting distance of him, and yet ignorant of the fact that I was unarmed, determined to have no conflict with you, and so passed harmlessly on."

"That is hardly convincing, Nap. You would make me believe that your absence inspired terror in his breast, and that your presence would have resulted in my death."

"Exactly—perhaps in the death of both of us, but certainly in yours."

"It won't do, Nap!"

"It will do, and you will not deny it when I tell you, truly, that your gun was not charged! I recollected, when I sprang into the bushes, that you had not charged it before we set out, and I knew it was empty this morning."

This was true; and Jack was almost prostrated with the consciousness of the fact.

Silently they sprang upon their horses, dashed through the brook where they had first discovered the Irishman, and never paused until they were a quarter of a mile out in the prairie on the opposite side. Then they dismounted, Jack being now too feeble and unsteady to stand. The commotion of his blood had brought on a slight return of the ague, and he lay down on his saddle-blanket, until the fever which ensued subsided in a measure. Nap, in the mean time, had very deliberately loaded the gun.

They were roused by the trampling of an approaching horse, which came from an opposite direction to the one upon which their eyes had been mostly fixed. Upon turning, they perceived the rider was of the feminine gender.

"What's the matter? Why, it's you, Jack! How are you, my dear boys?" exclaimed she, checking her panting horse suddenly, and leaping to the ground. The horse began to graze about with the others, after the usual brief salutations with their noses. They were all trained to stay beside their masters and mistresses. And the girl, Polly Hopkins, whom Nap and Jack had almost as much feared to meet (alone) as the desperate Irishman, seated herself beside the prostrate young man. But she had no rifle, and did not wear a threatening aspect. Yet she, too, knew how to use firearms; and so Nap slyly uncapped his tube.

"What's the matter, Jack?" she again asked.

"I believe I had a slight chill."

"Let me see," said she, feeling his pulse. "You have very little fever—very little indeed."

"See if *I* haven't some," said Nap, boldly thrusting out his hand.

"Go off, my dear! You are not sick—not even love-sick," she continued, turning from him.

"I must get out of the sun," said Jack, "or I shall have a bad headache."

"You must, indeed. Come along with me, both of you. I have some medicine that will cure you, Jack,—and will keep *you* well, husband."

"Husband!" cried Nap. "You still hold to that, do you? Take care! You may get me in the humour, some of these days."

"The sooner the better. Say the word now, if you choose."

"Durned if she don't make me tremble, even out here by ourselves!" said Nap to Jack, but he was overheard by Polly.

"What are you afraid of? A girl nineteen years old, weighing just one hundred and thirty pounds; without speck or wrinkle; fair-skinned, blue-eyed, and hair only slightly auburn!" She might have added an oval face, a tall stature, and altogether a handsome person.

"I ain't afraid," said Nap, rather hesitatingly.

"Then just let Jack join our hands, and pronounce us man and wife. That's a lawful wedding in Missouri. After that I shall be yours, provided you treat me well. That's all I want, and it's what I'll have. Come now! I'm in the market. What do you say?"

"Let me speak," said Jack, amused. "I pronounce you man and—Stop, Nap! What are you running away for?"

Nap had taken to his heels.

"WIFE!" cried Polly, laughing heartily, and pursuing him.

"Keep off!" cried Nap, halting. "I won't run an inch farther. Stop—don't put your hands on me. I'm afraid of you—I'm afraid of myself—I'm afraid of Molly! You are prettier than Molly, and if I hadn't pledged myself to her, I tell you candidly there would be some danger of my falling in love with you."

"Pledged! What man ever yet cared for a pledge? Won't you break it, for me?"

"Then I might break my pledge to you, for the next handsome girl I met with!"

"If you did, I'd break your neck! But come," she continued, seizing his hand and laughing gayly, "let us return to Jack. We've had fun enough for one day, and you have a red face. Mount, Jack, and let us all ride up the country to our house."

"No, Polly, not to-day. We expect to see some men on business in the opposite direction."

"Well, if it must be so, it must," she replied, gravely. "But neither of you must be offended at my nonsense at the store, or out here. I get into girlish freaks sometimes, and resolve to do something that will be talked about and laughed at. My novels say that fine ladies do pretty much the same things in the great cities and grand places, only in a different way. They must have distinction, and so will I. I am as free as air, and independent as a swallow. They may call me odd, mad, if they please; but no one ever dared to cast a foul aspersion on my character. That I should fearfully avenge!"

This was true.

"Farewell, Polly," said Jack, mounting into his saddle. "We will call at your house soon. But to-night we must stay at Mr. Townley's, and to-morrow we go to the camp-meeting."

"Oh yes!" cried she, laughing mockingly, and springing with great agility upon her horse; "I understand: you are going there to be nursed by Miss Mary. You are going, perhaps, to make a proposition. She'll have you."

"No, indeed, Polly; I feel like any thing else than a

lover, now; and besides, to tell you the truth, I left my sweetheart behind me, as Nap did his."

"I know it. Oh, you are astonished that I should have heard it before! I can tell you her name. **Kate Frost.** We girls soon know all about such engagements. And I suppose, like Nap, **you** could not be induced to violate your engagement? **Take care! Mary may** bewitch you, as I intend to bewitch Nap. **Nap!** I give you fair **warning.** I have a design upon you. I will **meet** you at the camp-meeting. '*Meet me, meet me by moonlight, love.*'" Saying this, or rather singing the conclusion of **it, she** galloped away.

The young men proceeded at a brisk **pace** toward the residence of **Mr.** Townly, where, if they were not expected that evening, they knew they were always sure of having a hearty welcome.

"Jack," said Nap, after a prolonged silence, and checking his horse until he fell into a slow walk, "it strikes me that it would be serving Molly as she deserves, if I were to marry Polly Hopkins."

"But how would it be **serving yourself?**" responded Jack, dryly.

"Very well; I think Polly is a **very** pretty girl, and very spirited."

"Very. **That is, high** mettled. Don't be a fool, **Nap,** and marry that **girl.** If you **do, you will** catch a Tartar. You are the most susceptible person I **ever met** with in my life. When you **hear** Colonel Benton talk politics ten minutes, you turn politician; and although **you** don't belong to his party, you **repeat** his arguments, **imitate** his gestures, mimic his voice, and even reiterate his terrific denunciations. And yet **you are a** Whig in principle, although you call yourself a Democrat"——

"Stop, Jack—hear **me,**" said Nap, letting the reins fall on his horse's **neck. With** his left hand he grasped a white handkerchief **in the centre, and waved** the corners gracefully to and **fro.** All **the fingers of** his right hand were doubled up, excepting the middle one, which was pointed stiffly toward his companion. This was in exact imitation of the Rev. Mr. Darling, an eloquent preacher whom he had recently heard at Tyre. "Hear me, Jack. I own that I am a tariff-man, and an advocate of internal improvements. I believe in Adam Smith and Henry C. Carey; but"——

"But what? How the deuce, then, can you be called a Democrat?"

"I'll tell you, confidentially, as Mr. Benton told it to me. I would rather be the follower of an irresistible monster than its opponent. I would rather hold a mad bull by the tail than the horns." While Nap spoke, his handkerchief was gracefully waved, and the middle finger of his right hand pointed more stiffly than ever.

Jack gazed at him, recognising without difficulty the gestures and even the tones of the preacher. He was aware that Nap's mimicry was involuntary, and knew that such habits were incurable, for they had been practised by him in Kentucky. Hence he affected not to mark the ludicrous finger pointed toward him.

"But, Nap, if one calls himself a Democrat, and is yet a Whig in principle, might he not be deemed a hypocrite in politics, nay, a vile demagogue?"

"Don't let us talk politics, Jack. That was not the subject. It was Polly"——

"The Tartar?"

"I think not. She is handsome"——

"And so is a wildcat, a panther, and a skunk."

"Nonsense. She would soon become tame enough, like other married women, or I'm much mistaken. But then, truly, I am virtually pledged to Molly Brook. In the glow of enthusiasm, or rather in the zeal of admiration, when inspired by the presence of this girl, I am sometimes tempted to break my word—but not at other times. If Molly were to die, or to marry somebody else, I am sure I could not resist Polly Hopkins; but, as it is, whatever else I may be called, no one shall ever reproach me for having committed a dishonourable action. I may be impressible, indeed I am too susceptible, as you charge me; but I am honest." As Nap said this, he thrust forward his finger, and wiped his eyes with the handkerchief in the other hand.

"You are, Nap—you are!" said Jack, heartily.

"Yes, I may be a fool in a thousand other things—and no doubt I am—but I'll die an honest man!" Here Nap flourished the handkerchief again before his moistened eyes, and poked himself on the breast with his middle finger.

They rode a mile farther in silence, which brought them in front of Mr. Townly's house. The dogs came barking at them when they paused, but were quickly followed by Mr. Townly himself, who drove them away, and requested the young men to dismount. They did so, and when the negro boy took charge of their horses, they were about to follow Mr. T. into the house; but hearing him say that his wife and daughter were absent, and would not be at home for an hour, Jack requested his host to show him over his farm. Both Jack and Nap had been admiring the arrangement of the fields, the good condition of the fences, and the fine appearance of the stock; and having expressed their admiration, their host took great pleasure in giving them all the information on the subject they desired. As they strode over the premises they learned the following particulars of the preceding year's crop:—Mr. T. had sold fifteen tons of hemp, at ninety dollars per ton; five thousand pounds of bacon, at eight cents per pound; three yoke of oxen, at sixty dollars each—all equal to one thousand nine hundred and thirty dollars, besides supporting his family, numbering, with the negroes, thirty-one. There were three hundred and twenty acres—which he had purchased originally for one dollar and twenty-five cents per acre—but which was worth more than ten times as much then, for the place was highly improved, besides having a commodious brick mansion on it.

Nap was in raptures, and might easily have been persuaded to become a farmer. He thought of his host's pretty daughter Mary—but then he likewise thought of his honour.

Mrs. Townly and her daughter Mary reached home before Mr. T. had got through with showing the young men over the farm. And when Nap and Jack entered the house, they were not only greeted by the smiles of the hospitable ladies, but they beheld evidences of the good cheer which had been already provided for them.

Mr. T. was not a seeker of popularity. He wanted no office; he desired no praise from natural fools or crafty fanatics; and he belonged to no temperance society, though strictly temperate himself. He was content to work for his living, as God designed mankind to do. He scorned to solicit subscriptions to employ lazy temperance lecturers, or to lecture himself, and levy contributions from a pack of deluded simpletons. He left that mode of distinction, and of obtaining a beggarly support, to the worthless vagabonds and idle hypocrites whom he heartily despised. Therefore, no denunciations could restrain him from practising the old-fashioned hospitality of placing some spirits before his guests, "for the stomach's sake." And as the dew had fallen upon them, our brace of young gentlemen sipped moderately and temperately, to withstand the vicissitudes of the climate, and to temper their systems to the atmosphere.

Afterward they partook with the family of a sumptuous repast; and then, in the good old way of our ancestors, they ranged themselves around the blazing fire, made agreeable by one of those cool evenings which sometimes follow a sultry day in Missouri.

The chairs they sat in were likewise the comfortable old-fashioned split-bottomed ones, and the young men felt and acted as if conscious that the more they enjoyed themselves, the more they would contribute to the enjoyment of their entertainers. They joked, told amusing tales, and laughed heartily. And Mary sang several old-time love-songs for them, until Nap's sighing, and enthusiastic admiration convinced Jack that he was in danger of receiving a new impression. But yet he could not entirely divest himself of his favourite Mr. Darling's gestures. Mr. Darling was a perfect model, in Nap's eyes, of elocution and captivating manners. Hence his left hand waved the handkerchief, and his right pointed his remarks with the usual finger.

Jack grew excessively tired of seeing that finger protruded on the delivery of every sentence; but he felt that it would be indelicate to venture any remark on such a nuisance. So he determined to gaze at the offensive member every time it was thrust before the company, and endeavour to stare it out of countenance. And he succeeded. For Nap, observing that his friend's eyes were fixed upon his finger so often and so steadfastly, at length, and for the first time, looked at it himself. He perceived, with shame and confusion, that it was not only a very long, thick, and rough member to be flourished in a timid young lady's face, but that it had been blackened with powder when he charged the gun, and he had afterwards neglected to wash it. Then he sedulously strove to conceal it, after every one present had seen it a hundred times. As is sometimes found to be the case in the best regulated households, there was a smart rent in the bottom of the chair he occupied: and as the finger still would remain straightened from long habit, he determined to hide it in the fracture of the seat. So he thrust it in the hole under the skirt of his coat; and although, in the progress of an animated discussion, it would occasionally reappear and assume its accustomed attitude, he would, as soon as conscious of its offensive presence, by a spasmodic effort, hurl it down again to its place of concealment.

Upon one occasion, when the finger descended through the bottom of the chair, it was seized by one of Mary's pets—a beautiful white tomcat. Nap started slightly.

He had seen the cat playing with Mary's apron-string, and was at once convinced it was not a rattlesnake tickling him. Besides, puss was gentle, and did not pain him by a severe infliction of his claws. Hence, to avoid attracting the notice of the company to the point assailed, Nap bore the annoyance for some minutes with the stoicism of a philosopher. But in his quiet efforts to thrust or frighten Tom away by the motions of his finger, he seemed to render the animal the more violent and pertinacious in his assaults. And yet poor Nap was content to bear a few smart punctures rather than make another exhibition of his great blackened finger.

Mary, however, had observed the exercises of the cat; but she never dreamed the projecting object that puss was attacking could be a man's finger. It struck her it must be quite another thing; and that supposition made her altogether as ill at ease as Nap himself. A pig had been slaughtered on the farm that day, which was to be sent over to the camp-meeting as a neighbourly contribution to the daily feasts in the woods; and as Mary had seen one of the little negroes playing in the yard with the pig's tail, she felt convinced that it must have been brought into the house, and had somehow become wedged between the slits of the chair.

For many moments Mary strove to entice the puss away, but without success. Then embracing an opportunity, when her mother was entertaining the young men with an amusing anecdote of the early times in Missouri, she glided unobserved out of the room. She hastened into the kitchen and seized a pair of tongs from the hands of the fat cook, who was tumbling the blazing fagots about in the capacious fire-place, where every thing was kept nearly at a white heat. Thus provided, she tripped lightly back, and entered the room softly on tiptoe. None of the company observed her, as all of them had their faces turned toward the hearth.

Thus encouraged, Mary noiselessly approached Nap's

chair. Stooping gently down, she applied the heated tongs to the supposed pig's tail.

"Scat! hem!" said Nap, quivering convulsively, but still suffering his finger to remain where it was. The cat, retreating before the heated tongs, sprang from under the chair, and ran across the hearth.

"Scat!" said Mr. Townly, at the same time aiming a slight blow at Tom with his foot.

"That is Mary's pet—don't hurt him," said Mrs. T.

"I was not aware that you disliked cats, Nap," said Jack, "for we have one at the store, and I do not recollect ever seeing you drive it away."

"Oh no; I don't dislike cats; I like them very much"——

"Except in your sausages," added Mr. T., laughing.

Meantime, Mary, during this colloquy, had desisted momentarily from her attempt to remove the pig's tail, and stood, half stooping and breathless, fearing to be discovered. However, no one having seen her, and the cat having retreated from the room, she made one more effort to pull away the tail, and a more determined one than the first. Grasping the tongs with both hands, she again seized the devoted finger, which she pressed most resolutely and endeavoured with all her strength to remove. She pulled, and Nap pulled. Of course he could not bear this in silence.

"Murder!" cried he, springing up, and overturning the chair. The old gentleman and lady, as well as Jack, sprang to their feet in great alarm. The tongs fell from Mary's hands, and she fled to the kitchen. Her mother pursued her.

"What's the matter?" demanded Mr. Townly. "What was she doing with the tongs?"

"She had me by the finger—and the tongs were hot!" cried Nap, holding up the wounded member, and at the same time making a wry face.

Just then an explosion of merriment was heard in the

kitchen. Mr. T. ran thither, followed by Handy. A moment after, Nap heard them all uttering shouts of laughter, for Mary had told them the whole truth.

Mary then flew to her chamber, declaring it would be impossible for her to confront her injured victim again that night. Her mother undertook to make an explanation, and to apologize for her. But she was incompetent to the task; for when she came to the pig's tail, she was so violently convulsed with laughter, as to be unable to utter a word more. Jack then undertook it, but with no better success; while Nap looked and listened in embarrassment and pain. Mr. Townly alone could accomplish it; and he did so very gravely, and in his usual dry manner.

"It was natural—it was nothing to laugh at," said Nap. "I admire her delicacy in quietly attempting to remove what she supposed to be the tail of a pig. An apology is not at all necessary."

At the urgent solicitation of Nap, Mary was then sent for; but she declared she could not make her appearance again that night, being so excessively mortified at what had happened. Nap then begged for pen, ink, and paper, and addressed her the following note:—

"My Dear Miss Mary,

"I entreat that you will not be mortified at the unintentional mistake you committed. I appreciate your motive, in attempting to remove the supposed offensive member without disturbing me. I am only sorry that I allowed myself to be agitated, and that I was the cause of agitation in others. Had I known what was the nature of the instrument which held my finger, and that you had guided it, no such startling exclamation should have escaped my lips. I pray that you will pardon me, and believe me truly, your friend and admirer,

"N. B. Wax."

According to another ridiculous habit Nap had fallen into, or had been induced to adopt several years previously by a wag, he signed his name, as usual, about midway of the paper, instead of placing it at the right-hand side of the page.

The note was sent up by a negro girl, and was, contrary to the expectation of every one, promptly responded to. Mary, although she could not forgive herself for committing such a blunder, was willing to contribute any thing in her power to alleviate the pain of her victim. The idea of affording relief to the sufferer, having once occurred to her mind, all the shame and mortification she had experienced vanished from her breast. And so she quickly reappeared, with a bold visage, holding in one hand a linen rag, and in the other a cake of beeswax.

"Won't you melt it, while I make some lint?" she asked of her mother, placing the wax in her hand.

"Is that good for a burn, child?" asked her mother.

"I suppose so. He requested me to bring him some."

"Nap, is that what you were writing about?" asked Jack.

"No, indeed!" exclaimed Nap, in great surprise.

"I beg pardon, then; for I must have misunderstood the nota bene. I supposed it meant that you desired me to bring you some wax to apply to the wound," said Mary.

Oh, I understand it. Nap signs his name in so peculiar a manner as to make any one suppose it to be a mere postscript; and in this instance, when you were probably conjecturing what might be the proper remedy to apply to the wound, the word 'wax' very naturally suggested the idea that he desired to have a salve made of that substance."

"And it was no bad idea," said Mr. Townly, dryly; "for it is an excellent remedy, when mixed with softsoap Get some, Mary, and tie up his finger."

"And Nap, I would advise you hereafter," said Jack, "to write your name differently, so that it cannot be mistaken. Write it in full, **Napoleon Bonaparte Wax**; or if you like it better, sign yourself as the ancient **Romans** did, making an initial stand for the first **part of** the name, and write the balance in full; **for** instance, N. Bonaparte Wax. Cicero **signed himself,** M. Tullius Cicero; **Brutus,** M. Junius Brutus; Cæsar, C. Julius Cæsar. Why should not we Americans imitate the Romans?"

"**I'll tell** you why," said Nap, flourishing his handkerchief, **and** unconsciously extending his bandaged **finger.** "**But the reason is** not original with me; I had it from Colonel Benton. He says it has become a preposterous habit with silly parents to bestow upon their coxcombs in politics, and shallow **fops** in literature, the names **of great** men, as if a mere appellation **could** be a substitute **for brains.** He says he has been flea-bitten a hundred times **by the assaults of** Washington, Clay, Jackson, Madison, and Hamilton; or rather by Mr. G. Washington Snooks, Mr. H. Clay Pippin, Mr. A. Jackson Squib, Mr. J. Madison **Pumpkin,** and Mr. A. Hamilton Squash—scribblers for the papers, or frothy declaimers from the stump. And he says that during **his** long **experience,** all **such insects,** sporting those grandiloquent names, have been too contemptible in his eyes to merit annihilation. He deemed it punishment sufficient for them to be doomed to bear, during their lives, such aggravating sponsorial curses. From that moment I determined to sign myself simply N. B. Wax. I will never be indebted to another man's name for any distinction **I may win."**

"**And** any man **may win** distinction," said Jack, "**by** perseverance. Water wears away the rock that obstructs its course: so man may mould **his own** fortune into any shape he shall **resolve upon, provided** he is not diverted from the path that leads to the object he desires to attain. Wax may be made to assume as imposing a shape as even that of Bonaparte."

"That **is true,**" said Mr. T., with a serious visage, "for I have seen **it.** There **was a** show of wax figures in this county last year, and they had Napoleon, Josephine, Wellington, &c., as large as life, and twice as natural, as they told me."

Fortunately for Nap, he did not hear this. His head had gradually declined against the mantel-piece, and a gurgling sound issued from his nose, which Jack knew to be the prelude to something more startling. He therefore aroused him by a smart slap on the shoulder, and begged permission of his host for them to retire, alleging the fatigues of the day, and the exhausting laughter of the night, as an excuse for making the request at such an early hour. The petition was granted; and Jack then intimated to Mrs. T., in a whisper, that as his friend habitually snored very loudly, she would do well to send her guests to a room as remote as possible from the part of the house occupied by the family.

She did so; and acting upon Jack's suggestion, with some care for his own comfort, she had the young men placed in different rooms. The chamber Nap occupied was a spacious one, and was usually slept in by four or five children, who, on the present occasion, had been required to relinquish it for the benefit of the guest. But one of the boys, who had visited a menagerie which had been recently exhibited in the vicinity, having garnished the wall with one of the large show-bills, the eyes of Nap rested upon it on entering the room, and for a long time he was strangely rendered incapable of finding his accustomed rest. He read every word; he gazed at every figure, and he wondered how it happened that he had never witnessed such an exhibition. He could distinctly remember half a dozen of such shows being exhibited in the neighbourhood of his abode, and yet he had never beheld any of them. He had never seen an elephant, lion, zebra, or monkey, in all his life. It was truly remarkable. He then ran over the obstacles which had prevented him from being present on such momentous occasions to boys and curious young men. They had been the result of accident in every instance, which no foresight or precaution on his part could have prevented. On one occasion a little cousin had been taken suddenly ill, and he was sent several miles over the country in pursuit of a doctor; on another, his father died; on a third, he was ill himself; and on the recent one, which he had resolved to avail himself of, his horse, that was usually suffered to browse at liberty near the store, being frightened by the whistle of a steamboat, took to his heels and ran away. When he succeeded in capturing him, it was too late to ride such a distance with any hope of seeing the exhibition that day—and that day was the last of it.

Nap dwelt on these things, and for a long time found it impossible to sleep. He concluded there must be something significant and mysterious in such a series of accidents, tending to the same result, and his mind was troubled. But by slow degrees slumber overpowered him; though not till he had paced the room a great many times in much perturbation; nor until he had cooled his throbbing temples near an open window, before which a fine forest-tree had been tastefully permitted to stand.

No one heard him snore that night, though doubtless he snored as loudly as usual when he sank to repose. It was late when he awoke the next morning. The sun was shining brightly through the window, the sash of which had remained up all night. Perhaps it was the violent motion of a branch of the tree near the window, and a scratching sound at the casement which had awakened him. And upon gazing steadfastly in that direction, he beheld a large monkey that had escaped from the itinerant showman. It was dressed in scarlet, and wore a three-cornered hat, which, though fastened to his neck by a string, he could remove at pleasure. Thus, when Nap stared at it, it lifted the hat, as it had been trained to do, and after bowing very low, replaced it on its head.

"Well, my little nigger," said Nap, smiling, "that's

polite. And that's a pretty dress they have furnished you with, just to wait upon me. What's your name?"

The monkey uttered a chattering sound, and jumped up smartly once or twice.

"I don't understand such gibberish. Perhaps you're a Guinea negro, and don't understand our language. Well, pour me out some water, and then black my boots."

The animal looked him saucily in the face and winked his eyes repeatedly; but did not evince any inclination to obey the command.

"Why don't you do what I tell you, Sambo? What did you come here for, if not to wait on me, you rascal. Didn't your mistress send you to do something?"

Nap uttered these words somewhat angrily, as he rose from the bed and proceeded to put on his clothes. But the change in his tone only had the effect to make the monkey leap about more violently than before, and to grin and snap his teeth.

"Why, what sort of a negro is that?" exclaimed Nap, pausing in the act of pulling on his breeches. "I never saw such teeth in a negro's head before. He must be a raw Guinea negro. See here, my chap, if you behave in that manner, I'll slap your jaws. Don't give me any of your impudence!"

The monkey only responded by several loud stamps on the floor, and other menacing gestures and grimaces. It then walked to the washstand and poured some water into the basin.

"I'm glad you can understand me, you little rascal, though I can't make out the meaning of your squeaking jargon. Hello! What're you doing there, you infernal African?" Nap uttered this upon seeing the monkey lift up the basin and drink heartily of its contents. "Put it down, you nasty, dirty imp!" he continued.

Jacko, however, instead of obeying the mandate, danced toward Nap with the basin in his hands, and when within couple of paces of him, dashed the water in his face.

"You black devil, you! You, you impudent scoundrel! I'll **beat** you half to death for this!" cried the enraged Nap, running **around** the room in pursuit of Jacko, who eluded him with ease. Sometimes he dodged between his **legs, and** at others he sprang over his head. **At** last the monkey retreated to a corner and seemed to bid defiance **to** his pursuer. As Nap approached, Jacko indicated by a display of his teeth what would be the consequence if assaulted in that position.

"You don't mean to **say** you'll **bite me, do you?**" asked Nap, advancing. "If you do, I'll knock **you down** with my fist, and it's a heavy one!" Saying this, Nap attempted to throttle Jacko **with his** left hand, which was immediately seized by the animal's formidable array of white teeth. True to his threat, Nap doubled **up** his fist, and at one blow knocked **the** monkey some fifteen feet from the corner where he was standing. He fell heavily on the floor, and after a convulsive quiver, and a spasmodic motion of the limbs, remained perfectly still, for his neck had been dislocated.

Nap looked at him in alarm. He turned him over with his foot, and perceived that he was dead.

"Good gracious!" said he, trembling. "**I** believe I've killed the infernal negro. What did the fool bite me for, when I told him I would knock him down if he did so? What will they do with me? Goodness! I'm afraid they'll hang me—at least try me for murder." And for several moments **he** quivered violently, being desperately alarmed

Then hastily completing his toilet, he descended in silence to **the** breakfast-room. His troubled visage soon attracted the notice of Jack.

"I hope, Nap," said his friend, "since it was out of your power to disturb any one else last night, that your snoring did not interfere with your own slumber. Yet you do not look refreshed."

"I trust the little occurrence with the tongs, for which

I am to be blamed, did not deprive you of your rest," said Mary.

"Oh no," said Nap, laconically.

"Then why don't you eat?" asked **Mr.** Townly, **who** observed that he scarcely tasted any thing.

"Every thing is very good—only, somehow, I have no appetite this morning."

"No *occasion*, he meant to say. You'll see what an immense quantity **he'll** eat before he rises!" observed Jack.

"Perhaps he **had bad** dreams, or has seen a ghost," remarked Mary. "I hope he don't suffer much pain from the wound I gave him."

"Oh, not at all; it's quite well, I thank you. But as to dreams and ghosts, I can assure you I've seen an awful sight this morning!"

"What was it? Pray tell us!" exclaimed Mary.

"Why, Nap, you *do* look excited, just as you did after our moonlight hunt. But what's that?" continued Handy, seeing the wounds made by the monkey's teeth on his friend's hand. "That was not done by the cat or the tongs. It was the finger of your right hand which suffered last night."

"I know it. **And the** sight I saw this morning, you may be assured, was no fanciful vision; for the thing I beheld bit my hand."

"What was it?" asked Mrs. Townly.

"A negro."

"**A negro!** Impossible. Not one of them durst go into your room without being summoned thither," said the hostess.

'But I assure you one did come in, and a very impudent rascal he was, **too.** And yet when I came out of my room, I confess the door was bolted on the inside, just as I had left it before lying down."

"**Then** it was a dream, sure enough," said Mr. Townly.

"Then these prints of his teeth are nothing but imaginary punctures."

"But, Nap," said Jack, "you don't mean to say a negro boy bit your hand with his teeth?"

"He didn't do it with his nose. You see I've been bitten. Well; I say a negro boy did it in my chamber since I awoke this morning."

Mr. Townly laid down his knife and fork, and leaning back in his chair, gazed steadily at his guest, as if in doubt of his sanity.

"What else did he?" asked Jack.

"Why, when I told him to pour me out some water, he dashed a basinful in my face. You see my shirt is wet. This is no mere fancy."

Mary covered her face with her handkerchief, declaring that her coffee had scalded her.

"Then what did *you* do?" continued Jack.

"I'm afraid I did wrong—I knocked him down."

"No, sir, you did right—if a negro of mine had the impudence to throw water in your face."

"I might as well tell all, Mr. Townly, for it must be found out. He did not get up again! Oh, sir, will you forgive me? Do you think they'll try me for murder?"

"Did you kill him?"

"As dead as a door-nail. He never kicked, though I struck him only once, and that was when he bit me."

"You say the door was bolted?"

"Yes, sir; and I saw him get in at the window."

"How was he dressed?"

"In a red coat, and a sharp-cornered outlandish hat."

"They won't hang you, I'll answer for it. Eat your breakfast as quickly as possible, for I must laugh soon, or burst."

"You are sure I won't be tried?"

"Quite certain. I'll stand in your shoes for a sixpence."

"Thank you!" said Nap, at length beginning to eat

heartily. "I forgot to tell you," he continued, between the enormous quantities of savoury food he conveyed to his mouth, "that there was a remarkable feature about the negro which I never before saw on any human being."

"What was it?" asked Mary, quickly.

"A long tail. I didn't discover it until after I had knocked him down."

"Jacko! It's the lost Jacko, they were hunting the other day," said Mr. T., now giving vent to a hearty peal of laughter.

"Jacko? Was that his name?" asked Nap. "I called him Sambo; but he didn't answer me."

"Is Jacko up-stairs?" asked Mary, rising. "Run, Peyton! don't let him get away. Get the ladder and close the window."

"Don't be uneasy," said Nap, in the midst of his tremendous repast. "You need not fear he will escape. Put yourself to no inconvenience. If ever he runs away from his master again, I'll agree to eat him."

"They do eat them in South America," said Mr. T., "and they say their meat is very palatable."

"What, negro meat?" exclaimed Nap, dropping his knife and fork. "I'm done with the pig's ribs for to-day. Eat negro meat?"

"No, I didn't say so. I said monkey's meat."

"Monkey's meat? Mon—I never saw one in my life. Mon—I'll be durned"——

"Why, Nap," said Jack, with difficulty maintaining a grave face, for he now fully comprehended what had happened, "do you know what you are saying? Are you aware there are ladies present?"

"Pardon me, ladies; but—durn me if—if—blast me if I don't believe if it was a monkey I killed! Mr. Townly, did you ever know a negro to have a tail?"

"No, I never did. But that don't prove they never have them. There's a Yankee lady gone over to England, who knows more about such things than we planters in the

South. If she tells the duchesses and countesses they have tails, the wise people of the old world will believe her; and then I'd advise you never to go very far North to buy your goods, for they might snap you up and hang you. At all events, they'll have you in the papers, and call you a monster and a murderer. And that will not be all; they'll anathematize the entire white population of the South."

"What, because I killed a monkey?"

"They'll magnify him into an oppressed, persecuted individual, and subscribe money for the benefit of his kindred, friends, and defenders."

"Jack!" said Nap, rising abruptly, "do you know a monkey when you see him?"

"Oh yes."

"Then come with me up-stairs."

"Lead on; I'll follow. Perhaps he's not dead after all."

"Then I'm no judge of death, when a body's cold and stiff."

When they entered the room, followed by the family, they found poor Jacko just where Nap had left him, and quite dead. Nap, when assured beyond the possibility of a doubt that his victim was truly a monkey, was quite as merry as the rest. But he begged them not to tell what he had done; at least never to divulge his error in supposing it to be a negro. They promised to keep the secret —and performed it faithfully.

CHAPTER VI.

The Camp-meeting.

It being Sunday, Mr. and Mrs. Townly and Mary accompanied Nap and Jack to the camp-meeting. When they arrived in the vicinity, the horn, as they called a tin trumpet, was sounded for the people to assemble within the area of the hollow square formed by the temporary huts. Upon the ground where the pulpit, the altar, and the benches were placed, there grew a number of fine forest-trees, whose foliage, still green, served to shelter the host of worshippers from the heat of the sun, or from the damp of a passing shower. On one side, the ground was bounded by a sparkling brook, which came from a delicious spring of refreshing water in the immediate vicinity; on the other was a pleasant grove, beyond which the high undulating prairie was perceptible.

The horses of our party being tied securely to the bushes, they proceeded toward the stand whither the great mass of the people were collecting, and secured seats on a rough bench in front of the pulpit.

In the pulpit were several venerable preachers, who had been engaged for many years in the great work of conducting repentant sinners to the fold of Him to whose service their lives were honestly devoted. Beside them were the middle-aged and the more youthful labourers in the field. Among the latter, Nap had the satisfaction to recognise his especial favourite, the reverend Mr. Darling. But if he expected to witness any of his rhetorical flourishes, or to hear any of his thrilling appeals to the passions of the people during that day, he was doomed to be disappointed.

The most grave and venerable minister present arose and began the morning exercises. He was tall, pale, deliberate, and dignified. His white hair was combed smoothly back, and contrasted strongly with his black coat, having, as usual, its sharp, short collar. He made no effort to sweep away the hearts of his hearers by a hurricane of impassioned declamation. On the contrary, his text was announced in an orthodox manner, and faithfully adhered to throughout. He did not even recite an anecdote to excite a smile, or relate some thrilling semi-supernatural occurrence to startle the minds of his auditors with visions of agonizing horrors. But he laboured to convince the understanding and to subdue the heart, by the manifest truthfulness of his demonstrations, and the undeniable policy of always discharging one's duty to God and man.

Nap frequently remarked that it was an excessively dull meeting; and expressed a wish that they would come to the exciting part of the entertainment. But he was informed that the scene he desired to witness would not be exhibited before night; and so he embraced an opportunity to escape from his company, for the purpose of exploring the tents, and visiting the booths in the remote parts of the grove, where some extra refreshments might be had for the money.

Jack remained and listened. He listened to the sound of the aged preacher's voice, but did not always mark his words. He had heard him in Kentucky, in infancy, in boyhood, and now in manhood; and reminiscences of the past crowded upon his memory. The few straggling rays of sunlight that streamed upon the altar before him, and the shadowy outlines of the quivering leaves that flitted fairy-like at his feet, seemed by their magic influence to transport him back to the days of his early boyhood, when sitting beside his father he had witnessed a similar spectacle, and heard the identical voice then sounding in his ears. And now his father reposed among the dead, having departed exulting in the truth of the doctrine expounded by the venerable speaker before him.

A deep and lasting impression was made upon his heart, if not upon his understanding, and he had a strong inclination to enlist in the great army of the zealous followers of Christ. Although the venerable preacher did not aim to become impassioned, yet he had succeeded, from the associations he had produced in the memory of Jack, in rousing his feelings almost to a state of enthusiasm. Every now and then a tear would steal silently down the young man's cheek, and an electric thrill would shoot with the velocity of lightning through his breast. But he remained still and silent like the rest. What he had heard was only the distant, heavy artillery, which precedes the fury of the conflict. And he was yet to witness the contest with the hosts of the evil one, at close quarters, and in the whirlwind of frenzy. The victory might be on the side of the devoutly inclined ministers and the truly pious soldiers of the cross ; but the triumph, perhaps, was not to be without its sacrifices, wherein certain victims were to fall, and to become the trophies of the evil one.

During the day there were four argumentative sermons preached, each a little more impassioned than the last. This was in strict accordance with the consummate skill of the generals, and sanctioned by the commander-in-chief, Mr. Green, the presiding elder. As the day drew near its close the work became warmer and the scene more exciting. The presiding elder himself opened his effective battery upon the obdurate portion of the congregation, in point-blank range of him ; and although he was naturally dry in his remarks, and ordinarily unpoetical in his ideas, yet on the present occasion, as the critical moment had arrived for the commencement of a grand demonstration, he made extraordinary exertions to emit the spark which was to ignite every heart, and finally wrap them all in flames of holy fervour. For this purpose he displayed unusual animation. His gestures became nervous, his sentences terse, and his tones emphatic ; and at the conclusion of every paragraph there were shrill "Amens!" responded by the zealous brethren.

At the conclusion of the sermon there was an invitation given to the religiously inclined auditors to go within the altar and be prayed for. They were invoked to come forward during the singing of a hymn, and to kneel down before a bench placed in front of the pulpit for the purpose.

The sober countenance of young Handy had been observed by many. Brothers Steele, and Nave, and Black had watched his serious aspect with the solicitude with which it might be supposed they would regard the phases of the physiognomy of an anticipated convert of surpassing influence. And Nap, from sympathy and example, likewise became spiritually endued, and was quite ready to accompany his comrade into the fold. Hence, when the pressing invitation was given, several of the lay brethren, and as many sisters, all customers at Tyre, contrived to be as near as possible to the young men, so that they might encourage them with words of entreaty, and stimulate them by the happiness expressed in their own countenances, to press forward into the holy place.

But it so happened that the arch enemy likewise had one of his emissaries posted in the vicinity. This was the notorious Tom Hazel, an incorrigible sinner, and pertinacious scoffer of the pious portion of the community. And when several females and one or two of the other sex arose and boldly advanced toward the "anxious seat," as he termed it, he exclaimed in an undertone, but which was heard, as it was designed to be, by both of our young gentlemen—

"Now, they're coming to the rich licks! Jewhittikin! there goes a drove of 'em! There's Sally Weighton, old Mrs. Fennel, Tom Turner, Araminta Fall—all stoolpigeons, every one of 'em! Every year they're the first to go up. They do it just to lead on the green ones. Strangers think they're new ones, that's just been convicted; but they've been convicted a dozen times, to my sartain knowledge. **I'll swear to it! Catch** who? You can't come it **over me,** with that sort of bait! I've seen 'em down in the straw twenty times!"

Nap and Jack were deaf to these detractions, or rather loathed such irreverent expressions in such a sacred place. Brothers Nave, Black, Green, and Steele, besought them to go within the altar, and see if it would not result in their salvation. If it failed, no harm could ensue; if it succeeded, they would for ever bless the hour in which their friends prevailed on them to take a step fraught with so many happy consequences. Thus they urged them in tones of the utmost kindness, and with tears in their beseeching eyes.

Jack's feelings were deeply stirred, and he could see no impropriety in going within the enclosure to be prayed for; and Nap, becoming more and more excited as he beheld the animated face of Miss Sally Weighton, thought that he too was not, perhaps, past praying for. So the young men arose and followed the line proceeding toward the altar. Now, Jack and Nap were known by nearly every one present; and as the merchants are generally supposed to be rich, of course much importance is attached to their actions, and the influence they wield is considerable. Hence, when our brace of excited young men repaired to the altar, old Mrs. Fennel, the little old shouting woman in a black hat, clapped her hands violently together and shouted "Glory!" Then the penitents prostrated themselves **at the bench** within the charmed circle. The singers enunciated **the words of** the hymn they were singing **more energetically,** and several of the preachers, thanking **their** Maker parenthetically between the pauses **of the song, descended from their elevated** stand and mingled with the "seekers," **as well as among** the congregation at large, **shaking hands alike with saint and** sinner, old and young, **male and female, black and white.**

At the conclusion of the **hymn,** a solemnly exciting

prayer was uttered by the presiding elder, which was responded to throughout, and at the conclusion, by hundreds of emphatic "Amens!"

At length the hour for refreshment arrived. Supper had been prepared at each of the fifty tents or huts that surrounded the place of worship, and our fascinated young men were literally overwhelmed with pressing invitations to partake of the most savoury viands and the rarest delicacies which the country afforded. It had been arranged for them to return with the Townlys and spend another evening with them; and the Townlys were now mounted on their horses, and impatiently awaiting them. But the many religious friends of the young men would not allow the arrangement to be carried into execution; and Mary, seemed to be somewhat chagrined when Jack expressed a disposition to stay. Mr. T. warned him not to be snared and made a fool of by the drunken hypocrites—drunken with frenzy—as he expressed it. And so the T.'s rode away, leaving their susceptible young guests to their fate.

Nap followed Sally Weighton to her father's tent, while Polly Hopkins, at a distance, looked daggers and made mouths at him. Jack was swept with the tide into another tent, where he was surrounded by the women and preachers. Tom Hazel and Jackson Farnes, the latter with a bottle of brandy in his pocket, mounted unperceived up in one of the huge oaks which overshadowed the pulpit and altar, where they regaled themselves and plotted mischief.

CHAPTER VII.

The dark tents, and mistakes of the night—Nap and Jack squeeze hands—Polly Hopkins appears—She lectures Nap on the subject of excitements—Sal Weighton—Nap and Jack not "through"—Spiritual manifestations.

TWILIGHT was deepening over the scene. The repast was ended, and yet no candles were lighted within the tents, for the floors of all of them were thickly covered with straw, and if lights had been used, there would have been great danger of an accidental ignition. Besides, the costumes of the ladies were to be frequently readjusted, and if lights had been taken into the small sleeping apartments allotted for that purpose, the irreverent glances of the curious gazers without would not have failed to wander through the innumerable interstices of the frail structures. As it was, many mistakes were unavoidably made. Pious brethren, and even occasionally an inspired preacher, might be seen retreating hastily from those private apartments, having inadvertently turned to the left when they should have gone to the right. A word of pious explanation and apology sufficed to reassure the startled dames. But into others of these sleeping huts companies of young ladies and gentlemen were ushered for the purpose of preliminary exercises. They groped their way to the rude benches placed for the purpose, and sat indiscriminately together, attuning their voices in sweet accord preparatory for the duties of the evening. As there were no lights, of course their books were not opened; but in the far West the girls and boys commit to memory all the hymns they sing in public.

Into one of these felicitous circles Nap and Jack were ushered, and each found himself under the necessity of squeezing down upon a seat in a very narrow space between two young girls, who seemed to strive desperately to make room for them. Who they were, our young gentlemen had no means at first of ascertaining, for it was as dark as Erebus, and as hot as—there was any necessity for. But soon the one that separated the boys, she being immediately on Nap's left and on Jack's right, was recognised by her voice. It was Sally Weighton, and she sang like a nightingale. As Nap was likewise a famous singer, she had determined to have him at her side; and as Jack seemed to be moved with spiritual influences, she deemed it requisite to have him near at hand also, that he might receive the full effect of their holy symphony. Hence she contrived to be between them. In the rear, on a parallel bench, for benches were placed across the contracted floor within a foot of each other, at the suggestion of the presiding elder, who intimated that the greater the number of persons present, the greater would be the safety, sat the famous Polly Hopkins, in demure silence, and preserving for some unfathomed purpose a strict incognito. And in front, but with his back to our party, for they sat with their faces the same way, was Mr. Darling, Nap's precious model preacher.

As the exercises progressed, if the devil had unvailed the party, and with flaming torches had exposed the thoughts and attitudes of the black sheep which had found admission into that little fold, no doubt every pious minister witnessing the spectacle would have betaken himself to his legs and abandoned the field. Black sheep are found in every flock, and more than one was present on that occasion. In the house of prayer, in the pulpit, at the altar—wherever the pious may assemble—the devil is sure to be among them. And it seems that at such places his most strenuous and desperate efforts are made to resist the influences of his Master. If he meets with no success at that point, the crisis is over, and the soldier of the cross may exult in his hard-earned victory. But the experience of thousands will attest that the great

Deluder does not **always fail to** snatch **his** subjects from the very brink of salvation.

A ray of light, ignited **at** the pulpit where the people were assembling, gleamed through a crevice of the hut, **and** revealed momentarily to the astonished eyes **of** Nap, a picture which really astonished him, and filled his **perturbed** breast with additional emotions. Mr. Darling, who **sat** immediately in front of him, either had his arm around the waist of Mrs. Dickson, or else Nap's eyes deceived him. Mrs. Dickson was a handsome sister **in the** church, that had not pleased her husband, who was in the bond of iniquity, by going some fifteen or twenty miles from home to live a week in the woods among strangers. Nap rubbed his eyes; but when he sought to reassure himself, some interposing object had vailed the scene. But he could distinctly hear some one behind him give vent to a **low** mocking utterance.

It is a habit at camp-meetings, and in other **religious** assemblies, for the brethren, when they become sufficiently excited, to indulge extensively in the shaking of hands. The preachers themselves set the example—and doubtless it might be a very innocent example, if its indulgence could only be kept within the bounds of moderation. But to see one of the masculine gender grasp a fair plump hand **between** both of his, and rub it, and squeeze it, long retaining it without resistance, and only relinquishing it for **another** with mutual reluctance—if it be an evidence **of brotherly love and sisterly** affection, furnishes **at** the **same time,** without doubt, an opportunity for the devil, who is always at one's elbow, to insinuate **a modicum of his** infernal heat **into the** throbbing **veins of the unsuspecting** parties.

Such an example was extensively followed in the dark **tent** occupied by our young enthusiasts. Jack somehow, **for** he was unconscious of the manner **of it,** found Miss Sally's **hand** within his. **But we do assert that** it was only a holy zeal that inspired him. He was incapable, as yet, **of being** actuated by any other motive than that of a strictly religious character in such a place and on such an occasion. It may have been the same with Sally; but she being of the weaker sex, we will not venture a positive assertion. But certainly gentle pressures were given and returned, and no offence was taken. And Nap's hand had wandered in the same direction. It was dark, and hymn succeeded hymn with an unceasing fervency; and the pervading enthusiasm had wellnigh reached a climax, when Elder Green's voice was heard at the doorway, as he pulled aside the counterpane, saying, "Come, brothers and sisters, sons and daughters, let us repair to the stand. The candles are lighted, and they are about to sound the horn. Evil spirits may come amongst you in this darkness."

Instantly all within arose to their feet, but both Nap and Jack had their hands grasped more closely than ever, and each of them felt that it would be uncharitable, if not rudeness itself, to be the first to extricate his member. It was only a pledge of Christian brotherhood and sisterhood in the estimation of those present; and so they would feel no particle of shame on being discovered in that attitude. But when some anxious mothers entered the hut with lights in their hands, our young gentlemen made a discovery which surprised them exceedingly, and it was fortunate that the eyes of only one besides themselves perceived the extent and source of their mortification. Instead of each of them having a hand of Sally, it appeared that she had extricated hers from both of them, and that the boys were now actually grasping the hands of each other! It is needless to say that they instantly detached themselves.

Jack led the way out to the stand, with Sally undisguisedly holding him by the arm, while Nap instinctively followed, with his elbow protruded on the other side. It was seized by Polly Hopkins!

"See here, Nap," said she, "I don't like this business. You are getting upon a spree, and there is no telling what may come of it."

"A spree, Polly?"

"Yes; you are getting intoxicated, and you may commit some dreadful crime before you are aware of it."

"What crime can I commit?"

"Oh, *I* can't tell; but Satan might."

"Satan! Why he has no business here. It is altogether a religious excitement. I am excited, I admit—but it is with religion."

"And it might just as well be with wine, or politics, or anger, or love. I have been reading an essay on excitement. When one is excited to a certain extent, he is insane, and not conscious of what he is doing. When excited with wine, one is ready for any violent action; with politics, he will foolishly hazard his fortune on the success of his candidate; with anger, he will stab his best friend; with love, he would destroy an angel; and with religion, the writer says, he may commit every thing I have enumerated. He declares it was undue religious excitement that the devil made use of to strew the plains of the Holy Land with human bones; to arm nation against nation, and disgrace Christendom with innumerable outrages and crimes. It was this which plunged thousands within the flames at the stake. This it is which sows dissension between man and wife; the one making use of his power to punish, and the other taking refuge in the arms of a more congenial protector. It is this which is founding, on a gigantic scale, on the banks of the Great Salt Lake in the wilderness, a community of beastly bigamists. Nap, take a wild but guileless girl's advice, and turn your back on this pack of pious inebriates and over-righteous fools."

"I can't do it, Polly. It's pleasant. It may be as you say; but so far I have had no evil thoughts, and have been in no danger."

"Then how came your hand to be interlocked with"—here she was overcome by laughter, and her utterance failed.

"Oh, ay!—interlocked with Jack's. It was Jack's hand."

"It was not always Jack's hand. I saw you have Sally's. How was that?"

"Upon my soul, I don't know."

"I believe you."

"I don't know how it happened. But I had no evil thoughts—I am sure of that."

"No doubt. I will not deny it. In the moment of excitement, or in the glow of religious enthusiasm, and without being aware of it, you pressed the hand of the tempting girl at your side. And the reverend Mr. Darling encircled the body at his side. Neither of you had any evil thoughts. I am willing to admit it. It was the inspiration of the moment. And so an irremediable crime might be committed, and what would it avail afterward to say you had no evil thoughts?"

"Oh, there's no danger."

"Then go on."

"I will. That is, I'll follow Jack. I know he meditates nothing evil."

"No; he does not. But I'll wager more than I'll mention, that this religious drunkenness will cause you both to commit extravagant absurdities, which you will be sorry for, and which will bring many a tinge of shame to your cheeks in after life, whenever you shall chance to recall them to memory."

Nap had lingered outside of the limits of the ground whereon the people were reassembling during this dialogue, and when the first hymn was sung, the prelude to the services of the night, he moved forward and joined young Handy, who sat within the small enclosure in front of the stand, or pulpit. Polly declined accompanying him up to the altar, alleging as a reason that she was not yet prepared for the sacrifice, and that she had not faith in the authenticity of the calling of Mr. Darling and one or two other young ministers then present. But she said she would be an auditor of the performances.

After the hymn and a prayer, Nap's great model, Mr. Darling himself, arose to preach. He commenced in a key of such altitude that in a very brief space of time he was soaring above the clouds among the cherubim. Amens! Glorys! and Hallelujahs! were responded at every pause by the sympathetic crowd beneath, and by none more vociferously than Sister Dickson, who occupied a seat immediately in front of the seemingly inspired speaker. The growing enthusiasm manifested on all sides, and which was without doubt sincerely felt by hundreds of truly pious and happy mortals, was shared by the aged preachers on the stand, who smiled an approbation of the effective discourse their talented young coadjutor was delivering. Devoid of guile themselves, they could not suppose that beneath the manifestation of so much Christian zeal and pious eloquence in the speaker, there could possibly be concealed a stratum of worldly wickedness.

So great was the effect of Mr. Darling's sermon, that at its conclusion, many hands were clapping in irrepressible holy exultation, and many voices were shouting unrestrained hosannahs to the Lord. With some this was the natural and unavoidable consequence of inordinate and ungovernable excitement; with others it was the force of habit and example; but doubtless there were many who indulged in such excesses in the absence of an involuntary impulse, and with motives of questionable propriety. Nevertheless, such a scene was calculated to have a powerful influence on the younger portion of the vast congregation; and if the invitation to approach the altar had even then been given, many a startled sinner would have flown thither for refuge. But the critical moment had not yet arrived. The mere warmth which animated the breasts of the multitude was to be fanned into a glowing flame, pervading and irresistible.

Exhorters, mostly youthful and inordinately zealous,

were now pushed forward, until the common ejaculations usually responded to eloquent speakers were changed to boisterous exclamations and spasmodic groans. Tearful eyes fixed in adoration upon the heavenly vault above; seraphic smiles beaming from wrinkled faces, and endearing epithets mumbled from toothless gums; these, together with uplifted hands, and robust forms writhing in uncouth contortions, exclusive of the howling pandemonium encompassing them **on every** side, were quite sufficient to strike terror into the most obdurate hearts, and to induce especially the youthful auditors, not gifted with an extraordinary degree of courage, to flee to any asserted ark of safety that might be pointed out to them. And a hundred hands pointed to the enclosure around the altar.

When the speakers ceased their violent exercises **on the** stand, most of them descended to the altar, where, as had **been** anticipated, a great number of the seriously affected **pushed** forward to be saved. They were prayed for in strains of extravagant ebullition, which Polly **Hopkins** subsequently declared were enough to deafen the ears, and utterly disgust the one to whom the petitions were addressed. Be that as it may, a great number of the seekers of religion soon professed to have found it, and cried, and wept, and laughed, and shouted as well as the rest. These were pronounced "through," and **were** directed to disperse themselves among the hardened **outsiders**, to **assure them of the** marvellous effects of their precious conversion.

But neither Nap nor Jack were fortunate enough **to get** "through" so expeditiously. They were conscious **of the** weight of sin which burdened them. To confess that was an indispensable preliminary. But then all the **prayers** that had hitherto been uttered in their especial **behalf** did not seem to produce the miraculous change of feeling which others professed to experience, and which was declared to be requisite before a thorough conversion could be accomplished. If **Jack had** confessed **that** he felt a change within him, no doubt Nap would have done the same thing, for he could easily have imagined, if not felt, whatever sensation his friend might have experienced. For he was in such a whirl of excitement, that he was capable of fancying any thing, and doing any thing. But Jack would not utter a falsehood, notwithstanding the unremitting ministrations of Miss Sally Weighton, who repeatedly implored him to strive his utmost to obtain salvation.

When a temporary cessation of prayers occurred from the exhaustion of ideas, words, and voices, singing by the congregation was resorted to; and in that portion of the exercises, Nap could always perform a conspicuous part; for, as has been already intimated, he had a tremendous voice. So he arose, after a protracted effort to get "through," on his knees, and his voice was soon heard above all others, particularly in the chorus, which contained the joyful exclamation of "Oh, salvation!" But Nap, perhaps, from thinking of another species of felicity, invariably made a long pause after the *Sal*—and then pronounced the remainder very much like— *Weighton*.

It was while singing this hymn, and when moving about in the midst of the crowd, that Nap felt some one pluck him by the sleeve. On turning aside he beheld Polly.

"I forbid you calling upon her name!" said she.

"Calling upon whose name?" demanded Nap.

"Sally Weighton's."

"I haven't been calling her."

"You have. You thought, perhaps, it was 'salvation,' but it was Sal—Weighton. You needn't think she can save you; burnt brandy wouldn't do it, if you stay here among these noisy fools. You have no idea how ridiculous you appear. Just step with me, and I'll show you the other side of the picture." Saying this, she led him around to the rear of the preacher's stand, where the discordant voices and spasmodic motions of a motly crew attracted his attention. It seemed that a score of egroes of both sexes, not being admitted to seats in front, had congregated at this place for the purpose of getting or enjoying religion among themselves. One or two white exhorters had joined them, and even some white women, originally from Massachusetts, of the fanatical school, had thrown themselves among them, and contributed to the extravagance of the scene. Some were rocking to and fro, incessantly shouting "Glory!" Others clapped together their hands, and merely laughed vociferously. Some prayed, and some improvised a sort of jargon about rapping-spirits, hoe-cakes, and cracking corn, to which others appended an irregular and inapplicable chorus. Thus the medley of sounds was kept up, until a big fellow, as black as Satan himself, could no longer restrain his pent-up feelings, and he gave vent to them by divesting himself of his coat, and springing in the midst of his converted brothers and sisters, where he danced violently, alternately slapping his hands together and patting his thighs in unison with the motions of his feet. He had not long been exercising himself in this manner before the contagion of his example spread among the sweltering women, and several of them joined him in the dance.

At this point Nap turned away in disgust.

"How do you like it?" asked Polly.

"It's the ugliest sight I ever beheld!" said Nap.

"There are worse scenes than that enacting on the ground, if one could behold them. Why not, then, turn your back on the whole concern?"

Before Nap had time to reply—and there is no telling whither the mischievous girl might have conducted him—Jack confronted him, with Miss Sally Weighton still attending at his side.

"Oh, Mr. Wax!" said Miss Sally, "they are hunting for you everywhere. Do not abandon the altar until you are renewed. And you, Polly Hopkins, if you will only go in with him, I will get down on my knees and pray for your conversion."

"I thank you! But wouldn't you like to be prayed for yourself? And wouldn't you prefer to have a handsome young man perform that office?"

"Oh, for shame!"

"No such thing! And depend on it, your calling and election cannot be sure until you have such a one to pray for you."

"Monstrous! You judge others by yourself! You outrageous"——

There is no telling what might have been the issue of the rising anger of the two young ladies, had they not been interrupted in their charitable intentions by the appearance of the reverend Mr. Darling.

"One more effort, brothers!" cried he. "Go in once more, and resolve not to rise from your knees until your desire be accomplished. Perseverance will succeed, take my word for it."

"I suppose you speak from experience," said Polly.

"Ah, Polly!" said Mr. Darling, endeavouring to take her hand, which she prevented, "every one has heard of the wild and reckless spirit within thee. How gladly would I wear out my knees in wearying heaven"——

"Stop, now! Don't weary me; and if you should ever kneel for me, don't do it in my presence, nor let me know any thing about it. When I want any of your kneeling for me, or to me, I'll let you know it."

"Come!" said the preacher, placing his hand, in which was his soiled white handkerchief, familiarly on Nap's shoulder, and turning away from the contracted brow of Polly, which could just be distinguished by the dim red glare of the candles and torches.

"Jack, have you got through?" asked Nap, turning in hesitation to his young friend.

"No. I can't say that my feelings have improved any since sundown. But I will freely go with you. They promise that the next effort will bring about the miraculous change."

"Come on, then!" said Nap, half angrily. "I'll try it once more. And if I don't get through this time, Mr. Darling, durn me if I try it again!"

"What, what!" said Mr. Darling. Polly laughed outright. The reverend gentleman then began to utter a rebuke of the wild girl, as the probable cause of the expression which had just fallen from the lips of Nap, when she whispered something in his ear relative to Mrs. Dickson, and he was stricken dumb.

When our party arrived at the place appointed, they were met by other stragglers from the fold, who had been hunted up and brought back by the active messengers sent in quest of them. Once more the singing, the praying, and the shouting resounded through the forest. True to his promise, Nap got down on his knees with a firm resolution to remain in that posture until the promised change had taken place, or until he should despair of any such miraculous revelation being vouchsafed him.

"Now, brother, bewail your sins in tears!" said a famous exhorter, by the name of Snorter, who knelt by the side of Nap, and placed his arm around his neck.

"I can't cry!" said Nap.

"My dear brother, consider the enormity of your sins, and how great was the goodness of your Redeemer, who suffered death to atone for them."

"I haven't committed any very enormous sins, that I know of; but if I have done so, didn't our Saviour suffer death before I committed them, and before I was born?"

"Your sins have been the consequence of the fall of Adam; they were entailed upon the human race, and your Redeemer suffered upon the cross as an expiation for all mankind."

"That I believe; it is a quotation from Wesley. I am thankful for it. I acknowledge the infinite debt of gratitude I owe him. I worship him, I adore him, and I rejoice in his loving kindness to me, a poor frail mortal. But wherefore should I weep? I tell you again, I can't cry and howl."

"But you must repent of your evil deeds."

"I do repent them. I say I do, and I tell the truth. But what's the use of blubbering about it?"

"Ah, my dearly beloved brother, when you have heartily repented and obtained forgiveness, you will shout for joy in spite of yourself. Your eyes will open upon a new scene, your heart will expand, and your joyful feelings will find expression like the rest."

"Well, when that takes place I'll believe in this sort of conversion. Those who have been converted tell me the same thing, and I have been waiting to see it and feel it. I could jump up as high and tumble down as hard as the rest; but then it would not be an involuntary business. I am waiting to be moved by the Spirit which they say moves them; but it hasn't come yet."

"Have faith."

"I have—that is, in the Christian plan of redemption, which the Bible teaches."

"Remember the manner of St. Paul's conversion."

"I do. He was knocked as blind as a bat. Let some great change similar to that happen to me, and then I'll swear genuine miracles are not ended."

"Be not obdurate. Beseech your Saviour to pour down a flood of light from heaven upon your understanding."

"I will. And I would prefer that to total blindness, if any sudden change *is* to happen."

Mr. Snorter grew weary of his impracticable subject, and withdrawing, ascended the pulpit and commenced thundering from the stand. His discourse consisted mainly of marvellous occurrences he had partly witnessed himself, and partly learned from others, and all of them were sufficiently authenticated to obtain ready credence with a majority of his hearers.

It was during the delivery of this vociferous exhortation, that Nap was accosted by Brother Keene, who had for some time been kneeling silently at his side—for many knelt during the exhortation, seemingly engaged in prayer. But Brother Keene had not hitherto addressed a word to the anxious seeker, nor uttered a syllable audibly in his behalf.

"Nap," said he, at length, in a low tone, "what do you think of brother Darling's gray mare?"

"I've never seen her but once; but I think she's a fine animal." Nap had the reputation of being an excellent judge of horses.

"How much boot do you think I ought to give with my bay horse for her?"

"What, has Mr. Darling offered to swap?"

"Yes."

"To-day?"

"No, that is, he merely wished me to make up my mind by to-morrow. He says he wants a horse. And I want a large mare to breed mules."

"Well, I wouldn't give him more than ten dollars."

At this juncture, Mr. Snorter became intensely interesting, and riveted the attention of every one present. He was upon the subject of spiritual rappings, table-moving, &c. He declared that a child five years old had moved a large table from room to room in his house, with himself and wife standing on it, and that the spirit of Wesley had commanded him to go forth and exhort. He therefore spoke in the name of John Wesley, and no doubt the spirit of that great saint was then present in the assembly. He besought him to manifest his invisible presence by some sudden emotion in the hearts of his hearers. This was responded to by a simultaneous outcry of approbation. The speaker declared it was the voice of Wesley himself speaking by the mouths of the congregation. But he warned his hearers to beware of evil spirits. "There are, my beloved friends," said he, "evil spirits as well as good ones. There are fallen angels as well as the pure angels of God. The evil spirits speak by the same mediums and to the same people that the others do. It is hard to tell them apart. But you may detect them by their falsehoods, for they are the greatest liars that ever existed. One of them said I had thirty pieces of silver in my pocket, when I solemnly declare that in one pocket there were only a few copper cents, brought with me from Pennsylvania, and in the other there was nothing but a hole, the bottom being entirely out of it. I said nothing at the time, and only smiled; but now I utter my emphatic contradiction, and defy the evil one to make good his words. As I have appealed to the spirits of the good to bear witness of the truth of our cause, so I now pronounce condemnation upon the evil ones, and defy them to dispute what I have said in this holy place. Let any one of them dare"—— He paused abruptly. The torch at his elbow had emitted a blue flame, and a sulphurous odour seemed to spread around the pulpit. Again it was seen. Once, twice, thrice, in quick succession. The thunderstricken exhorter stood rooted to the spot, staring with wide, protuberant eyes. Meantime Jackson Farnes and Tom Hazel maintained their gravity up in the tree. Drop by drop the brandy from the hands of one fell upon the torch, while the other sprinkled down the pulverized brimstone.

The aged preachers adjusted their spectacles and stared steadily at the unexpected spiritual manifestation. Snorter continued entranced, his nostrils extended, and his body quivering with terror. The anxious seekers below, still on their knees, looked up and turned pale. A profound silence ensued. For a long space of time not even a whisper was uttered. At length, Brother Snorter made a desperate effort to speak, and succeeded in uttering only these words:

"I—I acknowledge I had some bank-bills sewed in the hem of my under-shirt!" At this confession, instead of vanishing, the blue lights flamed still higher.

"This is most extraordinary!" said the presiding elder, rising up, but not approaching the light.

"It's getting to be a serious business," said Mr. Snorter, "and I shall have nothing more to do with it." He withdrew hastily, and was followed by many of the congregation, who dispersed precipitately.

One glance had sufficed Nap. He broke away and ran into the bushes as soon as he beheld the blue blazes and scented the brimstone. Jack and Polly endeavoured to follow, but soon lost sight of him. Sally Weighton swooned. But the presiding elder and the aged preachers remained upon the ground, with sufficient valor to do battle bodily with the devil himself. So they at once plumped down on their knees, and called upon all present to do likewise. They then appealed to their great Master, the Captain of their salvation, to manifest his power by rebuking the evil spirits, if such there were, then obtruding in that presence. And soon the spirits ceased to appear, for the brandy had given out. Then a yell of triumph rang through the wilderness. The owls flapped their wings and vanished from the tallest boughs, and the wolves in the distance ceased to howl.

In the mean time, Jack and Polly traversed the most intricate paths, overgrown by plum-trees entangled together by densely clustered vines, whence temptingly hung ripe and luscious grapes. But they did not pause. They continued the search for Nap. Presently they heard voices in the deepest obscurity of a grove on the left.

"Is not that Nap, praying?" asked Polly.

"No; it is not his voice," said Jack. "Besides, there are two voices. Neither of them resembles his." Here Jack stumbled in the bushes, making a considerable noise. The voices were instantly hushed.

"Polly," continued Jack, upon regaining his feet, "what do you think caused the blue blazes?"

"Burnt brandy, which may often be regarded as the worst of evil spirits that afflict mankind, or rather that men afflict themselves with, for the spirits could hurt no one if let alone. Jackson Farnes and Tom Hazel did it. They were up in the tree."

"And none of them had the wit to look upward."

"None but me."

Footsteps were now heard approaching from the direction whence the voices had proceeded, and a moment after, instead of beholding Nap, the reverend Mr. Darling appeared before them.

"Is it possible!" exclaimed he, upon recognising the young couple. "Remember, there is a heaven above"——

"And an earth beneath," said Polly, interrupting him.

"And darkness, however impenetrable, cannot obscure any thing from the vision of the one whose eye never slumbers nor sleeps," continued Darling.

"And you suppose that the evil-minded love the darkness?" asked Polly.

"Yes. And I have the sanction of holy writ for it."

"Then," said Jack, "why did you seek the darkness?"

"I came to pray."

"And was your prayer answered? Suppose we intend to do the same thing?" responded Polly.

"But come!" said Jack. "We are in quest of Nap. We fear some evil may have befallen him."

But he was forcibly withheld by Mr. Darling as he attempted to pass him in the narrow path.

"He is not there. I know it. I saw his horse at nightfall tied to a sapling over yonder near the spring. No doubt he mounted his beast and whipped for home."

Jack and Polly turned in the direction indicated, and the handsome orator approached the encampment.

"What's that?" asked Polly, as they drew near the spring.

"That's Nap!" cried Jack. "That's his snore: I would know it among a thousand."

"And he does snore, then?" said Polly, archly.

"You can listen for yourself."

"It is not unmusical. Let us pause a little and listen. He is safe."

"But he must have been very sleepy. I am sleepy, myself. It must be near daylight. We are in a strange place at such an hour. Are you not afraid of snakes?"

"No more than they should be afraid of me," said she; but she really did seem to cling somewhat closer to young Handy. Jack broke through the bower of leaves and blossoms by a violent effort, and they stood over the prostrate form of Nap, whose head was pillowed upon the neck of his horse, and both were sound asleep.

Nap was no sooner aroused than the three were confronted by several aged women on horseback, and among them was Polly's mother. They declared they would stay no longer at the encampment, and insisted upon Polly and the young men accompanying them home. The whole party emerged a moment after into the cleared space in the vicinity of the encampment, where they paused until the horses of Jack and Polly were brought forth.

The aged minister was still triumphing over the expulsion of the evil spirits, and hundreds believed that the cessation of the annoyance was owing to the divine interposition. But while they gazed upon the scene, it happened that Tom Hazel was overcome by drowsiness. He nodded, and his hat fell down from the tree, and singularly enough lodged upon the head—a bald one—of the devout minister in the midst of his prolonged prayer, if prayer it might be called, but it was in reality a command dictated to God, directing what should be done, and what should be left undone by him.

All eyes were now directed toward the source from whence this missile had fallen, and the whole secret of the disturbance flashed upon the congregation. A rush was made toward the tree, and vengeance was threatened against the offenders. But in the melee they escaped.

CHAPTER VIII.

An intercalated year, and a short chapter.

WE must leap over a whole year in the life of our hero, subsequent to the adventures upon the camp-ground. We must pass without special notice those periods in the career of Nap which were not marked by any very striking events, and hasten to those occurrences which particularly merit the attention of his biographer.

A brief recapitulation of the ordinary events of the year which is skipped over, may, however, be necessary for the more perfect elucidation of the extraordinary ones to follow.

The young merchants then, had succeeded handsomely in their business. It could not be otherwise in a new country, where any degree of business talent was employed. Everywhere the secret of accumulation is the art of preserving what has been acquired. Anywhere one may gather sufficient wealth, if he can only devise the means of retaining what he receives. Thousands are poor who have made fortunes; and most of the rich men in the world have become so merely by dint of a pertinacious determination not to spend.

In that portion of the State of Missouri selected by our young merchants as the field of their operations, there were no inducements to spend; nay, scarcely a possibility of squandering what they made. The expense of boarding and clothing did not exceed one hundred dollars per annum, and with the exception of a few demands from itinerant philanthropists, and donations for the building of places of worship, which included school-houses and the salaries of teachers, there were no other sources of disbursement. Hence the merchant's profits were added to his means, and were continually swelling his capital and enlarging his sphere of business.

Nap's original plan of commencing business on his own account at Venice had been modified; and the style of his firm was now N. B. Wax & Co. Joseph Handy was his partner.

Jack Handy had likewise gone with a small stock of goods from the head-quarters at Tyre to the projected capital of a new county in the interior, some distance beyond Nap's point of business.

Another brother of the Handys, Benjamin, had come out from Kentucky, and was the clerk of Joseph, in whose school he was quite sure to learn correctly the mystery of fortune-making.

So much for the merchants. Among the rest of the characters of whom mention has been made, Mr. Darling's parenthetical history demands some notice. The mare he had disposed of to Brother Keene, proved to have fallen short of his description in some essential particulars. In truth she was quite a worthless animal, and bore no mules at all; and Brother Keene, feeling that he had been cheated, and having obtained witnesses to prove he was made the victim of a deception, resolved in his indignation to bring the reverend jockey to trial. The result was a suspension from the ministry for two years. Mr. Darling had likewise some kind of a personal difficulty with a Mr. Rogers, the nature of which no one seemed to be acquainted with. It occurred in the street of the village where Mr. R. lived, and late in the night when no witnesses were present. High words and the report of a pistol were all that any third party ever heard of the particulars of the occurrence. Mr. Darling was found standing alone, while Mr. Rogers, was seen retreating briskly to the inn. Who fired the pistol no one could tell, since the parties themselves would say nothing on the subject But it was surmised that the preacher had fired at his assailant, else why should the latter have been seen hastily retreating? At all events, the occurrence did the parson no good at his trial; and he submitted silently to the verdict passed upon him. He then became a temperance lecturer, and advocate of the Maine Liquor Law.

Tom Hazel still prowled about the country, hunting and fishing, and some said co-operating with the "bogus" money manufacturers. Jackson Farnes had not been seen since the night he acted as a medium at the camp-meeting. Neither had Mr. Snorter's fine horse been heard of since that eventful night. Farnes, it was supposed, had stolen him and made his escape into the Indian territory, or beyond the limits of the State in the south, where the horse thieves and counterfeiters were supposed to have their head-quarters.

Polly Hopkins had frequently appeared on the tapis, always the same in spirits, and ever delighting in her peculiar species of feminine adventure. On more than one occasion she had wellnigh induced Nap to forget his honour and forego his Molly. Even Jack had been more than once half bewitched by her, though firmly resolved never to commit himself to another until he had once more beheld his first love, the absent Kate. But, as Polly had foretold, both he and Nap subsequently became heartily ashamed of the parts they had enacted during the hurricane of excitement at the camp-meeting. Jack especially avoided Sally Weighton ever after, because she reminded him of the extravagances of that night, and, indeed, had contributed to promote them.

CHAPTER IX.

The new city in the West—Nap hunts a turkey and kills **a bitch—Tried** by Squire Nix—The barrel of mackerel.

THE sun arose in great glory, and cast its magnificent horizontal rays upon the tall spires of Venice—the western Venice—the majestic spires being those of nature's own production, viz. the oaks, the elms, the pecans, and the cottonwoods. And it must be owned that Nap's city in the swamp could not as yet boast of more than three houses. One of them was the store, another was the tavern at which he boarded, kept by Mr. Samuel Marsh, a great stutterer, and the last was a blacksmith's shop, owned and worked by the reverend John Smith, a Campbellite Baptist preacher. Nap had given Smith and Marsh a title to the lots, upon condition that they would build upon them and occupy them. If they abandoned them, the property was to revert to the original owner, together with the improvements erected thereon.

They called Nap a fool when he bought the ground, for it lay between a slough and the river, and its limits were bounded by them. But he, having a hint from Colonel Benton, cared not what all the world besides might say. And in pursuance of the hint from the great man, he caused it to be known that every alternate lot was at the service, "in fee simple and for ever" as it was termed, of any one would undertake to erect a building thereon.

But on the morning that the sun shone so resplendently upon the trees, Nap was absent from the store, about half a mile distant, in pursuit of a flock of wild turkeys, which had run past his door when he was sweeping the litter and dust from the steps into the street. Every time he attempted to take aim at them, it seemed they dodged, or thrust their heads down and ran along under cover of the sheltering bushes. He pursued; but ever when he had overtaken them, and was upon the eve of pulling the trigger, down went their heads again entirely out of sight. Thus they had led him so great a distance from the store, and he grew quite angry at their conduct; for a day or two before, a fine buck had stood perfectly still while he shot him from his own door.

He followed the "contrary gobblers," as he termed them, across the narrow tract of bottom or alluvial land, and ascended the bluff in the vicinity of Jack Grove's cabin on the summit. Jack Grove was not Nap's friend, and did not deal with him, but preferred riding to Tyre for his goods. The reason of this enmity or coldness was simply because Grove wanted to buy the land that Nap had purchased, but lacked the money to pay for it, and hence he considered himself an ill-used man. And when Nap passed near the little cornfield, Grove's brindle cur bitch ran at him and attempted to bite him. Nap thought her master had set her at him, for Grove himself was in the field, accompanied by Brother Keene, who had never forgiven him for divulging what had passed between them on the campground in relation to Darling's mare, (and which had ever since been a standing joke at K.'s expense,)—and by Tom Hazel, whom he had offended because he would not trust him for three yards of blue satinet to make him a new pair of breeches. Seeing these persons standing by the side of Grove, and being incensed at the perverse conduct of the turkeys in so long eluding him, he became inflamed against the bitch; and as she persisted in the attempt to seize him, he levelled his gun and fired at her. She fell instantly. Her master approached, uttering awful maledictions, while Nap charged his gun with as much expedition as possible, and retreated homeward.

When he arrived at the inn, he informed Marsh and Smith of the occurrence, and although they were both rejoiced to hear of the death of the bitch, because she was a notoriously dangerous animal, yet they feared the implacable nature of Grove would probably lead him into litigation; and they knew from Nap's description of the locality that the affair must have taken place on the land belonging to Grove. If it had been in a public thoroughfare, the shooting would have been justifiable.

And, in effect, before they had risen from the breakfast-table, the arrival of Grove was announced. He was accompanied by Brother Keene, Tom Hazel, and Squire Nix. Nap, attended by Marsh and Smith, met them in bar-room. The principals were sullen, and their friends silent. Not a word was spoken for several minutes; but all sat quite still, mutely looking at each other or on the floor.

"Boys, let me pint out the way that'll settle the hash betwixt you," at length proposed Squire Nix, a tall, gaunt, gray-haired old woodman. "I'm both your friends, and would as lief as not be both your fathers, if you'd take a notion to some of my darters. What say you? Heads or tails—a friendly fixin' of it up, or a right-down cat-a-mouse law-fight? If a reg'lar jury were to gin you, Jack Grove, twenty dollars damages, it would cost you ten dollars of it to pay expenses. I know it would. My law experience proves it. No jury in this here county would gin you damages and make Nap pay costs too, because it was an unpopular dog"——

"Wouldn't they go according to law?" asked Grove, interrupting him.

"*And* justice—law and *justice*," said the Squire.

"Th–tha–that's *it!*" said Sam Marsh, the innkeeper. "If they gin yo—you d–da–*dam*–ages, they'll g–gi–gin him c–co–costs." The last words were jerked out violently.

"Say, boys—heads or tails!" and the Squire threw up a dollar.

"Heads!" said Nap.

"Heads it is!" said the Squire. "Now if you don't agree, Jack, you won't even git damages."

"Heads let it be, then. You know the law, Squire. Here's my witnesses. Swear 'em. But mind, there's to be no costs."

"No; I'll not charge any thing for my sarvices. All I want is to make peace 'twixt neighbours. Come, Brother Keene, and you, Tom Hazel, come here and kiss the book." And the Squire swore them both on the Bible.

The witnesses swore positively that they had seen Nap kill the bitch; and that it was done on Grove's premises.

"Now, Nap, it's your turn to hear my speech. You have been guilty of a high trespass in going on his property and killing his bitch without leave or license. The law is agin you, as sure as you set there. And if this scrape was to git into the hands of the lawyers, they'd be sartain to pull a double X out of you—ten for fees, and ten for damages. You couldn't git out of it no way you could fix it. Now I don't insinuate that you done it a *malicious propensity*—no, durned clear of it. It isn't in your natur. But you done it—the witnesses swore to it pine-blank. Well, now, what can I do? I don't wish to have you mad with me—I don't want to stop gwien to your store o' Saturdays, and buying my fixens as hitherto-fore. You won't be mad, will you, Nap?"

"No, Squire. Say your say, and I'll submit to it as a good citizen ought. And then I want you to go over with me and see a barrel of fish opened. Your wife, I know, likes mackerel."

"To death! She does! Yes, you *are* a good citizen—an honest man, and a smart man. I'd vote for you to go to Congress. But Nap, I must do my duty, though it goes mightily agin the grain this time. I'm mighty sorry—but you've got into a scrape. You're in the mud, Nap; another step forward, and you'd be in the mire. Retreat, Nap; let me help you. I'll lift you out as easy as I can. Only one foot is in it now—if you were to go on, both feet would be in it. This lawing is a durned dirty business. Well, Nap, with a clean conscience, the best thing I can do for you, is to say ten dollars."

"Thank you, Squire!" said Nap. "I'll pay it, and will never think the worse of you."

"I know'd it!—Nap, you're a noble fellow! and if Grove don't shake hands with you, I'll lick him the first time I catch him where there ain't no witnesses."

"Here's my hand," said Grove.

"And here's the money," said Nap, paying it. "But before I knock open the barrel of mackerel, I want to see where I struck the bitch. Stay here, Squire, till I come back. Won't you go with me, Sam?"

Nap returned with Grove to his house, accompanied by Sam Marsh, Brother Keene, and Tom Hazel. And, to their utter astonishment, they found the bitch alive, and lying in the yard, whither she had come without assistance.

"N–no–now, Nap!" said Sam, plucking Nap aside, after they had been gazing some time at the wounded animal. "N–Na–Nap! n–no–now you've g–got 'em on the hi–hip! S–su–sue 'em f–for p–per–perjury!"

"I will! See here, Brother Keene, Tom Hazel, and the whole batch of you! You swore I killed the bitch. She's alive! 'Twas perjury. You know where I can send you to, now!"

"To Jef–Jef–Jefferson C–ci–city, I th–thi–think!" said Marsh. Keene and Grove were temperance men, and Marsh wouldn't trust Hazel at his bar.

Grove and his party thought of the penitentiary. They turned pale, and trembled a great deal.

"L–l–let me to–toss up, and m–me–mend it all," continued Marsh, taking a small coin from his pocket.

"Go ahead!" said Keene and Hazel.

"Heads!" said Grove.

"He–a–ds it is!" said Marsh.

"Honour bright! Now Marsh, make peace betwixt neighbours," said Grove.

"P–p–pay him b–ba–back the t–ten d–dol–lars, then!"

It was done. And declaring he was satisfied, and pledging himself not to prosecute any of them for perjury, Nap returned with Marsh to town, where they were soon after joined by the discomfited party, who required a written obligation not to prosecute them. It was given, and then they retired seemingly well satisfied.

Nap proceeded to open the barrel of mackerel. Both Nix and Marsh eagerly awaited the result. Nap, in full confidence of the superiority of the article, a great luxury in the West, spoke in high terms of its quality, as he was in the habit of doing of every thing purchased of Joseph Handy at Tyre, whence this barrel had been procured. He had indeed selected it himself, a few days before, from among many barrels in the wareroom.

After some vain attempts to loosen the hoops with a hammer, Nap seized the axe, and with a desperate blow knocked in the head. But such was the impetuosity of the blow, that the brine was splashed in every direction, and of course upon the clothes and in the faces of all present.

"Never mind that!" said Nap, removing the fragments of the heading; "it shows how well the fish have been preserved. Sometimes we find them uncovered and dry, and of course they are good for nothing. I'll show you these." He then threw off his coat and rolled up his shirt-sleeves. "Look here," said he, thrusting in his hand. But he caught no fish. "They are farther down," he continued, plunging his arm deeper, and feeling about in every direction. Still no fish. He even reached the bottom, but with the same result.

"Well!" said he, withdrawing his arm, streaming with the liquid. "That beats all the brine I ever saw or heard of. It is the best that ever was made. Just think of it! It was so strong it ate up all the fish!"

His auditors stared in wonder. Then Marsh, taking up a piece of the heading and scrutinizing it closely, succeeded in deciphering the following words: "TRAIN OIL."

"What! Let me see!" cried Nap, taking the heading

and reading the words. "Well! it wasn't brine, after all. What a mistake! And now we have no fish."

"But we have a mighty good *fish-tale*," said Squire Nix. "Well, give me some powder and lead, and I'll let you off this time."

CHAPTER X.

Spouting on Temperance, and political speeches—The "Jackson Resolutions"—Colonel Benton on the stand—Major Jackson replies—A telegraph despatch—Colonel B. on National Conventions—A rat killed.

THE next day was Saturday, and a great crowd was to be in town to hear Mr. Darling deliver a lecture on the subject of Temperance. Such gatherings are always promoted by the merchants and the politicians. Mr. Darling was the favourite and friend of Nap, and the appointment to speak on the subject above mentioned was in pursuance of the latter's suggestion. Many pounds of tobacco and yards of calico are sold on such occasions.

But Mr Darling was likewise a Democrat of the deepest dye, and he had notified Colonel Benton, who was stumping the State against the "Jackson Resolutions," of the time and place of the meeting. And Marsh, who was devoted to the interests of Major Jackson, had likewise despatched information to him. While Nap, who owned he was a Whig at heart while politically preaching Democracy, for the purpose of contributing to the excitement and swelling the number of auditors, had secretly sent notes of invitation to Mr. Miller, of Boonville, the Whig candidate for Congress; to Claude Jones, the miscellaneous orator and poet, and to Colonel Birch, a famous and able anti-Benton stump-speaker.

At an early hour, Mr. Darling, with the entire approbation of Nap, seated himself in a commodious split-bottomed chair in front of the store, and leaned back against the wall of the house. It was a pleasant morning; a pearly sky without a cloud; while a delicious breeze gave a graceful motion to the elastic boughs of the trees. Directly in front of the store was a spreading oak, which served as a capacious awning.

"Nap," said Darling, as the fidgety merchant threw himself in a chair beside him, "it is just eight o'clock. Which will be the most to your interest, for me to begin early and finish soon, or to put off speaking until your customers get through with their dealing?"

"I think you had better begin to speak at ten o'clock."

"And continue how long?"

"Oh, I want it kept up till night. They'll listen awhile and trade awhile, and stay all day."

"It'll be a laborious effort to keep up speaking all day. But I think I may look for some assistance. I would not like to break down on the stand. But I should hate it worse if my audience gave out."

"Don't fear that; I'll keep them stimulated."

"Do you intend to keep open the back door of the wareroom?"

"Yes, to be sure. And you must not be hurt if you hear that I have been ridiculing your speech. Jim Rue will superintend the back department. And he is to assist me hereafter permanently." Jim was never known as an over-zealous champion of the temperance cause.

"But suppose I give out?"

"I'll stimulate *you*. I have a long green bottle, which can't be seen through, filled with fourth-proof. Put it in one pocket, and a large spoon in the other. You know the cholera is about. Take the medicine on the stand by the spoonful. You may take it as often as you please. No one will suspect it is brandy swallowed in such a place and on such an occasion."

"They'll smell it!"

"If they do, then you must have the diarrhœa. That'il be enough."

"Nap, I feel some symptoms now!"

"You do? Then come in and try the medicine. And you had better put the bottle in your pocket before the crowd arrives."

The first arrivals were Colonel Benton and Squire Nix. Nix was telling him about the occurrence of the preceding day, when they halted in front of the tavern.

"You did right, sir. Solomon in all his glory could not have rendered a more righteous judgment."

Such were the words spoken by the Colonel when he dismounted.

"W–w–walk in, Colonel. I'm g–glad to s–see you p–p–pop into our t–t–town accidently. Y–your h–horse and y–yo–yourself shall be f–fed, and both w–w–wel–welcomed at my N–n–north American Hotel, even if I am a–ag–agin you in p–p–po–politics."

"Thank you, sir. But my horse and myself have both breakfasted at Squire Nix's. I will take a seat on your porch, though."

"Do it, C–co–colonel! C–colonel, didn't I h–he–hear you s–s–say the Squire d–d–done right in de–de–ciding the bi–bi–bitch case yesterday?"

"Yes, I did say so. It was a neighbourly office, and a wise decision. Take my advice, sir, and keep beyond the reach of the fangs of the law. I am a lawyer, sir—a lawyer gives you that advice."

"I'm ob–ob–obleeged to you, Colonel. B–but haven't you h–hearn that the Squire's de–decision w–wa–was re-varsed?"

"No!" cried the Squire, starting up. "If any magistrate in the county has had the impudence to revarse my decision"——

"It w–w–wasn't a magistrate."

"Who was it, then? That's all!"

"The b–bi–bitch herself."

"How was that?" asked the Colonel.

'Not dead, by zooks! Wasn't that it, Marsh?"

'That w–was it, S–squire."

"Then Grove shall pay back the money! He shall do it, or my name's not Nix!"

Marsh related what had occurred, which satisfied the Squire, and amused the Colonel, who compared his own case to it. He said that when the "Jackson Resolutions" were adopted in the legislature, his enemies, the "Softs" and the "Rottens" believed he was a dead dog; but when they got to their homes, they found him alive and kicking. Nix yelled out an approbation of this speech with his whole heart.

Just then, Jack Grove, accompanied by Brother Keene, Tom Hazel, and Claude Jones, stepped into the porch. The latter, having heard the remarks of Colonel Benton, exclaimed aloud—

"If the dog ain't dead, I'll be shot!"

"What dog do you mean, sir?" said the Colonel, rather fiercely.

"Oh, the bitch!"

"It's true, Squire Nix," said Grove. "After we returned the money, to keep him from penitentiarying us for perjury, we went back to the house to see if the slut was badly hurt. And what do you think?"

"I don't know."

"Hanged if she wasn't dead, that time."

"I said the dog was dead—the bitch I mean," said Claude Jones.

"But the lion lives to grind the bones of his enemies!" said the Colonel, involuntarily showing his teeth. This sally produced a hearty laugh at the expense of Jones.

"What would you advise me to do now, Colonel?" asked Grove.

"Throw the bitch to the buzzards, and let Claude Jones wait upon them with napkins and tooth-picks!"

Convulsive roars of laughter followed.

"Oh yes!" said Claude; "but the lion must swallow his share." This was thought to be a good retort, and was heartily applauded.

"Do?" continued the Colonel, addressing Grove. "I'll tell you what to do. Bury the hatchet with Nap Wax. He did right, and the law will give you nothing. But go to work and scourge the nullifiers out of the country. Chase Fox Jackson, Birch, and Napton out of the prairies. They are worse than the Camanches. Ask Claude Jones why he appears here to-day"——

"I know why he is here: I invited him to come with me. He was on his way to the Springfield court"——

"Fudge! He was on his way to Venice, to make a speech against Colonel Benton—and he might as well speak against the bluff upon which your cabin stands!"

"Why are *you* here to-day, Colonel? This is to be a temperance gathering," said Jones.

"Because I saw proper to come. I have announced my intention to speak to every body of men I can find assembled together on any occasion. By what authority does Colonel Benton address Missourians? Sir, I made Missouri what she is! I made her respectable in the eyes of the world. She has had peace, prosperity, and no public debt. I have only to root out a few sprouts of nullification, and imprison some thieving bank officers, and the state will be purified again, as it was in the days of General Jackson—not this Fox Jackson. I use no subterfuges, sir. I am here in pursuance of my plan."

By this time parties were arriving from various directions—men, women, and children. And a proposition from Nap, that the speaking should take place under the umbrageous oak standing in front of the store, was readily acceded to by Mr. Darling, and acquiesced in by the Colonel. Boxes were piled up, and logs were rolled around, so that both the speakers and the listeners were accommodated.

Mr. Darling was the first to ascend the topmost box.

With his white handkerchief in his left hand, (a habit he got originally at Washington City, having once witnessed an oratorical display by Mr. Rives, in the Senate,) and waving the right to and fro as he warmed with his subject, and recuperated with his medicine, a large spoonful of which he swallowed every ten minutes, he contrived to inspire most of his auditory with an enthusiastic conviction that the use of spirituous liquors was baneful to society, and that the vending of them should be prohibited by law. Toward the conclusion of his address, his face grew red, and his elocution more animated. He complimented the distinguished statesman then present, averring that his surpassing vigour of body and intellect might be justly attributed to his uniformly temperate habits. This reference to Missouri's greatest man, undoubtedly produced the loudest outburst of applause that had hitherto been heard. Such an opportunity was not to be lost. And so the lecturer, finding his medicine was exhausted, and complaining that there was no subsidence of the "symptoms," declined occupying more of the time of his hearers. He requested, however, that some friend of the cause would take round a hat and receive a collection to defray the expenses of its champions, who contributed their time and energies for the benefit of the community.

A somewhat lengthy pause ensued, during which a stranger mounted the box, and after some pertinent remarks, for he was sincerely devoted to the cause, he threw a five-dollar bill into his own hat, and said he felt proud in being able to set so good an example.

"Who is he? who is he?" cried many voices, as the hat travelled about from hand to hand, receiving liberal donations.

"My name, gentlemen," said the stranger, "you have no doubt heard mentioned frequently. I am sure you will hear it often during the ensuing campaign—but I hope, nay, I believe, you will never hear it coupled with a disgraceful epithet. I am the nominee of the Whig party in this district for Congress."

"Your hand, sir!" said the Colonel, mounting up beside him. "Fellow-citizens, I know Mr. M—— to be a gentleman—which cannot be said of some of the renegade Democrats, who would sell you to the nullifiers and disunionists. And, Whig as he is, I would rather see him sent to Congress than any of the 'Softs' or 'Rottens.' Now, sir," he continued, "I have introduced you. You can make a speech. This is a mixed multitude, comprised of all parties."

It was not, it seemed, Mr. M——'s intention to make a speech on that occasion. He had been handsomely introduced, however, and was satisfied to rest upon the favourable impression he had made.

Not so the Colonel. He came there to make a speech. He avowed it. He had heard there was to be a temperance lecture, which he had no intention to interfere with. But he had resolved to address the people after the lecturer had concluded his harangue. And he always preferred to address *sober* men, for they would be better able to comprehend his meaning, and more likely to appreciate his motives. Then, for an hour, he played his tremendous battery upon the author of the famous "Resolutions," and all his aiders and abettors. After which he told the crowd what he intended to do for them. He said that just where he stood, perhaps—certainly not far remote from it—the greatest thoroughfare would run that ever belted any portion of the habitable globe. The importations from China would pass through Missouri to the East, to New York and Philadelphia, to London and Paris, and all the treasures of California and Oregon would be poured into their laps. Here the women held up their aprons, their imaginations picturing the heaps of gold which the Pacific railroad was to be the means of transporting eastward.

Then the people were startled by the sound of a hunter's horn, which was followed by the yelping of hounds, and the "hark away" of their master. Presently a thin, tall, straight man came galloping along the road, as if in pursuit of a deer. He seemed to have no intention of halting in the place, and really appeared to be urging his reluctant steed toward the upper end of the slough. But being recognised by some of the old hunters present, he was hailed, and finally constrained to dismount. A shout of triumph from the Antis attested their exultation at this unexpected and accidental arrival of their champion. It was Major Jackson himself.

Marsh having stuttered to him the substance of the Colonel's animadversions, with all of which he had been made familiar, he mounted the box quite prepared to launch forth a seemingly impromptu reply and defence of himself. Being a handsome man and a ready speaker, his reception was sufficiently flattering. Besides, neither Colonel Benton nor his satanic majesty himself had the power of intimidating him. He was a man of cool self-possession, and a first-rate shot.

The Major began by recapitulating the censures which *he had no doubt* were passed upon him in his absence. This elicited an affirmative response from the audience. Then he proceeded to refute them in a strain of earnest eloquence. He proved that he stood on the same Democratic ground he had always occupied; he had never appealed to the Whigs to help him; his Resolutions, which had been so much condemned, embodied the same doctrine that was held by Democrats in all the slave-holding States, and were not at all at variance with the Baltimore platform. He declared that Colonel Benton had openly opposed the wishes of the party in Missouri, by his opposition to the annexation of Texas in 1844. General Jackson, then living, [here Colonel Benton withdrew to the porch to the tavern,] had attributed his political aberration to an addling of the intellect caused by the fatal explosion on board the United States steamship Princeton. Ever since that event the Colonel had been like a buck shot in the eye.

He could not go straight five minutes together, but was continually bumping against trees and rocks, and running roughshod over his old friends and supporters. "He has repeatedly asserted," continued the Major, "in the presence of public assemblies, **that my Resolutions, adopted by the** legislature **of the** State, **were concocted by the** secessionists, and were the result of a **nullification plot—** Mr. Calhoun himself being **the** father. Fellow-citizens, I need not defend myself against any such charges. You know me too well to suppose such a thing possible. But you will, **I hope, permit me to read a** telegraphic despatch, which I have received from Washington, giving a brief sketch of the *Colonel's* secret plots. I do not vouch for the truth of the statements. I shall merely read them, so that if they be without foundation, the Colonel may **employ** himself in disproving them. **That will be much better employment** than manufacturing **charges against me. I will** merely state that the author **of the letter, the substance of** which was telegraphed to me, has been **in a** position which gave him an opportunity to obtain a vast amount of political information. **But I'll read the** despatch:

'DEAR SIR,

'Here is a lightning streak revelation of the secret springs of "Old Bullion's" conduct and position. First intrigue: Placing in Mr. Van Buren's **possession** documentary **facts** which resulted in the alienation of General Jackson from Mr. Calhoun. But **Van** Buren was afterward made President by General Jackson, Colonel Benton being repugnant to him, as he had a bullet from B.'s pistol then rankling in his arm. Intrigue second: Getting control of the columns of the Globe, making a fortune for himself, and marring the fortunes of others. For instance, when he intimated to Mr. Buchanan that he ought not to stand in Mr. V. B.'s way, Mr. B. remarked to a friend, "I withdraw. It is better to walk down stairs voluntarily and quietly, than to be kicked down." Intrigue third: To defeat the annexation of Texas in 1844 Intrigue fourth: To be made Lieutenant-General in Mexico—nipped in the bud by the Senate. Intrigue fifth: To have the Buffalo platform erected, and cause Mr. V. B. to get upon it. V. B. did so, because he had reaped the benefit of the first intrigue, and thought his prompter infallible. Intrigue sixth: Finding the last move a failure, resolved not to identify himself with it openly, but to have it secretly understood by the Quakers and Free-soilers that he was with them in principle. Intrigue seventh: To oppose the Democratic administration; condemn all nominating conventions; announce a book from his scathing pen to frighten the great party leaders; and finally to be an INDEPENDENT candidate for the Presidency, whenever the Whig party might be in the article of dissolution. To be the champion of the great Pacific railroad—whom Whigs, anti-administration Democrats, Free-soilers, Abolitionists, and Quakers will support. *And he will be elected.*'

"Such, gentlemen," continued the Major, "are the statements of this writer. I do not endorse them all, as I have not the means of substantiating them. If they be unfounded, they can be refuted. And I deem myself justifiable in bringing forward such weapons in my own defence. You have all heard his assault upon me and my friends. Now let him defend himself. Fair play is a jewel."

"Who wrote that letter? His name! His name!" cried the Colonel, approaching with gigantic strides, and with a flushed face.

"His name is signed at the bottom," said the Major, with an imperturbable countenance.

"I demand his name, sir! I demand his name!"

"You *demand* it? I intend to come down stairs when it suits my convenience. And as I am through with my speech, I will meet you face to face on the common level."

"Calhoun wrote part of it!"

"No, sir. Impossible."

"Did you not say you held yourself responsible for the writer's statement?"

"Did you not hear me say the contrary?"

"You are not responsible, then. I blow it to the wind like the thistledown. A mere catalogue of goundless surmises, sir. They cannot injure me. I throw them behind me, sir, like waste paper!" And before the Major could avow what he intended, the Colonel had turned away again and retired out of hearing.

Another accidental arrival. This was Mr. Winston, the Whig candidate for Governor. He came up the river-bank with a struggling cat-fish in his hand, which he had just taken. He seemed surprised to find himself in the midst of such a large body of his fellow-citizens, who deafened his ears with their plaudits. He was a famous hunter and fisherman, and was in the habit of traversing the State alone, and on foot, plunged in abstruse meditation. He was the grandson of the renowned Patrick Henry. Wherever he appeared he was welcomed by Whig and Democrat, although the latter would not vote for him; and his eccentric appearance anywhere never produced astonishment. They soon had him on the topmost box, where he spoke most eloquently for more than an hour.

The last arrival was Judge Birch. He had a bridle in his hand, and was in quest of his horse, which he said had escaped from him in the bushes. He, too, was a famous Anti-Benton orator, and one the Colonel looked upon with serious aversion. They had him up on the box, and he was vociferously cheered at the end of every sentence. [Mr. Darling having departed with the proceeds of the collection, there was a constant stream of spirits flowing at the wareroom in the rear of the store.] The Judge, having, as he confessed, once been identified with the Whigs, professed to know their principles; and he proceeded with great dexterity and logical precision to show that Colonel Benton differed from them in no material point. As he proceeded it was quite perceptible that the Whigs present evinced an unfeigned delight at the information, while the incredulous Democrats withdrew by degrees and clustered around their old leader in the porch of the inn.

This disposition of affairs being exactly such as the Colonel might have desired, he indulged in one of his characteristic conversations for the especial enlightenment of his friends. One of his partisans having asked him what he really thought of National Conventions, he replied—

"Humbugs! Humbugs, sir! National curses! A game of blindman's-buff! With their eyes bandaged they say who shall be President. To be sure, they see under the bandage, and cheat, like we used to do in the nursery. They take the one who agrees to give them the most sugar-plums. The purple is put up at auction. The highest bid takes it, sir! A humbug, sir! An infamous humbug! What sort of men do they nominate? A general? Washington and Jackson *were* generals, sir! They knew how to fight. They had the intellect and the nerve. What battles have the President and his Attorney-General gained? The first met with mishaps before engaging with the enemy; the last had his ankle twisted by his horse, or something of the kind"——

"No, Colonel," said an emigrant from Newburyport, "he wounded a Mexican—he broke one of the enemy's legs."

"He? If he did, it was a Donna's, not a Don's! A parasite, sir! In politics, a fungus springing from the ordure of national nightshade conventions. A virulently poisonous *boletus*, which is death to the party swallowing it. I sometimes eat the genuine mushroom myself; but my stomach turns at the deadly fungi which are coriaceous in texture, and have a membranous collar around the stem! They are poison, sir! No, sir! These generals came from the dunghill. They were not of the fighting breed. But a convention of conspirators against the people, gave them the first honours of the Republic. It is a vile humbug, sir. What speeches have they delivered? One of them made two in the Senate. I rose up and left my seat. My brow burned with shame, sir! One was in opposition to the claim of an old lady on the treasury, the other all about removals from office. Spoils, sir! Spoils! Taylor was a humbug President, sir,—and so was Harrison; but they were not humbug generals, sir! I can put up with single humbugs, sir; but not double ones."

"You are right, Colonel!" said the Baptist parson and blacksmith, John Smith.

"Right, sir? I know it, sir! Let us have Presidents and cabinet-ministers who have laboured for the country and benefited the people. And you are right, sir in building a shop and erecting the bellows in this town. The lot you got for nothing may be worth a hundred dollars per foot to your children. And these majestic woods and undulating prairies will bring one hundred dollars per acre. Missouri, supposed to be cast in the obscure and almost impenetrable wilderness, will be the most fruitful and wealthy State in the Union. You will live to see the time when you may take fresh venison and grouse to New York in two days. Your hemp, tobacco, and grain [speaking to the farmers] will be taken to market as quickly and almost at as small an expense as the products of Kentucky, where the land now sells for one hundred dollars per acre. Your land will produce double as much as theirs, with half the labour. So, every one of you who leaves a quarter of a section to his children will leave them a fortune. These things are to be done by the power of mind; but men must be gifted with brains before they can think. Humbug conventions must be abolished, and men of intellect be elevated to positions which will enable them to accomplish great results."

Thus the day was spent—the politicians speaking alternately from the box, some assailing, some defending Colonel Benton, while the Colonel himself sat in the porch of the inn and instructed as many eager listeners as could get within earshot of him. But if all this expenditure of eloquence was designed to be the sowing of seed which were to germinate at a future day, we must say that Nap's operations were of quite a different description. It was harvest-time with him. Both in the store among the dry-goods, and in the wareroom, where it was not so dry, there was a constant scene of activity and business. While the husbands were luxuriating in the idea of a vast increase of wealth being brought to their doors by the Pacific railroad, the wives were purchasing the material with which to array themselves in a manner becoming the high station they were to assume. The only unpleasant occurrence was a confusion which seized upon the intellects of poor Jim Rue, toward night. He said it must be the smell of the liquor, because the drinking of it never had that effect. After many trials he owned that it was impossible to count the money he had received correctly. He could not make the "pile" agree with itself, as he stated. The amount of cash he received varied between sixty-nine and seventy-three dollars, and no two countings made the same result. "There's two," said he, making a final and desperate effort. "No," said Nap, "it's only one." "Then," said Jim, "I see double; and that's the truth of it."

At supper, Nap was pleased to find himself in the near vicinity of the Colonel.

"Colonel," said he, "although I am a Whig in principle, I shall vote for no Anti-Benton man. I owe more to you than to all the politicians put together."

"That's not improbable."

"It is just as I say. In the first place I settled here because I once saw you put your finger on the map and assert that this point would some day be improved. It is a central location; and I am selling more goods than I supposed I would. But that is not all. To-day, while you were telling them about the increase in the value of farms and of town-lots, every now and then one of your listeners slipped out of the crowd and came to me to enter for a lot. I gave away ten, upon which they are to erect houses immediately; and I have sold a number to others who buy on speculation. I am to have five dollars a piece for them; and they will amount to vastly more than I gave for the whole town."

"How many lots have you remaining?"

"Oh, I suppose there are five hundred, counting the eighteen feet ones and all."

"Don't sell any more until you find you can't give them away. A lot given away, upon which a house is to be built, is better for you than to sell it for fifty dollars."

"I understand. I'll follow your advice, Colonel. But, Colonel, do you really think Mr. Darling was right in advocating the Maine Liquor Law? I admire him very much; but I don't think I can go with him that far."

"All humbug! They might as well enact a law prohibiting the sale of daggers, because men stab one another, and sometimes destroy themselves with them; or pistols and guns in time of peace, because men do murder with them. No! let them lecture the intemperately inclined against the danger of indulgence. Man is a free agent; and if he resolves to destroy himself, no laws, human or divine, can prevent him from doing it."

"Th–tha–that's m–my doc–doctrine!" said Marsh, his face glowing with enthusiastic approbation.

"It is undoubtedly a disgraceful and brutal habit to indulge in drinking to excess," continued the Colonel; "but the responsibility and the penalty must be with the one who does it."

"Th–tha–that's m–my doc–doctrine!" said Marsh, who had sold not less than one hundred drinks that day.

The Colonel retired early, as was his wont. No one

could induce him to break his rule. And **Nap** returned, much fatigued, to the store.

The full moon illumined the sky and the earth as soon as the sun descended below the western horizon. Objects could be discerned **almost as** distinctly as by the light of day. It was a brilliant, calm, pleasant evening. The mocking-bird **sang** incessantly; **and had it not been for** the **unharmonious** croaking of the frogs **up the slough,** one might have been enchanted with the scene and the sounds.

Jim Rue had fallen asleep on a bale of Chicopee D muslins, bought for **less than cost of a house** which made a fortune by discounting its bills and notes at the market rate. Nap had **not disturbed** him when the signal for supper **had been heard; and now he** found him in the same slumbering condition, and in **the same** attitude, not having moved hand or foot. The only change preceptible was that his chin had fallen more and his mouth was **wider** open.

Nap sat down beside him in a chair **and** leaned **back** against the counter. He smoked a cigar in solitude and profound silence. But the stillness soon brought **forth** one of those pests **of all** river **towns, a** large gray tom-rat. He galloped over the floor several times, smelling in different directions **for food.** Finally he paused **near the** foot of Jim, which hung pendent near the floor, and standing up on his hind legs, actually began **to** gnaw the leather. Nap noiselessly reached **back** and grasped **a** two-pound weight. **Taking a deliberate aim,** he struck **the** animal on the **head and killed it.** But the missile had likewise come in contact with Jim's **heel,** and awakened him.

"What's that, Nap?" he asked.

"A rat. He wanted to make a supper of you."

"Let him rip. He'll have tough chawing."

"I've killed him. Here he is," said Nap, holding him up by the **tail.**

"He's a whopper!" said **Jim.** "Throw him out, and I'll take another **nap.**"

"Hadn't you better eat your supper first?"

"No, I'm not hungry. Mrs. Marsh sen; me a roasted prairie-hen to-day. I eat it when you wen'; to supper."

The next moment Jim was again asleep, and silence once more reigned.

CHAPTER X.

Snoring and rats—Polly Hopkins **arrives when Nap is dreaming of** her—Nap kisses her in return for the loan of a **pistol—Nap hides his** treasure—He is robbed.

NAP watched for another rat. His success gave him a peculiar relish for the sport; but he thought it strange that he could kill only bitches and tom-rats. How long he sat watching we have no means of ascertaining. No other victim offered himself for his amusement, although an abundance of them could be seen in the street, or road, in front of the store. The door being wide open, Nap diverted himself watching their gambols. He hoped one (he did not wish for more) might come in and be killed; but being disappointed in this desire, he drew back once with the intention of hurling the iron in their midst. He restrained himself, however, when he reflected that he might lose his weight, as the lot opposite was covered by a dense growth of sumach and hazel bushes.

At last, overcome by the exercises of the day, physical and mental, he fell asleep. Of course he snored. The rats in the street paused in the midst of their moonlight gambols, and standing on their hind feet, listened to the sound. It was familiar to their ears; and no sooner had they recognised it, than they boldly entered the door. They ran under the chair in which Nap was sitting; and they sprang upon the Chicopee D bale of muslins, where

Jim was sleeping. They stood no longer in fear of losing their lives. Their present concern was how to sustain them. They mounted the shelves in the warcroom in quest of cheese; cut open the bags of dried peaches; and gnawed into a sugar-barrel. But this sort of forage did not content them. They sounded a tattoo on some dry beef-hides, and another old gray grandfather smelt Jim's heel.

At that hour, Nap, if he had been awake, and Jim, if he had been duly sober, might have heard the sounds of the hoofs of a horse galloping down the road. The rider sprang to the ground in front of the store, and hastily tying the horse to the rack, entered without further ceremony. The dim rays of the iron lamp suspended from the ceiling were not necessary to make it apparent that Nap was plunged into a profound slumber. The sound which proceeded from his nasal organ was not altogether unfamiliar to the ears of the visitor, who, approaching, and slapping the sleeper smartly on the shoulder, exclaimed—

"Wake up, Nap! You're wanted!"

"Why!" exclaimed Nap, spreading wide his eyes, his arms, and his fingers. Why—hello! It's Polly—durned if it ain't! I was dreaming about you!"

"Indeed! And pray what were you doing in your dream? Making me your wife?"

"No, not exactly. But sit down, and I'll tell you."

"I haven't time. Make haste and tell me; and then I'll tell you what brings me here."

"Well, as I said I wasn't exactly making you my wife; because I dreamt I had done it already. But about a month after we were married, I received a letter from Molly Brook, full of lamentations and reproaches. You saw me reading it. I was weeping in pity. You came behind me softly and looked over my shoulder, and when you saw who it was from, and what was in it, you snatched it away and put your foot on it. I stooped down to lift your leg away, but could not budge it. I said I had no idea a woman could be so strong; and you said a woman had a right to be strong after she was married."

"That will do," said Polly, laughing slightly.

"But what do you want to-night, Polly?"

"A pistol," said she, her lip compressed and her cheeks pale.

'No! Jim, wake up!" Jim drew a long breath and sat up on the bale, staring at Polly.

"Let Jim alone, and get me your revolver. I have been insulted. I have been spending the day with grandma Fennel, who is really a pious Methodist Christian, if she does shout. She don't know any better. She kept me till after supper, telling of her adventures, forty years ago, when the Indians prowled through the country. She was the only granny in this region, and was always kept on the move from post to post; and she travelled mostly in the night, accompanied by the husband of the next lying-in wife. She entertained me by relating many perilous adventures, until it grew dark, and then I mounted and cantered away. I had not gone a mile before I met an ill-looking fellow, whom I thought I recognised. He wheeled his horse and galloped at my side. I asked him who he was and what he wanted. He said he had many names, but no wife; and he thought I would just suit him. I attempted to spit in his face. He seized my bridle, and strove to lead my horse into the bushes. Just then a hound yelped close to us on the trail of a deer, and a moment after, a tall hunter, well-mounted, hallooed encouragingly to the dog. He was obscured by the bushes, yet he frightened my man away. I then put whip to my horse and continued on my way homeward. But soon the rascal overtook me, for he rode a splendid steed. I warned him to keep off, saying I had a pistol. He did not care for that, he said; and was about to seize the reins again, when we came in sight of Brother Keene's house. He cursed the house, and dashed into the woods on the right. But I had not gone a mile before he was at my side once more. He said he would let me off if I would dismount and give him a kiss"——

"The infernal scoundrel!" said Nap.

"If it had been you, Nap—or Jack"——

"Jack be hanged!"

"But let me go on. I wore out my hickory switch on my beast. The earth seemed to fly behind us. All at once the rascal drew back again, and disappeared."

"Why?" asked Nap.

"Because we were in sight of town, and he knew you would protect me."

"And I—I will!"

"No; I'll protect myself. Lend me your pistol. He'll be sure to overtake me again, and it shall be the last time!"

"Here's the pistol, Polly. But suppose I take out the bullets. If you let him see you are armed, it will do. If you were to shoot him sure enough—Who do you think it is, Polly?"

"Jackson Farnes, the thief and counterfeiter. I'll blow him through if he dares"——

"No, don't, Polly!" said Nap.

"Let her rip!" said Jim. "He's a double-purple madder-dyed villain!"

"If it's loaded with powder, and mustard-seed shot, it'll do. Polly, if you'd sting his horse with small shot the next time he comes up to you, he'd get a fall, and perhaps have a limb broken"——

"I'll aim at his heart!" said she, taking the pistol out of Nap's hand.

"Let her rip, I say!" continued Jim.

"I will!" said she. "And now, Nap, good-night. But keep an eye out for Farnes. He's back here after no good to any one. If *you* had asked me for the kiss," she continued, archly——

"May I have one?"

"I owe you thanks for the pistol. I feel secure, now.'

"But may I?"

"I must thank you, I say."

"Now, Polly!"

"Don't you understand? Take it!"

Nap *did*. It was the first time he ever tasted such a thing in his life, and it came near running him crazy. He trembled, flew about in every direction, and was speechless. Polly only laughed.

"Let him rip, Polly!" cried Jim, getting up with his feet on the Chicopee D bale, and towering above them both. "I'll see fair play."

"Do you get down again, Jim, and go to sleep!" said she. And before either of the young men could recover from the sudden confusion into which they had been plunged, Polly had leaped upon her horse and was galloping away. She soon slackened her pace, however, and then lingered along the silent road overhung with boughs and vines, through which the moon shone but dimly. But she was not molested. It was quite probable Farnes had heard every word that had been spoken in the store; and if so, he knew that Polly might prove to be a dangerous customer. At all events he did not persecute her any more. And when she reached the high prairie, and drew near her father's house, so confident was she of her entire safety, that she amused herself firing at a wolf that ran along parallel with the road.

Nap and Jim finding that no customers came but the rats, closed the door and retired for the night. Jim occupied a cot in the wareroom, like a sentinel at his post, guarding the spirits he presided over during the day. The rats never disturbed him. Even Nap's snoring was no molestation. Day or night, whether sitting up or in a recumbent position, if he remained perfectly still and silent for ten minutes, he fell asleep. Happy man! No pricks of conscience ever tormented him!

Nap spread his blankets on the counter. Then, with his thoughts dwelling upon what Polly had revealed in relation to Farnes, he made the door doubly fast, but neglected to secure the window. He usually left the shutters open, to enable him to see the first streaks of the morning. He always slept with his feet toward the window, and as his head was elevated by the pillow, of course his eyes opened upon the trees in front of the store. When his eyes were open it would be impossible for any one to present himself at the window without being seen by him. But he forgot that one's eyes, when one is asleep, are of no more use to see with than a couple of leaden balls.

And Nap had a considerable sum of money about the house, viz. one thousand dollars in silver, two hundred and fifty in gold, and two hundred and fifty in bank-notes. The silver, tied up in shot-bags, he placed in a nail-keg; and pouring a few pounds of eightpenny brads over them, suffered the keg to remain uncovered between others containing sixpenny and fourpenny nails. The gold he poured into the leg of a boot in one of Conrad, Thompson & Co.'s boxes. The paper money, in an old pocket-book, was shoved under his shirts and drawers, beside a long pistol, in a trunk from Haddock, Reed & Co., in which straw bonnets had been originally packed. His treasure thus disposed of, he thought there was no danger of being robbed. He was one of the many country merchants who believed there was more security in concealing the place of deposit, than in bolts and locks when the locality of the treasure was known. He scarcely ever used the same hiding-place twice in succession; and on one occasion, failing to remember where he had deposited his pocket-book, he believed he had been robbed. After searching in vain for hours, he scooped it out of a bag of coffee when selling a dollar's worth of that article.

At Tyre, at Venice, and at Troy, the merchants had been for weeks diligently collecting funds, which it was their purpose to concentrate at the first-named and most ancient city by a certain day, in anticipation of the arrival of several gentlemen from the East, who represented a number of the houses to which the three concerns were indebted. These gentlemen from the East, it must be noted, were not exactly on a dunning expedition; but they had been notified that a certain amount of funds would be paid them if they would call, which they were pressingly invited to do. They were agreeable companions, and not averse to the free enjoyment a new country affords. Among them were "Joe" T., Jno. P., (a famous singer,) M. J., Enoch H., S. S. C., and W. P. R.

It was after midnight. A solitary individual dismounted noiselessly from his horse some fifty paces distant from the store. He approached stealthily. There were no sounds without but the hooting of owls and the howling of wolves. Within, Nap was snoring as usual. Indeed, from the stillness around, the sounds of his untiring organ seemed to be unusually astounding and grating. Yet it was music to the ears of Farnes, who rose up boldly from under the window, where he had stooped down a moment to listen. He knew that Nap never dissembled in the article of sleep at that hour of the night.

With a stick prepared for the purpose, the burglar, stooping down again so that his head might not be within range of a bullet, slowly lifted the sash. This operation produced some little noise, and for several minutes Farnes remained quite still, and out of sight if any one should be awakened within. He listened intently. Nothing was heard but the continuous snore, and the occasional squeaking of rats. The burglar then propped up the sash, and placed one of the boxes which had been used by the orators under the window. He listened again. His guiding sound, the friendly snore, assured him there was no danger. So he entered. He knew exactly where the trunk was. Disguised with false whiskers, he had been among the crowd in the store during the day, and had seen Nap exchange specie for paper, and deposit the pocket-book in the trunk under the counter. And now the full moon poured a flood of light through the window, illuminating even the sleeper's features, and making the burglar's scene of operations sufficiently plain to him without calling in requisition the aid of his lantern. He stooped down beside the trunk. It was locked. He wrenched off the hasp, and again remained still a few moments, to listen if either of the young men had been disturbed by it. There being no such indications, he deliberately opened the trunk and removed the clothes. The long pistol first attracted his notice. He took it up, and running the ramrod down the barrel, smiled triumphantly upon finding it heavily charged. He retained it, to use against its owner if he awoke. But Nap did not dream of such a thing. He was smiling; perhaps supposing himself to be in the company of Molly or Polly.

Farnes next seized the pocket-book, which he deposited, without opening it, in his own pocket. He then proceeded to search for the gold and silver. He knew there was a large amount in the house. He had heard Nap say so, and that he wished to exchange it for paper, which would be more portable for Ben Handy when he came from Tyre on a collecting tour. And Ben was daily looked for. But the robber was balked. No specie was to be found in the trunk. One moment, and for a moment only, he had an impulse to withdraw and be contented with what he had secured. Relinquishing that idea, he determined to look further for Nap's treasure. He examined several drawers in which fine goods were kept; but to no purpose.. He then espied the end of the cash drawer under the counter. It was within a few inches of Nap's head, and one of his hands, extending beyond the edge of the counter, hung directly over the front of the drawer, and effectually secured it. It could not be drawn out while the hand remained in that position, without arousing the sleeper. Farnes stood a long time beside the unconscious Nap in deep and direful meditation. Once he cast a glance at the window to see that the way was clear, and then placed the muzzle of the pistol within an inch of poor Nap's temple. He paused with his finger on the trigger, and cast his eyes toward the door leading into the wareroom, which was open. He knew that Jim slept there, and Jim he knew to be as brave as Cæsar, although slow of locomotion. He then moved softly to the door, with the intention of closing and securing it. He was chagrined to find a barrel of sugar and a pile of log-chains would have to be removed before his purpose could be effected. This he could not undertake to perform. He glided back to Nap, and again stood beside him in deep meditation. Finally a smile played on his dark lip. He stooped down under the counter, and taking up a pin which glistened in the moonlight on the floor, punctured the obtruding hand. Nap moved slightly, and then slapped the wounded place violently with his other hand. Still the obtrusive member was not removed. Farnes applied the point of the pin again.

"Plague take the mosquitoes!" said Nap, turning over and catching violently at the supposed insect. But as his face was away now, and his hand removed, he was no more troubled by the mosquito, which, no doubt, he supposed to be killed. A few moments after he snored again. Then Farnes rose up and pulled out the drawer. He found nothing in it, however, but a few pieces of small change, a half-finished letter to Molly Brook, and a rough map of the embryo city. None of these were molested by him; and he concluded that it would be a fruitless search to hunt further for the specie. So selecting a fine riding-whip which hung near the window, he made good his escape. Mounting his fine horse, (stolen from Judge B.,) he set out at a brisk pace on the road leading to Troy, which was in the route to the boundary line separating the State from the Indian Territory.

At early dawn, as was his usual custom, Nap arose much refreshed. Jim was up too, sweeping the floor, and quite himself again, with his throat perhaps a little more than ordinarily thirsty. A quid of tobacco soon remedied that.

"Nap," said he, standing with the broom in his hand, "how did you happen to leave the window up all night?"

"I didn't know it," said Nap, looking in surprise at the raised sash. "I didn't leave it up! I'm almost sure I didn't."

"You must have done it in your sleep."

"No, I never walk in my sleep. That is, I never heard of my doing so. It must have been up all night, for I was cold this morning, and the mosquitoes came in and bit me. Look there at the whelks," he continued, showing his hand.

"This don't look right, Nap!" said Jim, perceiving the sash had been raised from the outside, and was still propped up by the pronged stick Farnes had used.

"Who could have done that?" exclaimed Nap.

"Nobody after any good. As sure as day, he was a double-purple, madder-dyed villain. A forger"——

"A burglar, you mean," said Nap, pale and panting.

"A madder-dyed rascal, anyhow! I'll bet a hundred dollars it was Farnes. Where's the money, Nap?"

Nap sprang to the nail-keg. All was right there. The gold was likewise safe in the boot-leg. But—alas! the clothes were tumbled out of the trunk, and the pocket-book missing!

Nap pulled a handful of hair from each side of his head, and threw himself down on the couch he had just risen from. He did not snore. He had a chill. Jim swore like a trooper, and spat every half minute.

CHAPTER XI.

Ben Handy, and longings for money—Jack and **Ben** Handy have a cash customer at Troy—Silver exchanged for paper—Ben arrives in Venice, and puts the people on the track of Farnes—The robber taken and the money recovered—Polly Hopkins returns with the revolver and frightens Ben Handy—Ben's horses run away with the specie—Dollars scattered in the dust.

BENJAMIN HANDY, the youngest of the family of Handys, as we stated before, had been sent for by Joseph to assist him at Tyre. And there he learned the rudiments of the art and mystery of merchandising. Little Ben, as he was frequently called, had by nature perhaps one of the best qualifications to obtain wealth of any of the family. He had stability. If he was not gifted with the same quickness and activity of mind that characterized some of his brothers, he had the faculty of pursuing steadily any object he designed to accomplish. Unlike most young men who fritter away their time and talents in the partial and ineffectual pursuit of a constant succession of new projects, never persevering to the consummation of any of them, he marked out deliberately a course to be pursued for the attainment of his desires, and unfalteringly adhered to it. If the constant water-drop will wear away the rock, what obstructions and difficulties can prevent the steadfast and undeviating efforts of a man from achieving fortune?

Just previous to the time when the arrival of the young gentlemen from the East was expected, Ben had been despatched by Joseph to bring in from Troy and Venice all the money that Jack and Nap might have on hand. As Troy was the most distant point from Tyre, Ben determined to go thither first, and to return by way of Venice.

On the morning succeeding the night of the robbery.

Ben was engaged with Jack in counting and tying up rouleaus of dollars, which were to be conveyed in his saddle-bags. He was, besides, to lead a pony from Troy to Tyre, and of course he had his "hands full." But he determined that the pony should bear the weighty saddle-bags. Jack, however, prevailed on him to remain till noon, hoping that he might have an opportunity of exchanging some of the specie for current bank-notes.

Several persons arrived in the town during Ben's stay, and very willingly made the exchange, for specie alone was taken at the land-office. Thus Ben's "load" was materially diminished, for Jack had accumulated a pretty considerable "pile."

But before Ben had completed his final arrangements, Jackson Farnes arrived and entered the store. Jack had never seen him but once, and then briefly and indistinctly, at the camp-meeting. Farnes had no fear of being recognised by him, nor did he care much whether he was known or not. He was certain the news of the robbery could not have reached Troy; and if it had, why should any one suspect him? So he entered the store boldly, with the stolen whip in his hand, and said he wished to purchase a pair of boots—the best in the house. Ben had a passion for selling goods to ready buyers, and believing from the appearance of Farnes, whom he had never seen before, that he was in "earnest," he volunteered his services in accommodating him with the article demanded. He sold him a pair of boots for six dollars, which had cost but three and a half. Farnes gave him a ten-dollar note to change.

"That's just into my hand," said Ben, holding the note. "I want paper money."

"If that's the game, stranger," said Farnes, "I can let you have a couple of hundred for the specie." And he displayed a large roll of bank-notes—the pocket-book having been destroyed.

"Agreed!" said Ben. "But while Jack is counting the money, I want to sell you something else." And he did sell him fifteen or twenty dollars' worth more. But inasmuch as the fellow never objected to the price of any thing, Ben began to scrutinize him closely, and to examine the money carefully. He was almost afraid that something—he could not conjecture what—was wrong about his careless customer. At last Ben's eyes rested upon the whip in the hands of Farnes, and he recognised the mark on the ticket, which the rogue had neglected to remove. "I'll bet I can tell where you bought your whip," said Ben.

"I'll bet you!" said Farnes.

"You bought it of N. B. Wax & Co., at Venice."

"Durned if I did! But what made you think so?" asked Farnes, becoming somewhat restless.

'Because I know the mark on the ticket. We use the same mark at all three of the places where we do business."

"I won't dispute that—and it mought have come from there—but I didn't buy it."

"You swapped for it then, or found it. Somebody bought it there."

"That's another thing. But I must be off. Good day." And gathering up the specie, which he had not taken the pains to count himself, the rascal mounted his (Judge B.'s) fine horse and cantered away.

"He's a singular genius," said Ben.

"He's either a fool or a knave," said Jack. "These are good notes, though."

"Let me see that!" said Ben, recognising the handwriting of Nap on the back of a ten-dollar bill. It was the name of Mr. Keene, which had been written there. "No doubt the fellow's been at Venice.. He may have got a large note or two changed there."

"I wonder he didn't get specie then," said Jack.

Ben, dismissing the matter from his mind, set out at the appointed hour. The distance to Venice was less than twenty miles, and he could easily reach it by supper-time without pushing the horses. So he travelled leisurely along, dwelling upon the great project which generally occupied his mind, viz. how he might some day make a large fortune for himself.

He reached Venice before sundown, and after having his horses fed by Marsh, presenting himself with his saddle-bags on his arm before Nap.

"I hope, Nap," said he, after the usual brief salutation, "that your money is not specie."

"Well, it isn't any thing else!" said Nap, dryly.

"I'm sorry for it. But have you much of it?"

Nap told him the amount.

"That'll break the pony's back. Have you no paper?"

"Not a rag!"

"That's strange! What's the matter?" continued Ben, observing Nap's extreme agitation.

"Ben," said Nap, very gravely, "I'd rather by a hundred dollars you had come yesterday."

"Why?"

"I—I was robbed last night!"

Ben heartily sympathized with him. Then the thought flashed upon his mind that the customer to whom he had sold the boots might be the robber. He got Nap to describe to him the denominations of the notes, and the banks they were upon, as well as he was able. And when he remarked that one of the notes had been paid him by Brother Keene, whose honesty he doubted, and in consequence he had written his name on the back of it, Ben brought down his hand so violently on the counter where Nap was sitting, that the specie in the drawer beneath rattled loudly. Nap started in surprise.

"What's to pay now, Ben?" he asked, quickly.

"See here!" said Ben, taking out the notes he had got from Farnes, and spreading them on the counter.

"These are the very notes I was robbed of!" exclaimed Nap, recognising them.

"If they ain't, I'm a Dutchman!" said Jim, likewise recognising several of them.

"Huzza!" cried Nap, almost dancing with delight. "Here's the money back again! Huzza for you, Ben!"

"Ben's a trump!" said Jim.

During all this time the imperturbable gravity of Ben's face manifested no change. He merely winked more rapidly than usual.

"How did you recover the money?" at length asked Nap.

"I'll tell you," said Ben, in so grave a tone as to repress Nap's rejoicings. He did relate the manner in which he became possessed of the notes; and once more Nap's chin fell despondingly. Jim was dumb and dispirited, and took a dram.

There were a number of Nap's friends and customers in the store; and when Ben described the man who bought the boots, and Nap related the conversation he had held with Polly Hopkins, they declared unanimously that it must be Farnes. Marsh came in, and upon hearing what Ben had narrated, stuttered out a proposition that a dozen men should mount their horses and go in pursuit. He knew where Farnes would stop in the Indian Territory, and volunteered to guide the party to the place. Arming themselves with pistols and butcher-knives, and several having their rifles with them, (a habit with many in the far West,) nearly all present seemed impatient to start in pursuit of the robber, under the guidance of Marsh. Nap alone hung fire. Ben, who was fatigued, offered to stay and assist Jim. But Nap declared he was ill. He was sorry for it, but he could not go. He said, however, as it was necessary for some one from the store to be in the pursuing party, Jim might go. Jim mounted with alacrity.

They rode all night at a rapid pace, and at dawn had passed the boundary line and were in sight of Dr. Weed's house. The Doctor was universally regarded as a desperate character. He had served a term in the penitentiary for robbing the mail in Pennsylvania, and was now supposed to be a member of a band of counterfeiters.

"Th–that's the pl–pla–place, b–bo–boys!" said Marsh. They halted and held a brief consultation. Then they separated for the purpose of approaching the house, which was in the midst of a grove of black-jacks, from different directions. Thus the premises would be surrounded, and the escape of the robber prevented. It was agreed that if Farnes could not be stopped in any other way, should he take to flight, he was to be shot down.

As had been concerted, the party approached from different points, and arrived at the house simultaneously. The dogs gave the alarm, and the lights were extinguished.

"He–hel–hel–lo!" cried Marsh.

"Who's there? What do you want?" demanded the Doctor, from an upper window.

"We've come for Farnes!" said one of the party.

"A–an–and w–w–we'll h–ha–have him!" said Marsh.

"He's not here!" said the Doctor.

"It's a d–d–d——d lie!" said Marsh.

By this time all the doors were guarded, and the Doctor was told there would be no use in attempting to conceal Farnes, or in resistance. Much bustle and confusion could be heard in the house, and it was quite apparent that more than the Doctor's family, consisting of himself and daughter, were within. The Doctor was ordered to light the candles and open the door. The command was reluctantly obeyed. The foremost of the party, accompanied by several of the boldest men, ascended the stairway, while the rest remained below and watched the doors and windows. Marsh opened a chamber door on his right.

"What do you want here?" cried a female, in bed, whose white cap, and the upper portion of her face, were alone visible. It was the Doctor's daughter.

"F–Fa–Farnes!" said Marsh.

"Don't you see he's not here?"

"B--b--but I w--wa--want to s--see that he *is* h--he--here!" replied Marsh, approaching the bed.

"Go off!" exclaimed the girl.

"G--ge--get up. D--do--don't be a--a--shamed. Y--you've g--got a go--gown on."

"I won't! *you* ought to be ashamed!"

"E--ex--cuse me, m--mi--miss!" said Marsh, extending his hand and stripping off every particle of the covering.

"You beast!" cried she, red with rage.

"G--get up."

"Well!" cried she, springing up. "Now what else do you want?"

"I--I'll s--see." Stooping down and thrusting a candle under the bed, they beheld Farnes lying on the cords. The bed had been placed on him, and the girl had got on the bed.

"J--Ja--Jackson F--Farnes, you're w--wanted!" said Marsh, throwing off the bed. And then turning to the frowning girl, who looked defiance, he said, "W--wasn't y--you a--a--shamed to g--get on t--t--top a--and h--hi--hide h--him?"

"No! I had a right to do it, for we were to be married lawfully to-morrow."

"W--wh--where's the m--mo--money, Farnes?" continued Marsh, turning to the cowed and unresisting captive.

"Whose money?" he asked.

"N--Nap W--Wax's."

"I haven't got it. Not a dollar of it."

"No, you double-purple, madder-dyed villain, you exchanged it with Jack and Ben Handy for specie!" said Jim.

"Prove it!" said Farnes.

"Here's the boots he bought of Ben!" said Jim, lifting them from the bed-clothes; "and they're mighty heavy." Turning them up, a quantity of specie fell out and rolled about the floor.

"You have no right to take Farnes here!" cried the

Doctor, rushing in. "This is out of the State, out of the United States, and I want to know by what authority you act?"

"J–Judge L–Lynch!" said Marsh. "B–be qu–quiet, Doctor, or y–you'll g–get into a s–scrape."

The money was gathered up and counted. Nearly the whole amount that had been stolen was recovered. Then, fearing the Doctor might soon collect a large number of his lawless band to attack them, the party mounted their horses and whipped back over the line, taking Farnes with them, his feet tied to the stirrups of his saddle.

Farnes, recovering his composure, joked and laughed with his captors as they rode along, and frequently bantered them for a race. He appealed to them to "give a fellow a chance," and let him have sufficient start of them to be out of reach of their rifles. He knew his horse was the fleetest one in company, and if he could only get beyond the range of their guns, he might easily make his escape. They encouraged him to believe they were relenting, and prevailed on him to confess he had committed the robbery. He said, the window-shutter being open, and Nap's snore distinctly heard from the road, the temptation was too strong to be resisted. He described the minute particulars of his operations, and dwelt upon those points which seemed to entertain his auditors the most. When questioned whether he really intended to use the pistol, he said that if Nap had opened his eyes he intended to shoot him through the head. This avowal dyed him "double-purple" again in Jim's estimation.

When they drew near Venice they met Judge B., who was hunting his horse. The Judge had purposely turned him loose originally, never supposing that he would be taken up by a rogue. Major Jackson, who was still sporting in the neighbourhood, soon after joined them, and testified that it was truly the Judge's horse, for they had travelled much together over the State, riding, as Colonel Benton said, pretty much the same hobby. The Judge took possession of his horse, and rode away with the Major toward the next place of meeting.

Farnes was escorted into town on foot by three horsemen on each side of him and as many in the rear. His hands were bound behind him, and all eyes were fixed upon him. Yet he did not seem to be abashed. Jim was the first to announce the capture of the robber to Nap and Ben; and when he displayed the money that had been recovered, Ben's features relaxed, and then, for the first time since his arrival, he laughed very heartily.

Farnes was placed in one of the upper rooms of the inn, and a watch set over him.

About this time, it being still early in the day, Polly Hopkins came in to return Nap's revolver, to buy some dimity, and to hear the news. She seemed much pleased at meeting Ben there, and to learn he was to set out in an hour for Tyre, because his course would be along her road. Ben only looked grave.

"But, Nap," said she, upon learning what had occurred, "didn't I warn you against Farnes?"

"Yes, you did; but I didn't think there was any danger. I thought he was after you."

"I wanted him to show me his face once more! If he had, he would not have drawn blood from you."

"Drawn blood from me? He didn't do it!"

"He did. He told Brother Steele, the constable, a little while ago, that your hand hung over the money-drawer, and that he ran a pin into it to make you jerk it away."

Nap, struck speechless, let fall the yard-stick with which he was measuring some alpaca for several ladies in the store, and stared in terror at the marks of the punctures on his hand.

"A mosquito saved your life, Nap!" said Jim.

"But it wasn't a mosquito!" said Nap.

"No matter. You thought it was, and that was the same thing."

"Come, Ben," said Polly, "there's stuttering Marsh at the door with your horses. Let us be off."

"I'm in no hurry!" replied he, rather coldly.

"You needn't be afraid of robbers, Ben," said Nap, "while you have Polly with you."

"I'm not afraid when I'm by myself," was the dry response.

"A--are you ar--armed?" asked Marsh.

"Yes."

"What with?" asked Polly.

Ben exhibited a very small pocket-pistol.

"That pop-gun wouldn't frighten a woman, much less a man!" said Polly. "Nap, I'll keep your revolver till I see you again."

"Very well; take good care of Ben, and take care of yourself."

"I'm in no danger, I thank you. Come, Ben," she continued, going out and mounting her horse.

Ben, after some hesitation, silently followed, and they rode away together. When they had proceeded about a mile, Polly abruptly turned her face toward her companion.

"Ben," said she, "I don't believe you were ever in love in your life."

"I know I never was!" was the half-angry reply.

"Why?"

"Because I don't care any thing about the girls."

"Nap and Jack both have sweethearts in Kentucky, and that's the reason they don't fall in love with me."

"They are silly for it."

"I think so too. You have seen Kate and Molly. Are they better looking than I am?"

"I don't know. I never noticed them."

"Then look at me."

"I don't want to look at any girl."

"Ben, I know you hate old bachelors."

"How do you know it?"

"Your brother Joseph was telling me last week that **you went** to school to a Miss E——, who was forty years of age; and once, when she lifted a switch to whip you, you became very angry, and called her an old bachelor. She laughed so heartily at your **mistake,** that the switch dropped from her hand."

"But she **was an** old maid, and not a bachelor," said Ben, smiling, **for he** had really made the ludicrous blunder. "**It was** an old maid I hated."

"You don't call *me* an old maid, I hope?"

"I don't call you at all! Keep your horse **out of my** way."

"Ben, I think I must be your first love, and marry you some of these days."

"**Get** out, with your nonsense!"

"How old are you, Ben?"

"Sixteen."

"A nice age for a pet!"

"I've got a young wolf chained at the store; you may have him."

"Never mind, you'll get older some of these days."

"And wiser."

"Yes. I'll teach you."

"I want none of your instruction."

"You're a fool, Ben!"

"You're another!"

A running dialogue of this kind was kept up until they reached the road which led to Polly's house, and there they parted. She could not persuade her impracticable companion to accompany her home and take some refreshment.

When **the** sun was about an hour high, Ben had reached within some seven miles of Tyre, where his horses grew excessively dull, and evinced an indisposition to pro**ceed farther.** He could not keep their mouths from the **rank** grass that grew along the roadside in the rich prairie through which he **was** passing. He kicked and cuffed them until he grew weary. He even fired his pistol occasionally at the flocks of grouse that continually flew up from the road, where they had been wallowing in the dust. But the jaded horses could not be startled. They did not even lift their heads when he fired.

He dismounted, opposite a low thicket. He transferred the saddle-bags from the pony, whose back had so long bent under their weight, to the strong horse on which he had been riding. Then, letting the animals browse together, he stepped aside and cut an elastic switch, with which he determined to make better progress homeward.

But no sooner did he display the switch, than the pony, which had hitherto seemed to be ready to fall with exhaustion, kicked up his heels and cantered away, followed by the old horse. Ben vainly cried "Whoa!" The animals only cast mischievous glances back at him, and increased their speed. He followed panting, and perfectly miserable. Presently he saw the saddle-bags tumble over and hang under the horse's belly. This made the animal spring forward more violently than ever, and soon after the last strap gave way, and the saddle-bags fell in the centre of the road.

The young man was certainly in an unpleasant predicament, and from his distressed expression of countenance, one might have seen that he fully realized his apparently hopeless condition. He could do nothing but follow the road the horses had taken until he came to the saddle-bags. But long before he reached the place where they had fallen, he perceived that a portion of the money had been jolted out and was strewed along in the dust. The first parcel he found was a rouleau of fifty dollars, the coins not having burst the paper enveloping them. Such was not always the case with the rest of the packages. For soon he espied Mexican dollars and five-franc pieces scattered promiscuously in the road. Of course he did not pass by any of them, but diligently collected all he could find, and placed them in a strong handkerchief. He progressed slowly. Sometimes the dollars lay several feet apart; in other places fifteen or twenty were found together, and occasionally he picked up an unbroken rouleau. It was just when he had reached the saddle-bags, that he espied a man riding across the prairie with a large buck before him on his horse.

"What are you hunting, Ben?" cried he, when he had approached within fifty yards of the young man.

"Money," said Ben, when he recognised Brother Nave, whose house stood on the road to Tyre, some three-quarters of a mile ahead of them.

Brother Nave was much astonished, and at first believed the boy had become demented, thinking of the placers in California. But when every thing had been explained to him, he dismounted and assisted Ben in the search. Not a dollar was found on the ground Ben had passed over. And when they arrived at the house, it was ascertained that nothing had been lost! Brother Nave sent a negro boy down the road to a small stream, which was then not fordable; and there the runaway horses were found standing in the ferry-boat, waiting to be rowed over. They were led back, and Ben yielded to the proposition of Brother Nave to remain with him all night, and make a fresh start in the morning. And the next morning the pony paid the penalty decreed by Ben for his misconduct. The saddle-bags were securely lashed to his back, and he was urged forward unmercifully under the stimulation of an elastic hickory switch.

A few days after, news came from Venice that Farnes had escaped, and had stolen Brother Keene's famous horse. He was pursued, however, and taken; and finally served a term at Jefferson City, sawing stone.

CHAPTER XII.

A foggy morning, but a bright day—Nap rides out to hunt deer with a party of Eastern merchants—Nap has a crooked gun—A buck started—Nap fires and kills Colonel Hopkins's bitch—And slaughters the prairie-hens.

THE day was just dawning. A dismal fog rested upon the broad river. The whippoorwill had ceased its song, and taken its flight into an impenetrable thicket. Even the wolves stopped howling, as if affrighted at the harsh sounds they made themselves on the motionless air. They slunk away into their dens, and sullenly rested with their heads pressed to the earth between their paws. And the great green frogs, which had made the slough loudly reverberate their deep bass notes, were likewise awed into silence, and sat with their heads stooped low, and their long legs drawn under them. The misty cloud which immersed every thing seemed to have robbed them of their spirits, and to have plunged them into a profound melancholy. Thus they remained for a brief space of time; and then, as if with a desperate resolution to end their woes—to rush away from the humid and sombre atmosphere enveloping them—they leaped, one and all, into the deep oblivious stream and sank to the bottom.

The cock, perched upon a persimmon-tree in Sam Marsh's garden, clapped his wings and crowed. An opossum, which had been foraging on the same tree, closed his eyes and fell to the earth; but immediately after disappeared, as no bones had been broken.

Nap was snoring away, as if sleeping against time for a wager. As he drew near the end of the race he seemed to be urged forward by whip and spur, for the sounds were uttered in quicker succession, and each louder than the last, till the final tremendous explosion awoke him. He sprang up, and aroused Jim.

"Come, Jim!" said he. "Be up and stirring. I must be off. The Philadelphians and New-Yorkers must not be upon the ground first. I am to be the pioneer in the hunt. I hope Polly will have some spinning or weaving to do, to keep her at the house. Captain Jewett will be here to-day with his new boat. Put all the produce on board, Jim, and have the bills of lading properly signed. Consign to D. T. & Co. Write them to sell for the most they can get, and keep the money till further orders. As for these confounded deeds," he continued, glancing impatiently at some half-a-dozen instruments of conveyance lying on the desk, "I'm getting sick of 'em. It's give, give, give—and I get nothing back"——

"You are selling a sight of hardware though, and other building materials," said Jim, pausing with the broom in his hand.

"True, Jim. That's a fact; and I make 'em pay a profit. But it seems to me that it's about time to begin to *sell* some of the lots. Very soon every man who wants to live here, or build him a shanty, will be supplied. Then when my alternate lots are put up for sale, there will be no buyers. I'm afraid Colonel Benton's advice won't do me any good."

"Let it rip, Nap! Go it blind! Colonel Benton can see about as far ahead as other men of his age can see behind 'em. I never could guess how the things he predicted were to come to pass; but they never failed to do it. And now if he was to tell me to give my horse away, I'd do it. Somebody would be sure to give me a nigger!"

In fact, ever since the time that Colonel Benton had told the people crowding around him in Sam Marsh's porch, that Venice would some day be a *real* town, Nap had been daily applied to for lots. And now, although scarcely a week had elapsed, some eight or ten wooden buildings were going up in the bushes. The sounds of axes, saws, and hammers began with the rising of the sun, and only ceased with the setting thereof.

Nap had sold all his nails, augers, saws, hammers, axes, hinges, locks, window-glass, &c., and had sent more than once both to Tyre and Troy for new supplies. But this was not all. The spirit of enterprise is always contagious. Many of the vacant lands in the vicinity were entered, and families hitherto in the habit of dealing at other points concentrated their business at Venice. They brought all their "truck" to Nap, and bartered for his "plunder." The shipment his faithful Jim was to make consisted of twenty bales of deer-skins, for which he had paid twelve and-a-half cents per pound; five thousand pounds of bees-wax, for which he had given a shilling a pound; otter skins at a dollar; mink at twenty cents, and several hundred "coons" at fifteen cents. All paid for in merchandise at seventy-five per cent. advance on the Eastern cost!

In truth, so multifarious were Nap's engagements, that he imagined he grew thinner and lighter. He certainly became more active. But a day having been appointed for him to meet the Eastern gentlemen on the famous hunting-grounds in the vicinity of Colonel Hopkins's farm, he had made preparations to join them with his usual punctuality. And that he might not be a mere spectator of the sport, he had provided himself with a double-barrelled shot-gun. He had swapped a rifle for it. The one (an itinerant pedlar) with whom he made the exchange, warranted the fowling-piece to be of excellent quality, and sure to do execution if aimed right. He fired both barrels at a mark himself, in Nap's presence, and placed, at a distance of thirty yards, some fifteen pellets in a paper not larger in circumference than a dollar.

Thus provided, Nap, after an early breakfast, mounted his horse and rode out to the place of meeting. The sun had risen in great glory, and he rejoiced to find himself the first one upon the ground. He was soon joined, however, by Colonel Hopkins.

"Nap," said the Colonel, "who's with these city folks? Who's to show them where to find the game, and how to kill it?"

"Joseph Handy is to come with them. No one else, I believe."

"And he'll be like the man in Scripture—the blind leading the blind. I heard him say last week he had not fired a gun since he's been living in Missouri."

"But I'm here!" said Nap, somewhat exultingly.

"You! You killed Jack Grove's bitch. That's all I ever heard of you killing. You don't know the first principles of hunting. See here. Before us lies extended one of the finest hunting tracts in the world. We can, from this eminence, see over five thousand acres of prairie, interspread with hazel and sumach thickets. Parallel ravines run through it, and small brooks of cold clear water gurgle along from a dozen springs. The whole ground is practicable for horses and hounds, and most of it for carriages. There never was a prettier field for sport; and I venture to say that within the same space there can nowhere be found a larger quantity of game. Deer, turkeys, and prairie-hens are there in droves"——

"I don't see one!" said Nap.

"Of course you don't. But I'll bet more than one buck and more than a hundred prairie-hens, are now looking at you. Perhaps a wolf's mouth is watering for a slice of your thigh."

"Durned if I like that, Colonel!"

"Pshaw! My Polly would chase a whole regiment of them!"

"You will stay with us, won't you, Colonel? You are an old hunter, and can teach the boys."

"Of course I will. I have my rifle, and will blow up my hounds. I intend to have you all at my house tonight, and I must provide some meat for you. But I shall have to kill it myself, I suppose. There is only one among the batch of the city gentry I saw at Tyre, whose eye looks as if it could draw a bead. That is R———ll. He has the right sort of an eye. But what can he expect to do with a shot-gun?"

"I have a shot-gun too, Colonel."

"Nap, I didn't think you were so green, after living as long as you have done in Missouri. Let me see it. Well! if you kill any thing with this gun to-day, I'll agree to eat it raw, hide and all!" continued the Colonel, running his eye along the barrels.

"Why do you think so, Colonel?"

"Because it isn't straight. It has a twist to the left. Some rascal has cheated you."

"You're mistaken, Colonel. I saw him try it. He fired twice, and hit the mark both times."

"He did? I'll——but yonder come the boys, some on horseback and some in buggies. Talking and laughing loudly, while the game is listening. Novice like. I'll blow for the hounds."

He sounded his horn, and immediately the dogs were heard yelping in the distance toward the house. They were led by an old negro.

The party approaching were yet a quarter of a mile distant; but their voices could be distinctly heard.

"Nap," said the Colonel, "if I were not here, what would you do first when the boys arrive?"

"We'd take stands at the other end of the ground, and put in two drivers with the dogs at this end."

"You would, would you? I thought so! And the standers might just as well be sitting in my porch. Not one of them would get a shot."

"Why, that's the way Sam Marsh, who is a good hunter, told me to do."

"And did he say nothing about the wind?"

"Oh yes, I forgot that!"

"What did he say?"

"Hanged if I recollect!"

"Ha! ha! ha! You have forgotten the most essential portion of your instructions. Don't you see the breeze comes from the other end of the ground?"

"Yes."

"Well. Every buck is lying with his nose to the wind, and not one would run toward the standers. They would turn and come this way. The drivers might have some shots, and that would be all. No, since the wind is in this direction, and as there are no good stands here, we must all ride over the ground parallel to each other, and about a hundred yards apart. The dogs must be kept in the rear to chase the wounded deer. If all the men have shot-guns, none of the bucks will fall, if hit, before running a long distance. We must ride among them and start them up ourselves. They will try to get around us, and if one misses, another may hit, as they run along the line."

When the party joined Colonel Hopkins and Nap on the eminence, from whence they could see over the extensive grounds, ever famous for their abundance of game, and for the rare sport which had been enjoyed there by hundreds of hunters, they were greatly charmed with the prospect, and unaffectedly eager to engage in the exciting diversion. All had shot-guns except the Colonel. His rifle was uncouth in appearance, long and heavy, but a celebrated instrument of destruction. It had been made by Daniel Thornton.

Mr. R——, or, as he was called, "Uncle Billy," was placed on the extreme left, and Colonel Hopkins posted himself on the right. They were about half a mile asunder, and the intermediate space was occupied by four of the city boys, the redoubtable Nap, and Joseph Handy. They were ranged about a hundred yards apart, and were formed in a straight line across the plain. The flankers, Colonel Hopkins and Uncle Billy, were some fifty paces in advance. The dogs were kept in the rear by the Colonel's negro man

Upon a signal from the Colonel, the party moved forward simultaneously at a brisk walk, each man having his gun in readiness to fire. Their guns being charged with buckshot, it was understood that no one was to fire at smaller game than deer. Uncle Billy was soon thrown into a state of nervous excitement. Scarcely a minute elapsed that he was not within pistol-shot of quails, pheasants, and grouse, which were continually flying up in front of the horses, and temptingly presenting their fat rumps. Sometimes they rose from under the horses' feet, and scarcely ever beyond the range of No. 5 shot. The truth was, they had never been fired at on the wing in that section.of the country; and such "small game" were rarely molested at all by the resident hunters. Resolving to pay his respects to these birds before he left the ground, Uncle Billy suffered them for the present to fly away unharmed.

"Look at him! See there!" exclaimed Joseph Handy, as a fine short-haired buck sprang up from his bed in the tall grass, within fifteen feet of him. As he arose, he could be heard expelling a long breath, like a disturbed ox with full paunch forced reluctantly to leave his comfortable quarters. He shook his ponderous and many-pronged horns, and threw up his tail as he leaped gracefully and without precipitation over the tall sumach-bushes to a bald spot in the prairie, about forty paces from his lair, where he paused and made a brief survey of the field.

"Shoot! Why don't you fire?" exclaimed half a dozen voices.

"I didn't think of that! I forgot I had a gun!" said Joseph, endeavouring to make his horse, which was a hunter and wanted to pursue the game, stand still while he fired. But when he succeeded in arresting his animal, and raised his gun to his shoulder, the buck was gone. The tips of his antlers only were seen, and the thumps of his hard feet on the dry earth could be distinctly heard; but he was beyond the range of Handy's lead. He ran down with the breeze a few moments and then made a curve toward the left of the advancing line of hunters. Not liking the "cut" of Uncle Billy's eye, as Colonel Hopkins expressed it, he carefully avoided his aim, so that when he turned his nose toward the hunters again, he converged sufficiently toward the centre to be more than a hundred paces from Uncle Billy's muzzles. At first he seemed to be inclined to charge through the line within twenty feet of Joseph Handy; and he really approached within a few paces of the bed where he had first been lying, notwithstanding the cry from all parts of the field to Joseph to "look out." He did look out; but not in the right course. His eyes were directed from one hunter to another as they successively uttered the warning cry. His horse saw the buck and pawed the earth impatiently, while the rider continued to look in every direction but the right one, until the deer, abandoning the slight curtain of blackberry bushes that screened him, and as if in mockery of the whole squadron of novices, started off deliberately at a measured gallop, in a parallel line with the hunters, from left to right, exposing his broadside to them, and within fifty paces of their guns. Joseph fired when it was too late. Joe T., M. J., J. P., and S. S. C. fired one after another, like minute-guns at sea, but without effect. The buck neither lowered his flag (tail) nor widened the distance between him and the inoffensive battery of shotguns.

At this juncture, an old bitch, the mother of the Colonel's pack, escaped from the negro in the rear, and entered the chase, although there were no indications that any one of the hunters had brought blood, or even touched a hair of the noble deer. Hearing the warning voice of this foe upon his track, the buck again paused to survey the field. He had just passed a diminutive wild-cherry tree, upon which were perched a dozen grouse. Nap had long been regarding the birds, and regretting that he was bound to reserve his fire for the deer. The young wild-cherry tree was directly in front of him, and not forty yards distant. But now there was no longer a restraint imposed upon him. The buck stood with his huge body fully and tempt'ngly exposed, some fifteen or twenty feet to the **right of** the grouse, having passed under the diminutive tree without alarming the birds. There he stood, in perfect defiance of **Nap.** Turning his head over his back, he merely marked the approach of the yelping old bitch. He was panting slightly from the moderate exercise he had taken —being very fat—but exhibited no symptoms of distress, or even of alarm. He could not have avoided seeing Nap; but he looked upon him and his endeavours with perfect contempt. He seemed to grow angry. He shook his horns, stamped his foot, and flashed his eyes, as he observed the progress of the old bitch on his trail. He suffered her to approach as far as the tree, and then he bounded forward without any extraordinary exertion or seeming affright. **But as** he sprang up in making the first leap, Nap, who had been striving to repress his agitation, (the "buck ague,") fired both his barrels at him. The report was tremendous, and horse and rider were both enveloped in a cloud of smoke, which, for several moments, obscured them from the eyes of the rest of the sportsmen. And when the wind had swept away the cloud, it was perceived that the horse and man were some twenty feet **apart,** standing face to face, and staring at each other in amazement—Nap, indignant at the horse for throwing him—the horse wondering why his rider had tumbled off. Nap stooped down and picked up his gun. It had evidently been overcharged, and had rebounded from his hands. His nose was bleeding, and his lip was slightly **cut.** In no good humour he approached his horse, which did not move a hoof. He succeeded in mounting him, and then cast a glance toward the tree, where neither birds nor buck now greeted his uncertain vision.

"I've killed him, Sam!" he cried to C., who was next **to** him in the line.

"How do you know?" asked Sam.

"Because I don't see him. He must be lying in the low bushes. I'll load my gun and go there. But I'm sure he's dead, because I don't hear the slut any more. Before I fired she yelped every second."

While he was charging his gun, however, the buck was seen by the rest of the company rising from a slight depression in the prairie, and approaching the extreme right of the line, evidently with the intention of turning the flank of his army of pursuers, and retiring from the field in their rear, and toward the river. But he was not destined to succeed. An eye was upon him of which he had no knowledge. Colonel Hopkins, in advance of the line of hunters, guarded the right flank. Sitting on his motionless horse, and entirely hidden by a plum-bush matted over with grape-vines, from which hung luxuriant clusters of the purple fruit, he marked every manœuvre of the deer.

Supposing himself to be beyond the reach of further annoyance, the noble buck now slackened his pace, and as he ran gracefully along, with his side exposed to the ambushed marksman, at a distance of about sixty paces, he cast a glance at the disappointed novices. Just then the sharp report of the Colonel's rifle was heard, and the noble buck, pierced through the heart, stumbled along some ten feet and fell to the earth. The dark blood gushed up in a jet, and in its descent sprinkled the grass around. A groan, a sigh, and life was extinct.

Without casting a second glance in the direction of the fallen victim, for he knew perfectly well the fatal effect of his unerring aim, the Colonel proceeded to reload his rifle, a habit always observed by hunters, before approaching the fallen game. And when he did draw near, his pace was without evidence of excitement or precipitation. He stooped down and cut the buck's throat, that any blood remaining might escape. However, but little remained. It had gushed through the orifice made by his bullet. He then blew his horn for the boys to assemble around him from all parts of the field.

Nap understood the signal, for it had been previously explained to the party. They knew a buck had fallen, and were anxious to have a close inspection of his proportions.

"Stop, Sam!" said Nap, to Mr. C., as the latter galloped past. "Go with me out yonder by the tree."

"Nonsense, man! We all saw the buck after you fired. You missed him, clear; but Colonel Hopkins killed him."

"Not a bit of it! It was another buck. I killed mine to a certainty. I had a good aim, and he was standing— that is, he began to jump just as I pulled both triggers. I had fifteen large buckshot in each barrel—thirty in all, and *must* have peppered him."

"You may have peppered him, but the Colonel salted him. I believe I hit him myself, and all the boys say they struck him; but shot-guns wont do; buckshot won't kill such large deer. Come on; you needn't look there!" cried Sam, riding straight on while Nap turned his horse toward the tree.

"Hanged if I don't look, anyhow," said Nap, riding to the spot where the buck had stood, and looking in vain for him. He did not even see a hair, or a particle of blood.

"What's that!" he cried, as he heard a fluttering under the cherry-tree. "There he is, by jingo! No it ain't!" he continued, on approaching, and finding it to be a grouse in its last expiring struggle. "How the deuce did I happen to kill you?" said he, dismounting and taking up the bird. "Jerusalem and blue blazes! See there!" he continued, as he discovered five more grouse dead upon the ground. "Well, that beats all! Six prairie-chickens at a time! I didn't aim at 'em. The buck was at least fifteen or twenty feet to the right, and I took a dead aim at him. Hello! What's this?" he cried, starting back. "Colonel Hopkins's old bitch! As I'm living, she's as dead as a smoked herring. There are three holes through her side. No wonder she **stopped** yelping! But I'm in a scrape. The Colonel swears he wouldn't swap **her** for the best horse **in the** country. He says **she was** imported **by** "Dinks," a celebrated **sportsman in the East,** and was **stolen from him by a Mormon** preacher. All the **good** hounds in the county came out of her. What shall I do? **That's the** question. **I'm** glad Sam C. **didn't** stop! She's **as dead as a** door-nail, **and stiff as a** poker," he added, turning her **over with** his foot. He then bent a tuft of long luxuriant grass **over the** body, so as to conceal it from any one happening to pass in that direction. He did not fear, if it were known he had accidentally killed the bitch, **that** the Colonel would prosecute him; but he knew her **death would be** regretted, and that her owner would be irritated, and might perhaps, **as he was not** usually fastidious in the choice of **his words, utter some sarcasms not pleasant** to be heard.

Having concealed the dead body with something **like a** feeling of guilt oppressing him, Nap mounted his horse **and** set out in the direction of the scene of the slaughtered buck, where the rest of the party had already assembled and seemed **to** be disputing for the honour of having slain him. The Colonel hearing several of the boys declare they **knew** they had wounded the buck, because they saw him stagger and **stumble (as** they supposed) **when** they fired, only smiled, **and covered the deer with his saddle-**blanket.

"Now, Joe," said he, "where did you hit him?"

"I aimed at the head," replied Joe T. Joseph Handy and Uncle Billy had no pretensions to the honour of having killed him"

"**I aimed** at his heart," said Sam C.

"**And I** at his flank," said Jno. P.; "**and I know I** struck him, because I saw him wince."

"Where did you hit him?" the Colonel asked of **Marshall J.**

" Nowhere. I thought I had surely riddled his short ribs, but since I have examined my gun, I find it didn't go off. I exploded both caps—real G. D.'s—but the powder was too coarse. When I went to load again, I found both barrels still charged."

" You are too candid," said the Colonel; " you ought to have been mum. How could they tell whose shot made the holes in the buck? There ought to be fifty shot in him at least."

" Besides the thirty Nap says he put in him," said Sam C.

" I was mistaken, Sam," said Nap, exhibiting his large bunch of birds. " I had been looking so long at the prairie-hens, that when I intended to pull trigger at the buck, the barrels *would* point at the tree. So I beat you all—killed six, and here they are." Uncle Billy examined them with the eye of a connoisseur, and regarded them with as much interest as the rest did the buck.

" Nap aimed well," said the Colonel. " He made the best shot of the whole party. I saw him when he fired at the buck, and watched the tree to the left"——

" Did you see me ?" asked Nap, upon the eve of making a confession.

" I did, and I saw the tree rain down prairie-chickens."

" Did you see any thing else?"

" No; I then watched the buck; for I knew if I didn't kill him we'd have no meat"——

" I beg your pardon," said Uncle Billy. " The grouse are better than venison; and these, with those I intend to kill, would make a royal feast."

" We don't often eat such small game. They are not considered very good."

" Because they don't understand cooking them. To-night, if you have no objection, I will show the cook how to prepare them."

" I shall have no objection, if you have no fear of the

poker and tongs, and Polly's tongue, which *can* cut sometimes like a razor; can't it, **Nap**?"

"She has a sweet voice," said Nap, amid the smiles of the party.

"But let us see who killed the buck!" said the Colonel, throwing aside the blanket.

They surrounded the prostrate deer, and of course found but one perforation, and that was made by the rifle-ball, which passed through the heart. All who had fired at him seemed to be struck dumb with disappointment.

By this time the negro who had charge of the hounds came up.

"Here, Grippa," said his master, "take this bunch of birds home to Polly. Where are the dogs?"

"Gone, Massa! I couldn't keep 'em back when dey heard such a tarnation shooting. Don't you hear 'em?"

They were distinctly heard chasing other deer in divers directions. When they disdained further control, they had rushed into the prairie and started perhaps a dozen, which they were now pursuing without restraint, and of course without effect.

"But where's Juno?" continued the Colonel. "I thought I heard her running after the buck?"

"She did run arter him, Massa; I couldn't keep her back. But I doesn't know whar she is."

"She's as deaf as a post, and can't hear the horn, nor the music of the other dogs either. Do you take the buck home. I'll carry the prairie-chickens, and see if Polly can't fix 'em right. Boys, when you get tired of the sport, you know the way to the house. I promised to kill only one, if you failed. You'll find me aiding the women to prepare something for your comfort. If you see my pied bitch, throw her into the buggy and bring her along. I wouldn't take a hundred dollars for her. She has *blood* in her."

"Not much," thought Nap, whose face was turned away, and who trembled with alarm all the time the Colonel was speaking.

CHAPTER XIII.

The boys hunt the deer again, and grow weary of the sport—Nap and Uncle Billy stay to shoot grouse—Uncle Billy's success—Nap fires at one and kills another—Slight dispute about a bird.

The young gentlemen mounted their horses again, and proceeded with the hunt. Not more than half the ground allotted for the sport had been traversed. But one of those sudden changes of weather for which Missouri is remarkable, had taken place since the slaughter of the noble buck. The wind had changed to the opposite quarter, and the sky was dappled over with clouds.

For an hour our industrious sportsmen beat the bushes and galloped over the plain, in the hope of being able to "duplicate" the buck "knocked down" by Colonel Hopkins, as they expressed themselves in mercantile parlance. But the hope was illusory. No one could get a shot at a deer within killing distance. They started numbers, some thirteen in all; but they invariably sprang up and ran away before the huntsmen arrived within a hundred yards of them. They had the wind now, blowing from the men to them, and were enabled to perceive the danger in time to avert it. If the dogs had not been recalled by the Colonel's horn, they might have driven a buck within reach of the guns; as it was, the boys were left to their own resources, which they very soon perceived to be of no avail. All of them, therefore, with the exception of Nap and Uncle Billy, turned the heads of their horses toward the hospitable mansion of their host, where they anticipated much sport with the wild Polly, whose fame was spread far and wide; and, indeed, for the sake of spending an evening in her company, the meeting in that vicinity had been originally planned.

"I'll stay," said Uncle Billy, "and have rare sport yet.

I'll carry to the house in my buggy the weight of a deer in grouse."

"You can't do it; they're all in the grass," said Nap.

"That's just where I want them."

"But you can't see 'em on the ground."

"I don't want to. I want to see them fly."

"They've quit lighting on the trees. Don't you see, when they fly up, they all pounce down in the grass again?"

"I'll shoot them on the wing.

"Can you? I'll stay with you and see it. I've heard of that kind of shooting, but never saw it. If you can do that, I'll show you plenty of birds, and pick them up for you when they fall. There's a blind road running near the spring branch yonder, that I never travelled without starting them up every ten paces. Let us get in the buggy and drive along there slowly."

This was agreed to. Nap sent his horse to the house, and got into the buggy with Uncle Billy. They drew out the buckshot from their guns and loaded with No. 5. At the urgent solicitation of Nap, Uncle Billy's pointer was compelled to keep his place in the buggy. Nap assured him there would be no difficulty in finding as many birds as they might desire to shoot at.

The road they were to traverse was a wagon-track leading from several farms across the country to a mill, and was never sufficiently used to destroy the vegetation. There were places, however, where the grouse found enough dust to wallow in, and they resorted thither for that purpose, as they were not liable there to frequent molestation. Within a few paces, and parallel to this track, ran one of those sparkling rivulets which have been alluded to. Those brooks had likewise attracted the attention of Uncle Billy, and caused him to recollect that before leaving the city he had put several finely tempered fish-hooks in his pocket-book.

When Uncle Billy and Nap were in readiness to proceed

over the grouse-covert, and while the thirsty horse had his mouth still thrust into the sparkling brook, where he had been suffered to pause a moment, two birds fluttered out of the bushes near the buggy, and separating when some twenty feet high, started off in different directions. But Uncle Billy's eye had covered them both before they had time to escape, and they were brought down flapping and dying in full view of Nap, who sprang out of the carriage and picked them up.

"Well!" said he, returning, "that's curious. I never saw that done before. They're both dead, and here are the shot-holes. I wish I could do it."

"It is easily done," said Uncle Billy, indifferently, but at the same time experiencing a thrill of inexpressible delight and proud satisfaction; for it was a feat not very often performed even by crack sportsmen, and one which he did not suppose he could accomplish at the first trial. However, the first trial is not generally the worst.

"Do you think I could do it?" continued Nap, with his gun to his shoulder, which he threw around horizontally, as if following a bird with it.

"After some practice and a little instruction, no doubt you could. Let me kill a few more, and watch me when I fire. That will teach you the rudiments."

By this time, two more arose near the horse as he walked along the road. Without checking him, Uncle Billy attempted to repeat the operation so handsomely performed before. He did not succeed, however; yet he brought one of them down, which Nap, a capital retriever, soon deposited with the others.

When a dozen birds had been killed in this manner, Nap thought it time to try his hand; and Uncle Billy, after bestowing some instructions on him, such as when the birds flew across, and were at a certain distance, to aim a few inches ahead of them, and not to be in too great a hurry to fire, leaned back and calmly awaited the result.

As usual, the birds seeming to be in pairs, two rose up

together and flew in straight lines away, presenting their **broad** rumps, the most vulnerable parts, to Nap. They were some fifteen feet apart, and Uncle Billy told his companion to fire at **both.** Nap pulled a trigger at the right hand one, and the other instantly fell.

"Why didn't you fire both barrels, and kill them both?" asked Uncle Billy.

"'Gad, when the smoke cleared away, they were a hundred yards off, that is, **the one** I **fired at. I was so** blinded, I couldn't see which way the other flew. But it was a clear miss, I suppose."

"A clear miss? **Not at all.** It was a capital shot. I couldn't have done it better myself."

"Then why didn't he fall?"

"He did."

"Did he? I thought I saw him fly away; but it might have been another. Won't you show me where he fell?"

"Look near the root of yonder persimmon-bush. The one with the grape-vine on it."

Nap, although half incredulous, leaped down and ran **to the place** pointed **out.** He stooped eagerly and picked up **a bird.** He paused and examined it in silence. He shook it. It was quite dead. **He smelt** it. **He** placed his hand under a wing.

"It's warm! Hanged if it ain't. It must have been **me** who killed it," he continued, joining his companion.

"**Oh** yes. I saw it fall when you fired. It was done very handsomely."

Nap felt inclined to exult in his success, but had a secret consciousness that he aimed at the other bird, which certainly flew away. But he said nothing.

At length a solitary bird flew up, and both fired. It fell

"I saw that fellow fall!" cried Nap, running to it. "I **aimed well** that time, didn't I?"

"I don't know so well about that," said Uncle Billy, gravely. "I am sure *I* aimed well at it."

"You! did *you* shoot, too? I didn't hear you."

"We fired together."

"But I saw him fall when I fired. It must have been me who killed it."

"We'll decide it in this way. You alone shall fire at the next bird. If you kill it, and I miss the one I fire at afterward, we'll say it's your bird."

"Agreed."

Of course Nap missed, while his companion was successful. Nap then fired without effect five or six times.

"Something must be the matter with my gun!" said he.

"Take mine," said Uncle Billy. It made no difference. Nap's excitement and anxiety had grown to such a pitch, that he was incapable of aiming well. And when Uncle Billy had fired his companion's gun several times to no purpose, he was quite ready to agree with him that something was the matter with it. But Nap, finding both alike in his hands, now defended his gun because it had done notable execution that day.

CHAPTER XIV.

The girls at the house upon their P's and Q's—The girls know single men from married ones—Tale of a wild boar—The pied bitch again—The Colonel proposes a game of poker—The women had forestalled the game—Catching a Missouri salmon—A bass—Nap and Polly steal away.

WHEN Nap and Uncle Billy arrived at the house their buggy was literally loaded with grouse. The prairies between the farms, half overgrown with bushes and vines, are always frequented by these birds in great abundance. They breed in such coverts, and remain in them until the frost destroys the sheltering leaves. Then they congregate in large flocks and remain together until spring. Late in the fall they consume uncounted barrels of the corn left ungathered in the fields; and in the winter they will attack the stacks and barns.

Contrary to what might have been expected, Nap found the company assembled in the house quite reserved and decorous. Polly had with her for the occasion Miss Sally Weighton and one or two other girls, the daughters of her neighbours, to assist in entertaining the company. But the capricious Polly, whom the gentlemen presumed would be found as usual in a boisterous and romping humour, was now the impersonation of modesty. Her sentiments were refined, her expressions delicate, and her words low and musical. Surprised and disappointed, the young gentlemen felt themselves to be in a helpless condition. The subjects they were prepared to discuss were not broached; the jokes they had composed for the occasion were not called in requisition, and their premeditated laughter was altogether suppressed. At least such was the case until the arrival of Nap.

Nap thought he never had beheld Polly looking so lovely. Indeed, she, as well as her female companions, were handsomely dressed, and in accordance too with the latest and most approved fashion. On the other hand, our gentlemen had left their best clothes in their trunks, and now surveyed themselves with no pleasure decked in their shabbiest costume. Polly perceived and enjoyed their disappointment, and as their embarrassment increased, she became more interesting, and slightly more familiar.

Nap stepped in with a large bunch of grouse in either hand, followed by Uncle Billy.

"This is Mr.—Mr."—— said he, forgetting the name of Uncle Billy, whose introduction devolved upon him. He was "dumb-founded," as he declared, the moment his eyes fell upon the ladies, and on Polly in particular. Uncle Billy bowed repeatedly and smiled graciously.

Polly advanced, bearing him a chair, and calling him by name.

"Why, Polly," said Nap, "you look beautiful"——

"Surely, Mr. Wax," said she, interrupting him and slightly frowning, "you are not going to offend me by such familiar language as that? My mirror may say such things, but only when we are by ourselves, and then in a low whisper."

Nap staggered back to a chair and sat down in dismay. It was the first time that Polly had ever called him Mr. Wax, and the only time she had ever rebuked his rudeness. He stared at her in silent amazement; but still he thought she was unusually beautiful.

Some how or other the girls seemed to have found out who of the gentlemen were married and who were single. Sally Weighton occupied a chair at Jno. P.'s elbow; Miss Nave, one beside Sam C., and Polly seemingly by accident, sat down next to Marshall J. Joseph Handy, Joe T., and Uncle Billy could not avoid perceiving that they were "shut out," like "poor men at a frolic." Now some of these, and particularly Joe, had promised themselves a large share of amusement. Joe was the cause of it in others, and had a keen relish for it himself. And upon finding himself thus unexpectedly thrust aside as it were, he was slightly disconcerted. And although not used to blushing, his face seemed to have a somewhat deeper colour than that of one in delicate health. Neither Uncle Billy's features nor colour changed. Nor was he stricken dumb. Turning his chair to the right and left, he spoke to any and all of the young ladies without hesitation, and was listened to with complaisance.

But Jno. P. and his girl soon became very voluble. Jno. never lacked words on any subject, and he was really one of the finest singers that ever entertained homesick stage-passengers at midnight on the mountains. Having learned that Sally was an enthusiastic Methodist, he became very pious, and thus unlocked her lips. Her tongue soon rattled without intermission, and her bosom rose and fell as she caught her breath, and manifested her inflammable zeal in the cause with the merits of which she seemed to be so familiar.

Sam C. made many ineffectual attempts to get started with Miss Nave, a short fat, dark-eyed girl of German descent. Accidentally he mentioned having stumbled over a pig in the bushes, which was cracking hazel-nuts, and the girl's lips were unsealed. She said the pigs were the pests of her life. They destroyed the hazel-nuts, the hickory-nuts, and the pecans, which were worth so much per bushel. They even rooted under the fence and got into her garden, where they destroyed her melons and squashes. But she had her revenge when marking-time came. She held them for her father. Sam pretended to be familiar with the subject, but soon found that his information was not quite adapted to that longitude. For when he spoke of the advantage of putting yokes on the pigs, as they did in the East, she shook her head and said the brutes were not worth the trouble. She would rather "knock their dratted brains out." More would come. They never missed any, though the wolves lived on them. They were born in the woods every day, and the only way they could know which were theirs and which belonged to their neighbours, when killing-time came, was by the marks. They never knew exactly whether those they marked belonged to them—neither did their neighbours; but they all marked enough to do them. To an inquiry whether all were marked that were born, she replied with serious emphasis that not near all were subjected to that ordeal. Hence the great number of new litters, and the dangerous quantity of wild boars in the woods, which the men had to thin out with their rifles every winter. And then she related an interesting occurrence which had happened once, when she was out in the woods gathering shell-barks, to trade at the store for silk gloves. A boar, with curled tusks as long as her hand, had treed her, and kept her up there two hours, while he was splintering the roots with his horrid teeth. She knew not what might have happened, if Strother Brown had not come that way and shot the monster. She owed her life to Strother. But she said he was already engaged to Polly Walker. Sam of course thought it was the most romantic and interesting adventure he had ever heard related.

If Polly Hopkins saw fit to be suddenly sedate and reserved, she met with her match when she cast her lot beside Marshall J. He seemed to be quite as indifferent to her charms as Ben Handy. He was pretty much of the same temperament, and was soon voted incorrigible. He was familiar with every subject usually broached in the West, and was prepared to discuss any question. He could likewise relate his share of anecdotes; but he was too cool and self-possessed to be captivated by the blandishments of any of the opposite sex. The girls attributed his *sang-froid* to the chills which had recently assailed him.

Perforce Polly had to relax her premeditated frigid propriety, and she mingled her remarks with those of Joe, Uncle Billy, and Nap. Nap was becoming deeply smitten with her charms, in spite of himself and Molly Brook, and began to feel symptoms of jealousy when she strove to emit some rays from the callous heart of M. J. Joe T. was full of fun and romance, and talked of sparkling eyes, ruby lips, and Cupid's darts. Uncle Billy, in his deliberate way, was not bad at an innocent innuendo. Joseph Handy was occupied apart, writing a business letter.

Thus they were engaged when the Colonel entered to announce dinner.

"Come," said he, "the venison and the prairie-chickens are ready. The old woman would suffer no one to interfere. She got out her Leslie cook-book, and did every thing right, as she thinks. Come! the proof of the pudding is in the eating. Nap," he continued, turning abruptly to the one addressed, "you didn't bring home my bitch."

Nap's head fell. Those who observed it supposed his embarrassment was caused by the mention of such an animal at such a time and in such a place. This was fortunate for poor Nap.

"Never mind it now," continued the Colonel; "I'll send Grippa out to hunt her. I wouldn't swap her for the best horse in the county. Hello, boys, don't elbow the girls that way. They know the road to the dining-room, and how to eat, when they get there. Go ahead, first, girls."

The boys had offered their arms to the ladies, the meaning of which was not exactly understood in that prairie.

At the dinner-table there was more hilarity. Anecdotes and hearty laughter enlivened the scene. The game, both venison and grouse, proved to be excellent; and the "native wine," with "something stronger," detracted nothing from the general animation. At length the time came for the Colonel to hint at the grand scheme he had meditated ever since the day's sport had been projected. He was a famous poker-player, and he doubted not the young gentlemen knew just enough of the game to be the victims of its fascinations. He little dreamed that his "old woman" and Polly had likewise meditated on the subject, and had forestalled him by communicating their wishes to Joseph Handy, whom they knew to be ignorant of the game, and seriously averse to seeing his friends engage in it.

"Boys!" said the Colonel, in fine humour, "when you are done with the girls, we'll have some amusement at cards. What do you say to it?"

They said nothing. But the girls looked as if they were not yet "done with." They were now all smiles and happiness.

"Joe," continued the Colonel, somewhat surprised at the unlooked-for hesitation to respond to his proposition, "you know how to play, I'm sure."

"Upon my word, I don't. I never could understand, when travelling on the steamboats, how a man could be 'blind' one moment, and then say he'd 'see' his neighbour. Sometimes I would hear them say they were all blind but the dealer. Then I supposed that was the end of the game. But no. The next moment one of the blind players would rake in the money. So I turned away, and if I could find a lady on board who would talk to me in a social way, I preferred her to poker."

The Colonel looked blank. Polly cast a quick glance at Joe. If his eye did not quail, a slight perspiration covered his high forehead.

"And what do you think your wife would say?" she asked.

"Good!" exclaimed Uncle Billy, leaning back and laughing. "He tries sometimes to pass for a single man. What business has he to be talking in a social way to the ladies!"

"Oh, *you* are no bachelor, I'm sure," continued Polly, turning her mischievous eyes on the crack shot.

"How can you tell?" asked he.

"Easily. But no matter how. It is my secret."

"And must not be pried into," added Joe, quite recovered from the discovery of his married condition, and as gallant as ever.

"I suppose I might as well confess I'm a married man," said Marshall J.

"If you did it would not be true. I know to the contrary."

"And how do you know that, Miss Polly?"

"Because you are not so enthusiastic an admirer of the girls as the married men, who appreciate them because they know their value."

This made amends. The married men felt whole again.

"But *you* know how to play poker, don't you?" asked the Colonel, addressing J.

"Not I, sir. I never saw it played but once, and then the young man who lost his money jumped over board. After that I always retired when the game was proposed."

"And sought a more agreeable game?" asked Polly, at the same time sending him an approving glance.

"I don't know what you allude to."

"I mean some amusement in which you could lose nothing. If it was the society of the ladies, of course you had nothing to lose."

"Oh, I lost my heart long ago."

"But *you* play, don't you?" persisted the Colonel, turning to Sam C.

"I never played a game in my life," was the prompt reply.

The disconcerted Colonel was silent a moment.

"Drink, then, all of you, and help yourselves. I'll go and hunt for the pied bitch," said he, rising and going out.

"Why didn't he ask me?" said Uncle Billy.

"Because you look like a contemplative whist-player, or sentimental angler, and neither would suit his impetuous humour," responded Polly.

"That's his character to a T," said Jno. P., whose sanctified visage and profusion of pious observations directed to Sally, but which had been observed by the Colonel, exempted him likewise from interrogation on the subject of playing. But he, too, had his negative in readiness.

"I am sometimes pleased with a game of whist," said Uncle Billy, "for amusement, and not for gain. I differ from those who believe it sinful to indulge in a little innocent play, when time is not to be more profitably employed."

"I know why the Colonel didn't ask me," said Nap. "He learned me how to play the game one night at the store. Sam Marsh was looking on, and was to give me the wink when to stop. Three hands were dealt me, and I won every time, but not much. The fourth deal I got four tens, and bet all I had won on them. The Colonel went five dollars better; and when I was about to go my 'pile,' Sam gave me the wink. I stopped short and rose from the table."

"You would have won," said **Jno. P.** "What did you stop for?"

"How do *you* know?" asked Miss **Polly**, in astonishment.

"Oh, I've heard it said that hand was a strong one."

"Sam," continued **Nap**, "told me afterward that the Colonel held four Jacks."

"So, Nap, you were willing to play a *winning* game only. Stick to that," said Joseph.

"There would be no amusement in losing," was the candid reply.

As the subject of angling had been hinted at, Uncle Billy, thinking of the brooks in the prairie, and the hooks in his pocket, inquired of Mrs. Hopkins if there were any trout in the neighbourhood. She replied in the negative, and said a deceased brother, who was well informed on the subject, had often remarked that there were no trout in the State.

"But surely there must be some game fish in such pure waters."

"Oh yes," said Polly; "I have frequently seen them. All the brooks come together behind the orchard, and form what is called Spring Creek. In it there are salmon"——

"Salmon! No, no, Miss Polly," said **Uncle** Billy, firmly, being incredulous.

"Yes, yes, I say. I have seen them taken out in a net —I have seen them under the ice—I have eaten them."

"I'll swear to it!" said Nap.

"What, the genuine salmon?" continued Uncle Billy, with more energy of manner than he had hitherto evinced.

"Yes, genuine Missouri salmon," continued Nap. "Sam Marsh had several on his table the day Colonel Benton dined in Venice."

"Won't they bite? Can't one be taken?" asked Joe, who was a keen angler, and felt an interest in the subject.

"No doubt," said Nap, "if we had hooks and the right sort of bait. The folks in Missouri don't fish much out of the great river, where they take 'cats' weighing from one to two hundred pounds, which is like lassoing buffalo. But these salmon, they say, won't bite often. I suppose the people don't know what sort of bait to use."

"I would give something handsome to see one," said Uncle Billy. "If they are game fish—salmon is out of the question—I know what sort of bait to use. Have they teeth?"

"They have! One's mouth rasped my finger. But they are not like the pike or Jack I've seen in Kentucky."

"Miss Polly, can you rig us up some lines?" asked Uncle Billy, taking some hooks from his pocket-book.

Polly said she could. And she did. Several very good flax-thread lines were soon in readiness, and one of the negroes brought as many reeds for rods.

"Now for the bait," said Nap. "What shall it be?"

"Grasshoppers," said Uncle Billy. No sooner said than done. The negro boy, in a brief space of time, had captured a score of them, which he imprisoned in his hat.

Nap and Polly led the way, followed by Joe T. and Uncle Billy, while Sam C. and Jno. P. remained with Sally Weighton and Miss Nave, singing hymns and psalms. Joseph Handy was making calculations about his business affairs, and had already covered several pages of foolscap with figures.

The "Creek," as they called it, was a very pretty stream of clear, cool water. It was some twenty-five feet in width, flowing briskly over a stony bottom, and fringed on either side by willows, wild rose-bushes, and hawthorns. There were alternately ripples and deep pools, just as an angler would have them.

After imposing silence, Uncle Billy and Joe T. moved softly to a spot just where the water tumbled over a pebbled descent into a deep pool. When they threw their lines above, that they might float down with the lively current, they were themselves obscured by the trees on the margin, while Nap and Polly remained a few paces in the rear, witnessing the operation.

Joe met with no success the first throw. But there was a slight splash at Uncle Billy's hook as it glided into the deep water.

"I've got him!" said he.

"A salmon?" asked Polly.

"I don't know. But he's game!" continued the practised angler, playing his fish. He yielded when it made a violent rush, just keeping his elastic rod sufficiently bent by the fish's weight to prevent the hook from getting loose in his mouth. Thus tightening the line and yielding it alternately, and sometimes following along the margin of the stream as his captive attempted to run up or down, he succeeded at last in landing his prize.

"That's a beauty!" exclaimed Joe, putting down his rod and joining his piscatory comrade.

"That's one of them," said Nap. "That's what we call a Missouri salmon."

"It is not a salmon; but it is a noble fish!" said Uncle Billy, carrying it a few paces back from the water, and placing it on the grass.

The fish was eighteen inches in length, with large beautiful eyes, and teeth resembling a trout's. But its scales were as large and as hard as those of a rockfish, and the shape not dissimilar. It was not, however, so thick, nor so deep from the dorsal fin to the belly, and would not weigh so much as a rockfish of the same length. Its colour when taken was silvery white; but when exposed to the rays of the sun, and when expiring, the colours of the rainbow seemed to flit along its sides. When dead, it grew dark and dull in aspect.

"I wish I had learned to draw!" said Uncle Billy, standing over his prize and witnessing its struggles. "I have a boy at home who shall take lessons. He shall never have cause to regret that that portion of his education was neglected. I wish it could be skinned or preserved some way, so **Frank Forrester** could see it." While he thus soliloquized, studying the form and features of the fish, Joe had stepped forward to the stream, and cast out his line again.

"I've got one, Uncle Billy!" said he, in very great excitement, effectually rousing his companion from his abstraction, who immediately joined him to witness the operation of landing another specimen of the Missouri salmon. Joe knew how it should be done, and in process of time he accomplished the feat. But it was not a "duplicate" of the other. Though quite as heavy, it was five or six inches shorter. This was the Western bass, a species not known on the seaboard, and it elicited almost as much admiration as the other. It was a game fish, hardly inferior to the trout, and much larger than the trout usually taken in the United States. It was broad across the shoulders, active and powerful, and of a light yellow colour.

For more than an hour the anglers enjoyed their delectable sport—the best, as they owned, they had ever experienced in their lives. So absorbed were they in the prosecution of their exhilarating exercise, that the absence of Nap and Polly had not been observed by them until their bait was exhausted.

CHAPTER XV.

Nap makes a declaration under the hawthorn-tree—Uncle Billy and Joe T. accidentally overhear him—Sour grapes—Joe Handy strikes a bargain with Nap—An eye to business—The Colonel's bitch again—Nap fires at a barn-door and misses it.

IT was when the anglers were in the midst of their sport that Nap wandered away. He paused under a hawthorn-tree, thickly matted over with tangled grape-vines. Then turning his eyes toward Polly, who watched in silence his mysterious departure, he beckoned her to join him. She did so unobserved by the piscatorial gentlemen.

"What is it, Nap?" she asked. "What have you found there to show me? Crab-apples? Or haws? They are worthless; besides, the thorns forbid that we should molest them. The grapes? They are too high and too green. They are sour, Nap. Then what *is* it?"

"Polly," said he, averting his face, and in an exceedingly grave tone, "I have been thinking a great deal"——Here he paused.

"Indeed, Nap! Well, I hope you are well through with it. Did you suffer much?"

"I have suffered immensely, waking and sleeping"——

"Nap, when you suffer in your sleep, do you snore?"

"Don't make fun of me, Polly! You see I am serious."

"Let me see. Why, yes, you are as grave as a weeping willow. Don't cry, Nap. Poor fellow! Can I do anything for you?"

"Yes."

"What?"

"Let me marry you."

"Nap—Napoleon Bonaparte Wax! Haven't I proposed it over and over again, and you wouldn't have me?"

"But now I would."

"Why would you now?"

"Because every time I set my eyes upon you, you seem to be prettier than ever; and to-day you are perfectly lovely. At the store, I can't add up a column on the ledger for thinking of you. And when I go to charge anything on the day-book, I am sure to begin writing your name, and have to rub it out again. You ought to see my blotter."

"What does all that signify? I'm not a witch, and don't know anything about it."

"But it's because"——

"What, Nap?"

"I–I'm"——

"You are what, Nap? Speak quick."

"In love!"

"Oh, I know that. You told me so the first time we met. Molly Brook would go into hysterics if she could hear you proposing to marry me."

"Not a bit of it! When she heard a letter read which described my miraculous escape from being shot, what do you think she did?"

"Didn't she scream?"

"No."

"Didn't she swoon?"

"No."

"But she turned pale?"

"Hanged if she did! She turned red, and bursted her corsets laughing. She said I resembled a bear so much, no wonder Jack was about to shoot me for one."

"That seems cruel, don't it?"

"It don't seem like any thing else."

"But it was something else. She knew the object of the letter. Kate had received a letter from Jack, giving an account of the affair, and stating that you would write to your mother. Kate and Molly went to your mother's house together, and agreed to laugh at your expense."

"She shall cry for it! I'm in love with *you*, Polly, and will marry you whenever you say the word. I will, upon my honour"——

"Your honour! Stop there, Nap! Recollect Molly has your honour in her keeping. You can have none, unless she returns it to you."

"Didn't she laugh at me?"

"What has that to do with one's honour? Laughter is an innocent thing. No one can laugh away another's honour. And if you have no honour, do you suppose I will marry you? What can any girl want with a man without honour? She'd much better let him alone, and remain single all her life."

"Hang it, Polly! Ain't you going to have me, after all your propositions and entreaties? You said you'd marry me at the drop of a hat! Once we were half married! And again, when I pleaded my honour, you said you would see if I couldn't be made to disregard it."

"And haven't I seen it?"

"Yes, but you made me do it!'

"And if your honour were pledged to me, wouldn't others, more captivating than myself, make you 'do it' again and again?"

"No, I'll be durned if they would. There isn't a girl living upon the face of the earth more captivating than you are"——

"Come, Nap, that's nonsense, and of a dangerous kind, too. Let us speak of Molly."

"Oh pshaw! I wish she was married—or"——

"Stop! I don't like that! If you ever loved her—did you?"

"Oh, yes. But she's not so tall, nor so fine-looking as you are."

"Nonsense, again! But, Nap, I say if you ever loved Molly, you would regret to see another marry her; and you would grieve to see her dead."

"I didn't say I wished to see her dead."

"You came very near it. I can read your thoughts."

"You made me say and think as I did."

"Nonsense, again!"

"But I'm sure I love you best."

"My husband shall love me *only!* Nap, hear me. Molly was your first love. If you prove recreant to her, no one else should trust you. I believe you have some sort of an attachment for me"——

"A most furious and powerful one!"

"That may be. But sometimes the largest flame is

soonest extinguished. Had you never loved and abandoned Molly"——

"I didn't. She abandoned me!"

"If you had never loved her, I might safely rely upon securing your affections."

"I loved her first, because I saw her first. If I had seen you first"——

"You might have loved her last. No matter, Nap; my resolution is fixed. I will not have you until you shall have seen her again, and parted, mutually contented, for ever. That is my decision."

"Why, Polly, I thought I could get you at a word, any time."

"But you see you were mistaken."

"I do see it. I feel it!" he continued, almost sobbing. "In fun you could have had me, Nap. But now it is getting to be a serious business."

"Yes, I'm in earnest."

"And so am I!"

"Polly, I hope you ain't treating me in this manner because those fine city gentlemen are at your father's house. They are all married but three"——

"Pooh, Nap. Don't think me so silly. I see through them. They want sport, not wives. The married ones would be quite as ready for a flirtation as the single ones, and the latter have no idea of marrying any of us—no more than I would of having one of them. I would rather have you, Nap, than any of the crowd. You are at home, and known. They are away from home, and unknown. No one can tell what they do in their travels, or how many broken hearts they leave behind. Married and single, it is all the same; men are not to be trusted."

"If I were married, I know I could be trusted."

"I pity the one that would trust you after you had been absent from your home a month. No, Nap; married men are frequently the greatest rogues that go unhung!"

This was said with great emphasis, and, a moment after,

two gentleman might have been seen gliding away from the vicinity in a stooping posture, so that the embankment of the stream upon which the tree and vine grew might hide them from view. They had followed the stream thither, unaware of the presence of the lovers.

"Uncle Billy!" said Joe, when they had returned to the place where the fish had been taken.

"What do you want?"

"I say, listeners rarely hear any good of themselves."

"So I've heard before."

"I know it now."

"Hush! They are coming."

"Well, gentlemen, what luck?" asked Polly, with her old flow of spirits.

"Capital," said Uncle Billy; "and it might have been better, but we had no more bait."

"We've been trying to get you more," said Nap; "and that's the reason we left you."

"Were there no more grasshoppers on the lawn where the negro boy got the others? I saw him going in that direction. You went there, didn't you?" asked Joe, marking Nap's blushes.

"No!" said Polly. "We crept along the margin to yonder tree and vine. But no success was met with there. It was not the right place, Mr. T."

"Joe!" said Uncle Billy, striking his elbow against his comrade's ribs, "she saw us or heard us. Let her alone."

"Are there not some grapes there, Nap?" persisted Joe.

"Yes, indeed," said Nap, in confusion.

"But they are very *sour*," added Polly, "and I would not commend them to your taste. You would not like them. Better let me have the fish prepared for your palate."

"I think so, too," said Uncle Billy." "Fish cannot be served up too soon after they are killed. Not so, however, with grouse; and I must bury one of the birds in the garden to-night for my especial benefit in the morning."

When the party returned to the house, they found the

young gentlemen and ladies still singing, and sitting very closely together. John P. and Sam C. had evidently improved the time and opportunity. The girls, from their languishing eyes, seemed to be almost taken captive.

"Sally," said Polly, addressing Miss Weighton, whom she called into another room, "how do you like these city beaus?"

"I declare Mr. P. has the sweetest voice I ever heard in my life. I never want to hear any other the rest of my days!"

"And you could listen to him for ever!"

"For ever and ever!"

"I won't say Amen to it."

"Why?"

"Do you suppose you could make a Methodist of him?"

"I'm sure he is a good man—he has such a heavenly voice!"

"Don't let his voice make a fool of you. Has he hinted any thing pleasant to you?"

"He says I sing with much *feeling*, and he likes to be tenor to my treble."

"There's no harm in that, so long as there is no bass in it. He'll be off in the morning, and you'll never see him again."

"I shall be so sorry! I shall ever think of him."

"And no doubt others do. From the cut of his jib, I should suppose he has pleased many a girl. But what do you think of your beau?" she continued, addressing Miss Nave.

"He smiles pretty, and he has nice eyes and hair; and he says he would like to be a farmer, and"——

"And you would like to be his wife! Go, girls, sing and be merry to-day, for to-morrow they leave you."

Marshall J. sat beside the broad hearth, smoking a sociable pipe with the old lady, and conversing familiarly on any subject she happened to broach.

Joseph Handy had completed his calculations and arrived

at a result. It was ascertained to his satisfaction that he might advantageously dispose of his interest in the concern at Venice. Already Nap had paid back to him more than the gross amount invested in the store, and the only claim that Joseph might now prefer was for his share of the profits. So, when he proposed to sell his interest to Nap, he found a willing listener. The sum named, in the absence of authentic data, as the estimated amount of Joseph's share of the profits, did not seem extravagant to Nap, who had an aversion to making inventories. He agreed to give it, and the arrangement was consummated at once. Nap had the money at home, and promised to send it to Tyre the next day.

This matter despatched, Joseph excused himself on some plea of business, and returned home that night. He had no taste for hunting or fishing, and no time to fool away with the girls. When he departed, Polly declared that they never would have got him to join the party at all, if he had not supposed he could accomplish something relating to business before separating again. She had no doubt he came there to strike a bargain with Nap; and she congratulated our hero upon becoming sole proprietor of the establishment at Venice.

Nap likewise felicitated himself. There was now no one who had a right to restrain him in any thing. He had money enough in hand to pay Joseph, and it was the only debt he owed in the world. The stock of goods on hand was small, but well assorted, and of more value than the original capital invested. He had likewise some notes for merchandise sold to solvent men on time. Besides, he had made that day a considerable shipment of produce to his commission-merchant in St. Louis. If that brought a fair price, he would be in funds to replenish his stock, and to increase it materially.

But that which contributed most to his satisfaction was the assurances of the young gentlemen from the East, that their respective houses would be happy to supply him with goods on the same terms they had sold to Joseph, viz. at six months, with the privilege of twelve, interest to be charged after the expiration of the first half-year. And they pressed him to visit Philadelphia that winter. Joseph, before departing, had said to them that they might safely credit Nap for any reasonable amount, as he had no bad habits, and was not likely to form any in his secluded place of abode. And they had learned that Venice would certainly become an important business point in a very few years.

"If you go to the Eastern cities this winter, Nap," said Polly, "I suppose you will have the pleasure of seeing your mother on the way."

"I will," said Nap, winking significantly.

"And I think Mr. Handy, or some one else, said, there was a Miss Molly he might desire to meet with," remarked Joe.

"Well!" said Polly, "he's an unmarried man, and has a *right* to see the young ladies."

"Oh yes," said John P., "a cat may look at a king."

Just then, Colonel Hopkins returned.

"I've not found my pied bitch, boys," said he. "The infernal Mormons have stolen her. They tell me a party of them crossed the prairie to-day. To-morrow I'll pursue them. I'll have my bitch or I'll scalp a Mormon. Nap, won't you go with me? You can prove she's mine, if we find her."

Nap was very much confused. It was not observed, however, by any but Polly and the two wedded anglers, the latter supposing they knew the cause of it.

"Upon my word, Colonel, it will be altogether out of my power I have to send a certain sum of money to Tyre to-morrow, and I am sorry I can't be absent from home. The animal was a valuable one, and the man who stole her ought to be punished severely. I would almost be willing to shoot him myself."

"Ha! ha! ha! Shoot *at* him, you mean. That gun of

yours is worth nothing. You couldn't hit my barn-door, with a rest."

"It's a first-rate gun!" said Nap, **who** really believed what he said. "Recollect the execution it has done to-day."

"I'll bet **a pound** of powder you **can't hit my barn-door**; **that is,** the left half of it, with a dead rest, **at forty yards.**"

"**Done, sir! Come on,** we'll see at once," said Nap, willing to venture a pound of powder on such odds.

The whole party followed the Colonel and Nap over the square lawn toward the barn. Two chairs were taken out, one for Nap to sit in, and the other for his gun to rest upon. The barn-door was some fourteen feet high, and ten in width. It was closed, and presented a broad enough surface to be struck with an apple thrown by the hand of a lad at the distance of forty yards. Nap was really incensed at the Colonel's confident declarations of his inability to hit so **large a** mark; **and he was** annoyed **to find** the witnesses looking on in mock gravity, as if half convinced that **the** Colonel would win the wager.

"Nail a piece **of paper** about the size of a half-dime on the door," said Nap. "I mean to drive **the centre.**"

"I'll put up two targets," said the Colonel, "one **for** you and one for me. I'll bet on mine. I'll wager lead for the powder that you'll come nearer mine than yours."

"Done!" said Nap, impatiently.

A paper target was affixed to the door, about eighteen inches from the left edge of it. Another was placed upon the plank fence, some fifteen feet farther to the left.

"Now fire away," said the Colonel. "The left hand **mark** is the one I bet on."

"But you bet on both," **said Jno. P.,** who had not clearly understood the particulars of the proceeding; "and if you lose **one, won't you** win the other?"

"No; I'll win both. I bet he'll miss the mark he aims

at, and hit the one he don't aim at, or at least will come the nearest to it."

"Well, I'll show you!" said Nap, sitting down and firing the right-hand barrel.

"Shoot the other barrel too!" cried the Colonel. "I'll give you a double chance."

"Very well," said Nap, "I'll spoil your barn-door for you." He fired again, and doubted not he had put some five hundred pellets in the door.

They all went forward to see the result, Nap assured that he had not missed even the diminutive paper, much less the huge barn-door. But the extent of his amazement could not be measured, when he failed to discover a single perforation in the door.

"Now let us examine my target," said the exulting Colonel. The surprise of Nap, and of the whole party, was quite as great on perceiving that the shot of both barrels had entered the plank in the vicinity of the Colonel's target.

"That's the work of the spirits," said Jno. P.

"Let me have a fire, Nap," said Joe. Nap gave him the gun in silence, for he was inextricably puzzled. He had been told by the Colonel that his gun was crooked; but he supposed it to be a mere joke. He had, moreover, killed the birds and the bitch since then.

Joe fired, and down fell the left-hand paper. He looked curiously at the gun, and gave it up.

"Now I know why I couldn't kill the grouse with your gun, Nap," said Uncle Billy.

"Then I wish you would tell me," replied the other.

The Colonel explained. He made them perceive a slight bend in the barrels, so slight, indeed, that none of them would have discovered it, nor even the Colonel himself, had he not been informed of the source from whence it came.

"I'll sue the rascally pedlar!" said Nap. "No wonder, I didn't hit the deer!"

"Oh, that's not the reason you missed the buck," said the Colonel. "All the shot-guns on the ground were not bent. But I have won a pound of powder and four pounds of lead. Now if I had only my pied bitch—blast the infernal Mormons!"

"Colonel, send out when you please for the powder and lead," said Nap, desirous of keeping his host's thoughts upon the winnings.

After supper, it being ascertained that the young gentlemen and ladies had sung themselves hoarse, innocent games were introduced, and they had a boisterous night of it. They separated at bedtime, (the hour being indicated by a startling snore from Nap,) mutually delighted with the entertainment. Sally Weighton being the only one, perhaps, whose lids were insensible to the approaches of slumber.

CHAPTER XVI.

Nap prepares to go Eastward, and adopts the costume to appear in—Jack joins him, and they go together—Nap repulsed by a belle—His revenge—Nap roused from his couch—Is the victim of a practical joke.

THE winter so far had been a mild one, and the steamboats had not ceased running. It was now the beginning of February. Nap was engaged packing his clothes in a trunk, preparatory to embarking on Captain Jewett's new boat, which was every hour expected to arrive from above.

Nap was singularly costumed for the voyage Eastward. Happening once to hear Colonel Benton, when upon the subject of apparel, describe the dress of Mr. C——s, of A——n, he had ever since imitated it. If he could dress as men of distinction did, of course he might be in some slight measure great himself. Fortunately, in this instance, the passion for adopting a novel fashion, was by no means attended with any extraordinary expenditure of money. But the dress the Colonel had described was one worn in the summer, which seemed to have escaped Nap's recollection, at least so far as his hat was concerned. And, being fat, and the weather not cold, he still retained his old palm-leaf covering. **The brim** had originally been a very wide one; but it had been shorn of half its proportions by the obtrusive mouth of Sam Marsh's cow. It was, **besides,** much stained **by** the dust which had settled around the band in moments of profuse perspiration. His coat, vest, and pantaloons were all of Kentucky jeans, originally brown, but now sadly faded. The vest was pinned together in front, and the buttons were off the coat. He **had** no suspenders to his pantaloons, and his nether garments might at times be observed where the junction of the waistband and the vest should have been complete. His **boots were of coarse cowskin, foxy, and ripped** open in **several** places.

While **engaged in** the process **of packing, as above** stated, Nap heard a horseman dashing up **the** road **at a more** than ordinarily rapid rate. He turned, **and beheld Jack** Handy.

"Hello, Jack!" cried he, "where are you bound for in such a hurry?"

"I thought I was **bound for the place of your** destination, and supposed we were to go in company. **But now I** doubt it."

"Eh? **Are** you going East, too?"

"**I am** going East. I am sorry you are not going thither also."

"Why, where do you think I'm going then?"

"To some rag-fair. What in the name of all the **pawn-brokers** are you dressed in that style for?"

"**The exterior** aspect of a man is of no importance, as Colonel Benton says. **Some** of the richest and greatest men in the nation go in plain garments."

"But not in ragged ones."

"Clothes will wear out, and the Colonel didn'**t say when**

they should be changed for others. But everybody on the river knows me; and those elsewhere who don't know me, will never suppose I have three thousand dollars in my belt."

"That's true, Nap. I didn't think of that. Have you another suit for me?"

"Jim has; haven't you, Jim?"

"No!" said Jim, gruffly, for he was pained to see his principal so shabbily attired. "And if I had," he added, "I'd give 'em to one of my daddy's negroes to hang up in the field as a scarecrow."

"Scarecrow! That's it!" said Nap. "Crows are thieves, and of course thieves are crows; and I think these clothes will scare them away."

"I'd carry a pistol, and let 'em rip, if it was me," said Jim.

"And so I will take my pistol. But, Jack, I thought your brother Joseph was going?"

"So he was. But he has heard that a stranger is coming, and he wants to be at home to receive him."

"Who is it? What's his name?"

"Oh, he's not named yet."

"Not named?"

"No; it's a *little* stranger, his wife intends introducing early in the spring, and probably before he could return."

"Let her rip!" cried Jim. "I always said that girl was a trump."

"And you are going in his place?"

"I am. I am to buy for Tyre and Troy both."

"Good! Jack, won't you go through Kentucky with me?"

"Yes, indeed!"

"Where's your trunk, man? The boat may be here in an hour."

"I have none; but I'll empty my saddle-bags into your trunk if you have no objection."

No objection was made. And the young men were in readiness to embark when the boat landed shortly after

Captain Jewett, who was intimately acquainted with Nap, as he was likewise with all the Handy family, and being by nature one of the most polite and accommodating masters on the river, gave our young merchants one of his best state-rooms—one, he said, which had been reserved for them. Nap, however, at first made some objection to it. He was fearful that so fine a room might betray him. To which Jack replied, that he would lodge there and nowhere else, and his companion might sleep with a party of Indians, if he pleased, who crept every night under the boilers. Nap submitted, after some hesitation.

They were rejoiced to meet with their Philadelphia friends, besides a number of others from the Eastern cities, to whom they were introduced, all wending homeward, to be on hand at the opening of the busy season. There were also many country merchants on board, going in quest of their early spring supplies. To these our brace of young gentlemen needed no formal introduction. They became personally acquainted with them without ceremony, as is often the custom with merchants from the same State.

There had been recently a considerable rise in the river, and the steamer made some twenty-five miles an hour down the "mad," impetuous stream. Her rapid progress was entirely in unison with the "fast" ideas of her living cargo.

The belle of ——— county, Miss Mary W., was on board, and she was the only lady among the passengers that Nap had any acquaintance with. With her he had been on terms of intimacy, having sold her many a gown, and bartered for many a piece of jeans of her making. After supper, he walked to where she was sitting, and spoke to her in his most winning manner. But to his surprise he received in return a cold and distant nod. Miss Mary was splendidly dressed, and did not choose, in his present predicament, to have it supposed by the fine gentlemen in view, that she was acquainted with one who made so mean an appearance in company. A very few efforts on the part of Nap to engage her in conversation, sufficed to convince him that she judged her bird by his plumage. He turned away and occupied a seat near Joe T. and Uncle Billy.

"The other Polly," said Nap, "is worth a thousand of such primroses."

"When a man's in love, Nap," said Joe, "he supposes his sweetheart to excel all other women. But you have two, they say. Which do you like best, Nap?"

Nap made a frank confession of his attachments, for his heart was full, and Joe had an open countenance, inviting confidence, the highest possible requisite of an accomplished salesman. But Nap candidly owned that he was not prepared to decide which of his two girls he loved the most. He would, however, soon ascertain.

"But," said Joe, "you will not give the Kentucky girl a fair chance."

"Why?" asked Nap.

"Because you won't appear before her in as fine clothes as you do sometimes in the presence of the Missouri girl. Look at Jack. He is one of the best dressed gentlemen on board."

"I didn't think of that, by George! But now I do think of it, Molly shall make choice of me in these rags, or not at all. She put me off when I had on a new suit, but precious little money in my pocket. Now I intend to appear before her in an old suit, with"—here he lowered his tone—"with thousands in my belt. But don't mention it to anybody. I have a thousand dollars with me now, and there are two thousand more at Tatum's, in St. Louis, for me."

Joe smiled, and said he wouldn't mention it. He had in his own belt upward of forty thousand. But he knew the nature of Nap's feelings, his hopes and fears, in his new position, and appreciated them. He had likewise observed the treatment Nap had received from the pretty little belle, and readily entered into a scheme the former proposed by way of retaliation. So he procured a formal introduction to her, and introduced his friend Mr. R. from Philadelphia. Nap sat by and witnessed the efforts of the belle to captivate one or both of her city beaus. He was now the happiest man on board the boat. He could easily perceive that Miss Mary supposed that she was displaying her attractions to bachelors, and that she was deluded with a conviction that an impression was being made, which might not be so easily obliterated. And it was his purpose to spoil her rest by whispering in her ear that the gentlemen were both already married.

But he did not accomplish his purpose. After sitting a long time watching the young lady and the poker-tables alternately, a curtain seemed to fall over his eyes, and the scene vanished from his vision. How long he remained thus he could not tell. But he was presently aroused by an uproarious explosion of laughter. He started up, and looking to the right and left, beheld only mirthful faces and merry glances from different quarters directed toward himself. He could not conjecture the meaning of it, and might have remained in ignorance until startled again, had not Mr. W., Mary's father, approached and asked him if he was in the habit of *snoring.*

This opened Nap's eyes. He saw it all then. And he immediately retired to his state-room. Being larger and heavier than Jack, who was still in conversation with the Philadelphians and New Yorkers, he took possession of the lower berth. He was soon snoring again; but the loud conversation going on in the cabins, mingled with laughter, and the rapping of knuckles on the tables, that occasionally jingled with the specie so often won and lost, seemed for a time to swallow up the sounds emitted from his nostrils. When the hour arrived for the games to cease, and for the ladies to be enclosed, by the shutting of the great folding-doors, within their own cabin, the nasal notes from Nap's state-room became more painfully perceptible.

Mary W. and her mother occupied a state-room next to the partition separating the ladies' from the gentlemen's cabin; and first on the gentlemen's side was the state-room in which Nap was snoring. Mary was just unlacing her corsets, which had bound her palpitating heart in too small a compass, and was beginning to breathe freely, when she was startled by the grating sound.

"What's that, mother?" cried she, stooping in a listening attitude, her soft dark hair falling over her shoulders. Her mother was sleeping calmly, having retired early. "Mother!" she continued, "what makes that horrid noise?"

"What's the matter, child?" asked the mother, opening her eyes.

"Don't you hear?"

"Yes, indeed! That's a man."

"A man? Mercy on us! Where is he?"

"In the next room, and in the gentlemen's cabin. A thin plank only separates our room from his."

"It's too bad! I can't sleep so near him."

"Pooh! he's asleep. What's the danger?"

"But I hear every breath he takes. Who can fall asleep with such a sound as that in one's ears?"

"Try, Mary. There is no remedy."

"I will **try**, but I know I **shan't** succeed."

She **did try**, without success. And her mother now fared no **better**. For hours they lay awake under the infliction; **and** Nap surely had his revenge without knowing it.

Jack, being **somewhat** fatigued, and long accustomed to the sound, had fallen asleep after tossing about impatiently for an hour.

But not so with the gentlemen and stewards in the vicinity. **As** they reclined one after another, some in their berths, **and some upon the** floor, (there being a great **many** passengers,) and when a comparative silence otherwise reigned in that part of the boat, the snoring seemed to grow upon them until it expanded into the terrific vibrations of a hotel gong. Hopes were expressed that the sound might soon cease. Jokes, at the expense of the snorer, were related. And finally some maledictions were uttered.

Mrs. W. summoned Ellen, the chambermaid. She declared it was impossible for any one to sleep within hearing of such a monster, and requested that something might be done to abate the nuisance. Ellen, proverbially accommodating, passed into the gentlemen's cabin, and made known the nature of the grievance to the head steward. The steward got up and listened some time with his ear near the doors of the two state-rooms. But so distracting and voluminous was the sound that he could not be certain whether it proceeded from Nap's room, or the one next to it, occupied by a Presbyterian clergyman, and Frank B., of B———. Both rooms were locked on the inside, and the only way in which he could interfere would be to awaken the sleeper by calling or knocking. He hesitated to do either, because he could not be absolutely sure who it was that snored. Ellen saw the difficulty, and promised to explain it to Mrs. W. But before withdrawing her head from the partially opened folding-doors, she told the steward she had heard that if some one were to whistle in the vicinity of the snorer, he would cease the annoyance. She then withdrew.

The steward, quite as incapable of enjoying his accustomed repose as the rest, tried the experiment of whistling. It had no effect, of course. Then, after listening some time longer to the discordant note, he lost his temper, as some stewards are sometimes in the habit of doing, and uttering a furious oath, hurled a chair at the door of the room occupied by the parson and young B. The crashing sound brought them both out in their night-garments.

"God bless me! what has happened?" exclaimed the preacher, with his hands uplifted, and trembling.

"I suppose somebody fell from the table," said B. "The boat's going ahead; that convinces me nothing serious has happened."

The steward confessed that some one (he did not say who did it) had thrown a chair against the door, to stop the snoring within. Now the snoring had ceased. Nap had sprung up, and was about to open the door, when he heard the steward's explanation. Of course he desisted, and laid down again.

"But I didn't snore," said the parson.

"I don't snore," said B.

"Somebody over there has been snoring like thunder!" cried a man in an opposite state-room. "I'm glad you stopped it, steward."

"You see the snoring's stopped," said the steward, really believing he had aimed the chair at the right door.

"It could not have been me," persisted the parson. "I am a married man, and surely my wife would have told me if I had been in the habit of doing it."

"D——d if I snore!" said B., forgetting the parson's presence, and turning in again. He was followed by the preacher, and the door was once more locked.

But before those who had been the victims of the annoyance could have time to sink into the repose they so much needed, the grating sound again saluted their ears.

Frank B. immediately opened the door of his room and came forth to vindicate himself.

"You see now, it was not me, nor my room-mate either; it is some one next-door."

The steward admitted his innocence, and said he would now find the guilty one, and move him to some other part of the boat. About the same time, a voice in the ladies' cabin was heard calling for Ellen. But Ellen had vanished, no one knew whither.

The rapping of the steward awakened Handy.

"Who's there?" he asked.

"Me—the steward."

"What do you want?"

"I want to see the man in the other berth."

"He's asleep. Is it a matter of importance?"

"Yes, sir; of very great importance."

"Get up, Nap—some one wants to see you," said Jack, shaking his companion.

"Well? What is it?" asked Nap.

"Some one wants to see you."

"Oh, your granny! What does any one want to see me at this time o' night for? Be kind enough to say I'm engaged."

"It is one of the officers of the boat; and you must get up."

Nap did so very reluctantly; and when he had drawn on his pantaloons, he strode forth in no very good humour.

"Well, what do you want with me, steward!" he asked.

"Some ladies and gentlemen, sir, say you snore so loudly they cannot rest; and they have asked me to request you to sit up and keep awake until they get asleep."

"Is that all? I certainly do not snore louder than the escape-pipe puffing off its steam, do I? Why don't they ask you to have the engine stopped till they get asleep?"

"Oh, they're used to that."

"Why don't they get used to the other? I hear several other persons snoring, now. Why do they single out me?"

"Yours is altogether a different snore. Sometimes it's like the sawing of planks, and sometimes it's like boilers bursting."

"Do the ladies hear me! What ladies?"

"Mrs. W. and her daughter are in the next room to yours."

Nap said nothing; but he felt rather gratified to learn that Miss Mary had suffered a little. However, being very sleepy, and deeming it uncertain when every one but himself might be oblivious of sounds in their deep repose, he proposed to lie down at the other end of the cabin. The steward ordered one of his boys to make him a bed on the table in the place indicated. Here Nap once more prostrated his relaxed body, and, as usual, his escape-pipe was heard again. Unfortunately, several gentlemen in the vicinity were not yet slumbering so profoundly as to be insensible to the infliction.

One of Nap's neighbours, a Mr. N. H., lying on the same table, (which extended nearly the whole length of the cabin,) had been unlucky at cards, having lost a considerable sum of money, and of course was in no good humour with any one, not even with himself. He execrated himself for "calling" a stronger "hand" than his own, when he might have won, as he generally did, by "strong bluffing." While pondering over this matter, and turning impatiently from one side to the other, his ears were assailed by the universally unpopular snore of Nap. He listened a few moments, and then smiled maliciously, utterly forgetting his ill-luck in his contemplated amusement. He reached down and awakened a cabin-boy under the table. He placed a quarter of a dollar in the little fellow's hand, and whispered something in his ear. The boy nodded assent, and disappeared by way of one of the doors leading out on the guards, while N. H. breathed deeply, as if in a profound slumber.

When every one seemed to be quite still, the rascally urchin reappeared with a pan of water in his hand. He strode stealthily toward the head of Nap. Looking several times from his position toward his couch under the table, as if calculating the distance, and the time it would require to reassume his late recumbent posture, he paused with the pan suspended in his hands. He then dashed its contents over the neck and face of Nap, and vanished under the table, concealing the pan among his bed-clothes.

"Hello! Ugh! Hello, I say!" cried Nap. "The boat's sunk! The boat's sunk!" He tumbled down on the floor, and rolled over on his face, kicking lustily with his feet, and striking out his hands, as if swimming in the river.

A simultaneous unlocking of state-rooms was heard, and a moment after the cabin was entered by many half-dressed male passengers. These were immediately joined by as many women in their night-gowns and white caps, who came pouring in from the ladies cabin. Screams and howls were heard in every direction; but N. H. and the cabin-boy seemed to remain fast asleep. Ellen now appeared and strove to calm the ladies, assuring them nothing serious had happened.

Meantime Nap continued his struggles on the floor.

"Seize his feet and hands!" cried some one, and it was done. Joe T. and Jno. P. held him.

"Hold me fast, boys; I can't swim. Don't let me sink!" cried Nap.

"How deep is the water, Nap?" asked Joe, smiling, and presuming it was only a bad dream which had frightened him.

"How deep?" iterated Nap, wiping his eyes and staring around. "It was over my head! My hair is wringing wet."

Captain Jewett, who approached the scene of confusion, suspected some trick had been played on him.

"Dick," said he to the cabin-boy, "you know something about this. Who threw the water in the gentleman's face?"

"I was fast asleep, sir! How could I know any thing of it?"

"What's this pan doing here?" continued the Captain, kicking it from under the bed-clothing.

"I don't know, sir. I didn't have it."

"You lie, you rascal! Mr. Wax, I'll punish the boy. But some one hired him to do it. Who was it, Dick?" Dick whispered who it was; but the Captain did not say any thing to N. H., not wishing to have any further disturbance, and secretly rejoicing at the occurrence, for he well knew Nap's habit of annoying others. So, after repeating his purpose of having the offenders properly punished, he led Nap to his own state-room, where he was permitted to snore *ad libitum* the balance of the night.

CHAPTER XVII.

Nap and Jack arrive at St. Louis—Their produce well sold—Buying exchange—Nap presents a check payable to his own order, and is incensed at the conduct of the teller—Taking passage for M——e—— They arrive at C—— on foot—Nap's meeting with old Brindle and with Sting—The young men conceal themselves till night at the inn— The hostess's news and advice.

WHEN Nap arrived in St. Louis, he found quite as much money subject to his order in the hands of his commission merchant as he had calculated upon. His beeswax had brought twenty-four cents per pound; his deer-skins, twenty; his coon-skins, thirty cents each; and his minks, fifty. Handy was also quite as fortunate in his shipment.

The next thing to be done was to procure bills of exchange, payable in the East. This, Mr. T. offered to obtain for Nap from Messrs. J. J. A. & Co. The drafts were to be drawn on the Messrs. S. P. & Co., while Mr. Wm. M. I., a true friend of the Handys, was to give Jack his own drafts on the Messrs. F. & Co., and on one of the Eastern banks, where he was in the habit of keeping funds on deposite.

But before Nap's business could be despatched it was necessary to present a check he had obtained from a tobacco agent at the counter of the Bank of Missouri. This Mr. T. intended to do for him; but that gentleman being called aside by some one with whom he was in treaty for a cargo of coffee, Nap took up the check and went to the bank himself. He placed it in the hand of the paying teller.

"This is good," said the bank officer.

"I know it," said Nap; "I gave gold for it. Just give me five hundred dollars of your bank paper for it."

"It is payable to the order of N. B. Wax," said the official. "It must be endorsed by him."

"Oh, I forgot that!" said Nap, taking up his pen and writing his name on the back of the check. "There," he continued; "now it is endorsed."

"Yes, it is endorsed; but we don't know who did it," said the money functionary, glancing at the shabby exterior of our hero.

"You don't know who did it?"

"No."

"Why, durn it! didn't you just see me do it?"

"Oh yes."

"Well, I'm N. B. Wax."

"I don't deny it. But I don't know it."

"Don't know it when you see me, and hear me say so?"

"I never saw you before. How can I know you are not somebody else."

"Somebody else beside myself! Colonel Benton's right. Down with the impudent banks, I say!"

"If some one were to steal a check from you, ought I to pay it to the thief?"

"No. But I am no thief!"

"Excuse me. I don't know that."

"Confound you"——here Nap checked himself, seeing the teller was perfectly cool. "I–I'll bring a man here, sir, you *do* know—one who knows me—and knows I'm no thief. I'll sue you, sir! Durn your bank! I'll never have any thing to do with it again. I'll bring a man who knows me, sir!"

The teller informed him that that was precisely what he wished him to do, and what he should have done at first.

Nap retired in a great rage. When he repeated to Mr.

T. what had taken place, that gentleman smiled, placed his own name on the back of the check, and sent it by a black porter to the bank, who soon returned with the money. Nap was not fully reconciled even when the necessity of the course adopted by the teller was explained to him. He could not see why payment should be refused to him and granted to a negro.

Meeting Jack at the office of Mr. M., whose checks were not quite in readiness, Nap proposed going down to the wharf and engaging a state-room on one of the Ohio river boats, and then having their baggage taken on board while Jack was adjusting his business. To this Jack readily agreed, and so Nap sallied out alone, and, at the water's edge, accosted the clerk of the B. F.

"What is the passage to M——e?" asked he.

"Four dollars," said the clerk, glancing at Nap's cow-eaten hat, and at his tattered garments.

"That's low enough. There are two of us; we'll take the same state-room."

"State-room? You want a cabin passage?"

"To be sure we do! Do you think we're deck passengers?"

"Oh, you can go in the cabin if you like; but it is eight dollars there—eight dollars each."

"So you meant a deck passage? I always go in the cabin, sir—and I'm always able to pay my passage, sir."

"Very well. I don't dispute it."

"But you were going to put me among the deck passengers! Do I look like a deck passenger?"

"I've seen as good-looking men among them. But I'm busy now, unless you want a row. I always take time for that!"

Nap didn't want a row. Nor did he like the laughter that ensued from the crew. So he said he would go on board and select a state-room.

On board he confronted the second or "mud clerk," in the office.

"I want to engage a state-room in the cabin, sir," said he, "for myself and friend. Let me see the register, if you please."

"It is locked up," said the "mud clerk," closing it before Nap's eyes, "and the captain's got the key."

"I thought that was it you just shut up," said Nap.

"That's another one," said the clerk, looking contemptuously at Nap's garments. "But if you want a state-room, I'll make a memorandum of your name and take the money. No room is engaged till paid for."

"Are there many rooms not engaged?"

"Only two," said the imperturbable "mud clerk," although the truth was just the reverse, for only two had yet been taken.

"Let me see them, if you please," said Nap, secretly rejoicing that he had not delayed his application until it was too late.

"Here's one of them," said the clerk, when he led Nap to the room opposite the wheel-house, on the right-hand side of the cabin.

"But it's dark, being against the wheel-house, where there will always be a furious knocking of the paddles. I don't like it. There won't be light enough to shave by."

"The barber shaves the gentlemen."

"Yes, at a dime apiece. He don't shave me!"

"Well, suppose you look at the other room. I think it will please you better."

It was just opposite, and precisely similar to the first. The only difference was, that it was against the larboard wheel-house.

"I don't like it," said Nap.

"It's 'Hobson's choice;' the only chance for a ride on the B. F."

"Well, I'll take the other. Let us go to the office and settle."

Nap had paid for the passage of himself and Jack, and was just departing from the office, when a finely dressed gentleman **stepped up** and asked if any choice state-rooms remained unengaged.

"Plenty, sir!" **responded the clerk.**

Nap paused abruptly. But after some hesitation, not wishing to get into a "row," he strode away, groaning as he thought of the indignities he suffered on account of Molly Brook. And he determined that when his interview with her was over, to show the world that he could wear as fine clothes as anybody else.

It was perhaps a fortunate thing for Nap that he was put into the dark room. It was certainly lucky for the rest of the passengers, as the continued thumping of the wheel in his vicinity prevented his snoring for once from being extensively heard. The voyage was without special incident to M——e, where the young men entered a stage-coach.

Arrived at M——g, Kentucky, our young men descended from the stage. They were now within ten miles of their early home, where their aged mothers still dwelt. Although they certainly were richer than when they set out in quest of their fortunes, yet they did not choose to hire a carriage, or even a pair of horses, to convey them the remainder of the distance. They resolved to make an early start the next morning, and go on foot to C——, their native village.

So, at the hour appointed, Nap and Jack, each with a small knapsack, trudged along, in happy companionship, on the great highway leading toward their parents and sweethearts.

Sometimes, communing only with their own thoughts, they walked for many minutes in silence. Often their sensations, as scenes of infantile delights were recalled to memory, seemed too sacred for expression. At other times, as reminiscences of the past crowded upon their minds, all their powers of **speech** were brought in requisition, and yet their tongues failed to keep pace with their thoughts.

However humble may have been one's early home, and few his comforts in childhood, still, if his absence be not too long protracted, he feels a thrill of pleasure—sad, it may be, but still a pleasure—upon returning to it. If there be no friendly faces to give him a kindly greeting, yet he feels a glow of affection for the trees, the brooks, and the hills where in boyhood he wandered.

Neither of our young men had enjoyed the luxuries of life during their abode in C——; poor and insignificant, no one had felt any interest in their welfare, save, perhaps, the members of their own families, and, it might be, the young ladies for whom they had conceived the passion of lovers. Yet, as they approached the town, every familiar object arrested their attention, and often exacted the tribute of an honest tear. They lingered under the tall sugar-maples, just bursting their buds, upon whose strong boughs they had once fastened the vine-swing, and whiled away many an innocent hour. They strayed through the pastures, draped in early green, which, when schoolboys, they had traversed so often and so joyfully. The lark which now sprang up from their path and soared and sang so blithely, seemed to be the same that had enchanted their youthful hearts. The brook that gurgled over its pebbly bed, although it certainly did not disport the sam waters, was nevertheless quite as pellucid, and seemed i. no manner changed since the time they were wont to cast their lines upon its surface.

Such were their feelings and impressions when they came within sight of the village. Hitherto, neither of the young men, although they had been met by divers persons whose faces they knew, had yet elicited a recognition from any human being. No wonder, then, their affection was the more intense for inanimate objects. They could not evince a desire to avert their faces from their old acquaintances, whether they returned with improved fortunes or as paupers. They neither stared them coldly in the face, nor frowned upon them with aversion.

"There's an old friend will know me!" cried Nap, running out on the common, and endeavouring to embrace old Brindle, his mother's cow, which he used to drive home of evenings, and which always permitted him to hold one of her horns, and caress her neck as much as he pleased. But Nap was mistaken this time. She did not know him. She shook her head at him, and shied around with her tail erect, her eyes gleaming with surprise and fear, mingled with anger, and her nostrils emitting a deep-drawn breath.

"Ah, old Brindle!" said Nap, bitterly, "I would have almost as soon thought of being repulsed by my own mother as by you! You nursed me! For years I subsisted on your rich milk, and I thought you could never forget me. But you have forgotten the nubbins you received from my hand, before I forget the many rich draughts that nourished me, drawn from your teats!"

"Nap," said Jack, "she don't know you in these clothes. And if she won't recognise you thus costumed, how can you expect to get a hearty reception from Molly? It is not right, Nap. At least throw away your old straw hat, and put on the cap in your knapsack."

"To satisfy you, Jack, I will. And I must own the old hat does cut too bad a figure. Here, Brindle, it shall be a peace-offering to you. One cow had a bite of it"——

"But then it was new," said Jack, seeing the cow turn away from the hat which had been thrown on the grass before her, after smelling it once.

"She's an old brute!" said Nap; "and I'll not drink her milk again. But yonder comes one of the family that I am sure will know me," he continued, espying Sting, his mother's terrier dog, which had been taught to follow the cow, and to drive her home in the evening. "Here Sting! come here, my little fellow," said Nap, endeavouring to place his hand upon him as he met him in the path. But Sting growled and snapped at his fingers. "Go, and be blamed to you, you rascally son of a b——!" exclaimed

Nap, red with anger. "I snatched that dog out of the pond, when he was a pup, but four days old, and carried him home. I placed him on a blanket, near the fire, and raised him with the bottle. Old Brindle's milk sustained him. We were like **brothers**. And **now you see his** ingratitude! **He's like** the viper. **He would bite the** hand that rescued him from death!"

"It's your old clothes, **Nap**. That dog thinks his master should make a more genteel appearance. **Nap, you must** put on your other coat before you go **home, or else** your own mother will be ashamed of you."

"If she is, I'll hang myself. But she **won't be**. I know **her** too well. If I stood under the gallows, it would make no difference with her. **But,** hello! here's Sting smelling about my feet **and** wagging his tail. Sting! don't you **know me?**" **He** did, at last. **He** now wriggled **his** tail faster than one would suppose it possible the motion of that member could go. He whined, he barked, and finally leaped up in Nap's arms, who hugged him affectionately, and wept over him truly like a brother. "Poor Sting! You didn't know me at first, **and** you couldn't help it. I forgive you. You **are** not ungrateful. **You** are not **a** rascally son of **a b——**. My poor Sting!"

"Put down the dog, Nap," **said** Jack, petulantly. "**He** has muddied your shirt-bosom, and torn your **vest. The** people will think **we** are crazy."

"Let 'em think **what** they please, Jack. Sting is my friend, and I am his; **and** I will not slight a friend to please idle spectators. But who's looking at us? I don't want it to get out before night that we have arrived. And then I'm sure, if Sting had the **power,** he would celebrate the event by an illumination."

"Let us go to the inn, then, and conceal ourselves. We know how to get in the back way, and Mrs. Rankin will hide us."

"Agreed. **But** how am **I to** get rid of Sting? You

see he won't leave me. And if he did, I'm sure he'd make the news known to my mother. She understands his looks, and can read every wag of his tail."

"Bring him along, then. We must make him a prisoner."

Mrs. R. did cheerfully undertake to conceal the arrival of the young men. She had water, soap, and towels taken to their room, they being much needed, and likewise sent them a bountiful supply of substantial refreshments. And before the shades of evening began to gather over the village, Mrs. R. presented herself at their door, and most graciously offered to impart any information she could in regard to the changes, present condition of the people, &c., in C——. From her Jack learned that Kate had no new beau. Her relative and guardian, General Frost, remained quite as frigid as ever, and never failed to chill away any young man who ventured to visit his house for the purpose of seeing his niece. Kate alone had the courage to face the old General, and to oppose his unreasonable exactions; and to her, alone, he was sometimes in the habit of yielding. She was the only relative he had in the world, her father having been his only brother. He was her guardian, and managed her little fortune, to which might some day be added his own, that was larger, provided she remained with him and obeyed him, or married with his consent. He was a tall, white-haired old bachelor. He had served with distinction in the war of 1812, and had been subsequently elected to Congress, and was once the Governor of the State.

Mrs. R., however, informed Jack, with a significant smile, that if Kate did not often have visitors at the mansion of her aristocratic kinsman, yet she was by no means compelled to remain at home in utter seclusion. From her earliest childhood she had been in the habit of visiting at will the houses of her schoolmates, whether haughty or humble, although but few of her friends had access to her guardian's mansion, and this habit she had not relinquished in womanhood. Many a social hour she **would** spend with Mrs. Handy and Mrs. Wax. She was on very intimate **terms with** Molly Brook; and Mrs. R. said, to her certain knowledge, the girls never met without talking of their **absent beaus in** Missouri.

"**In** misery?" asked Nap, who was near the window, shaving himself, and did not distinctly **hear** what was said. His thoughts might have also been partly absent, and dwelling upon Polly. "**If they** think I have been miserable," he continued, "they are mistaken. There **are as** pretty flowers in the prairie as in the town."

"In *Missouri*, I said!" replied Mrs. R. "**La me, you** mustn't think **they want to** have **their** lovers miserable! They want to make 'em happy. And they'll do it, too! **You have** no idea how the girls have changed. I think you'll both say they are the handsomest women you ever laid **your eyes on.** And so merry—they're always laughing."

"**That's** by no means an agreeable thing for us to hear," **said Jack**, folding a note he had written to Kate, which Mrs. R. had promised to have delivered.

"La, man, would it make you happy to see the girl you **love** always miserable?"

"No, not miserable; **but a little sad because I was** away."

"Oh, nonsense. They do right to keep up their sperits as well as they **can.** The more they laugh the longer they'll look young. Look at me. They say I've laughed every waking hour since I was born."

"**I don't** object to their laughing, **so** they don't do it in the company of the gentlemen."

"And do you run away from all the young ladies **you** meet with out in the wild Missouri?"

"**Do we, Nap?**" asked Jack, turning archly to his companion in love's fetters.

"That's neither here nor there. I intend to haul Molly Brook over the coals," said Nap, gravely.

"And if you do, you'll get your fingers burnt!" **said**

Mrs. R. "She's changed, I tell you. But she's prettier. She's full of sly humour, and looks serious when she's the most merry. She has jokes and all sorts of tricks at her fingers' ends. Take care you don't offend her, or she'll put you off a year longer than she intended."

"Let her. She may put me off for ever!"

"Now, Nap, I know that's no such a thing! Nobody that ever did love such a nice, interesting girl as Molly Brook, could ever wish that. You don't know how beautiful her complexion is with her second-mourning dress on, and how her dark eyes flash sparks of fire when she has something wicked in her head"——

"Wicked?"

"Oh, I mean innocent mischief. And she has the darkest and silkiest and glossiest and longest hair in the world. If I was a man, I couldn't keep my hands off of her."

"The deuce you couldn't! And perhaps some of the men don't keep their hands off?"

"'Gustus Smart, the lawyer's son, couldn't. He asked her if he mightn't pay his addresses in earnest."

"And what did she say?"

"Say? She slapped his face, and set Sting at him!"

"Good! Hurra for Sting!"

"I say huzza for Molly. Everybody praised her to the skies!"

"Everybody had better mind their own business!" said Nap, churlishly.

"That's true, Mr. Nap; and you had better attend to yours, if you don't want that trump of a girl to slip through your fingers. And the wisest thing you can do will be to put on your best 'bib and tucker,' before you show yourself to her."

"I'm determined to make my appearance in these very clothes."

"What? If you do, you'll deserve to be hissed!"

"The clothes don't make the gentleman."

18

"But they make the first impressions. We see them first, because they're outside; and the world often judges the inside by the outside, as they do apples. I know when a handsomely dressed gentleman sits down at our table, he gets a better dinner for the same money than a vagabondish looking one does. But it's time for me to be bustling about the supper. Good night. Remember my advice."

Saying this with a serious toss of the head, Mrs. R. withdrew.

Our young gentlemen soon after descended to the street and proceeded to the humble domicils of their aged mothers, while the stars blinked merrily at them.

CHAPTER XVIII.

Nap's mother criticises his clothes—Meeting of the lovers—Nap is repulsed by Molly's father, and insulted by Mr. Smart—Jack makes him send a challenge, and gets him out of the scrape—Nap throws off his rags and becomes a dandy—Polly's father learns he has money, and becomes reconciled to him.

WE need not narrate the particulars of the meeting of the young gentlemen with their aged mothers. How could it be otherwise than affectionate and happy? At the tables of both the fattest pullets were served up at supper, and specimens of the best preserves the houses afforded were displayed. For Sting, particularly, it was a jubilation. He frisked from one room to another, following his old mistress in her search for dainties, and appeared to sanction every thing she did in honour of her son's return. And even the old cow seemed to have caught the enthusiasm, for she lowed incessantly at the garden gate. Mrs. Wax said she knew it was for Nap, and that old Brindle would never see a happy moment until he forgave her for not recognising him.

But when the first transports of the meeting began to subside, as all transports must do, Mrs. Wax could not avoid looking from Nap's face to his clothes and his pitiable boots.

"Why, Nap," said she, "how travelling does wear out one's clothes! I'll run and see if your poor papa's black coat is not too much moth-eaten for you to put on. He left a good pair of boots, nearly new, when he died. I'll get them for you also."

"No; don't, mother," said Nap, with a firm expression of countenance. "I couldn't get them on."

"That's true! You are larger than your papa was. He had small feet, and was never fat like you. You take after me, Nap. But I'll send down to the Jew clothing-store. They'll fetch up the things to fit you out. Don't shake your head, Nap. I've got money enough to pay for 'em. I'm not so poor as some of the rich folks think. There's a hundred dollars in the old walnut desk." She said this in a whisper, so that the hired negro girl might not hear it.

"Never mind, mother; **I have a** reason for appearing thus."

"But, Nap, I have a reason for wishing you to appear otherwise. I am older than you, and have seen more of the world"——

"Not more of the world, mother."

"Well, more of life, then; and more of human nature. My reason is this. Some of the girls may come in presently. **They do it** at all hours, and without ceremony. You have no idea how many come to see me. They have comforted me a great deal in your absence."

"**It was** no comfort to me, mother, to hear that they—and **Molly** Brook among them—came here to make fun of my being taken for a bear, and being nearly shot."

"They wouldn't have done it, Nap, if it hadn't been for Jack Handy's letter, saying the guns were not loaded.

Why, I laughed myself, till the water streamed from my eyes."

"Jack's always forestalling me. He had no business writing any such letter. I wanted to see how Molly would behave, and judge whether she cared any thing for me."

"She does care for you, Nap. She's a splendid girl, and I hope you will do no worse when you marry. All I fear is she won't have you. Her father wants her to marry young Smart, because his father's making money, and because he always dresses so genteelly. I'll send for the Jew, Nap, to fit you out. I have no other use for my money. Providence will supply me with more."

Nap's mother had been kept in ignorance of his success in business. Or rather, not being aware of the profits realized in the far West on the sales of merchandise, his appearance had filled her with secret misgivings that he might have returned penniless, and perhaps even pinched with hunger.

"No, mother. You must let me have my own way this time. I have made a vow to meet Molly attired just as I am. I will be able to judge then whether she most admires the man or his clothes."

"But why not let her admire both? One's clothes don't set up to be one's rival. Well, have your own way—only my money is at your service."

"Money! Mother, I'm going to tell you a secret. I am not a beggar. I don't return worse off than I was when I left home."

"You had five hundred dollars, Nap, when you left home."

"Let me whisper something in your ear, mother. *I have brought back three thousand dollars!*"

This announcement was certainly gratifying to his affectionate parent; but it did not make so great an impression as Nap thought it would. The effect was not so thrilling as he supposed it might be. Her love would have been the same, perhaps greater, if he had been

clothed with her little savings. Yet she was pleased to
hear it, for she knew he had come by it in an honest way;
and she felt the pride and satisfaction of being convinced
that when his success was made known in the village, the
people would treat him with more respect than they had
been in the habit of doing. That was the extent of her
exultation. Riches had no intrinsic value, in her estimation, besides the influence they exerted over the minds of
others. Contentment was her motto; and she knew that
one could be happy with a mere sufficiency to supply one's
moderate daily wants.

"Then, Nap," said his mother, after some grave reflection, "let me send word to Molly that you have made
a fortune, if you don't choose to dress extravagantly."

"No—not for the world! That would spoil my stratagem!"

But Jack had already informed her of it. In his letter
to Kate, written at the inn, he had explained every thing.
And as he was not sure upon what footing he might be
received at the mansion of General Frost, he had begged
her to meet him at the cottage of Nap's mother, accompanied by Molly.

Just as Nap uttered the word "stratagem," the gate in
front of the cottage was heard to open, and the friendly
wag of Sting's tail made his mistress aware that some of
her familiar visitors were approaching. A moment after,
delicate, half-suppressed laughter was heard in the yard.

"There they come, Nap! I thought some of the girls
would be here. They come nearly every night to keep
me company. They are lively, good girls. I do wish you
had on fine clothes."

"Mother," said Nap, resolutely, "never mind my
clothes. I have a great design in appearing thus, and the
issue of my scheme may decide my happiness for life. Do
you go into the parlour, and give them the usual welcome.
Don't be excited and raise their curiosity. Molly may
not be with them. Just do as usual. Don't for the

world hint that I am here. I will come in at the proper time."

His mother left him to obey his injunctions. She strove to meet Molly and Kate in the ordinary manner; but she could not altogether conceal her happiness. The girls strove likewise to conceal their knowledge of the arrival of the strangers. But to do so they had frequently to avert their faces and indulge in uproarious merriment.

Mrs. Wax, however, could not avoid seeing that the young ladies wore richer dresses, and had their hair arranged with greater care and taste than usual on such unceremonious visits. And this again startled her apprehensions for the consequences, when Nap should make his appearance in their presence.

"I want a glass of fresh water, Mrs. Wax," said Molly, rising, "and will go for it myself. Don't you move."

"But I will! I'll get it for you, Molly. Sit still!" cried Mrs. Wax, seeing that the giddy girl was about to enter the room where she had left her son, and through which it was necessary to pass to obtain the water.

But Molly had already sprung through the door and was out of sight. She passed premeditatedly through the room in which Nap was sitting, without recognising him. She had braced herself for the accomplishment of that feat. She certainly saw him, and he perceived she did. But without raising her eyes to his, she merely paused a moment, as if in surprise to meet a stranger there, and then passed on without speaking, and before the petrified youth had time to recover his self-possession or utter one word.

Nap's temples burned with emotion of mingled chagrin and indignation. He thought if such was to be his reception by his early sweetheart, the sooner he returned to Missouri and married Polly Hopkins the better. And he wished that Polly could be transported in a moment to his presence, that he might marry her at once, and before the face of Molly, and thus he would be sufficiently revenged. He resolved now not to remain alone in the room till Molly returned, and so he joined his mother in the parlour.

Jack had soon followed the girls to the cottage, and his meeting with Kate had been mutually agreeable, and altogether such as they had desired and anticipated. And when Nap appeared before them, Kate, as had been preconcerted, gave him a most enthusiastic greeting, without once seeming to glance at his mean attire.

"You are a happy man, Jack," said Nap, when the salutation was over. "Kate is made of the right sort of stuff"——

"Of flesh and blood, Nap," said she.

"Of the best blood. I shall believe in blooded nags hereafter"——

"You talk as if I were of the imported stock!"

"And so you are—and of the highest quality too. They may say what they please about General Frost, and the aristocracy of your family; but I like it, because it is as true as steel, and never flinches for time, distance, or circumstance."

"Why, Nap, what does all this mean?" asked Kate, in pretended surprise. "Why are you praising me? Where's Molly?"

"I don't know. I saw her run into the kitchen."

"You've seen her, then?"

"Yes, I've seen her—and seen enough of her. But she wouldn't see me! She didn't know me in these clothes!"

"Ha! ha! ha! Was it any fault of hers if she didn't know you?"

"How did you know me? If it were not for Jack, and"——

"Polly?" asked Handy.

"Yes—I would offer to marry you on the spot!"

"You would?"

"Hanged if I wouldn't!"

"And what answer would you make, Kate?" asked Jack.

"Why, if, and if, and so forth, I would take the matter into serious consideration. What care I for one's exterior? The heart is the thing; and I'm sure Nap has a large one."

"Kate, I have! But it has been sorely tried."

"Don't let it break, Nap. Molly will make amends. Here she comes."

Molly came gliding in with a glass of water in her hand, and seeing Jack first, let the glass fall to the floor and ran to him. She grasped his hand, and declared she was glad to meet with him.

"Molly, have you forgotten Nap?" asked Mrs. Wax, pointing to her son, who had stepped back into an obscure corner.

"No! Where is he? Oh, I'm dying to see him! Is he in town?"

"There he is."

"Where? Nap! Is this you? Why, it is! Oh, I'm so glad! Why do you shrink away so? Won't you—won't you take my hand? There it is! Yes he will! How you have improved! Nap, you are a fine-looking fellow, now. I don't care for your travelling dress; I don't care for poverty—the heart, the *heart* is every thing among old friends!"

"There Nap," said his mother, her eyes streaming with tears of pleasure, "that's Molly! It is her way. She's a noble girl!"

"Molly!" said Nap, in a tremulous voice.

"Nap!" said she, smiling, and still permitting him to hold her hand.

"Molly—I—thought you had forgotten me."

"Why?"

"Because you wouldn't speak to me in the back-room, when you passed through it for the water."

"Was that you? I didn't look at your face. Why didn't you speak?"

"I couldn't; I was choked."

"And I couldn't look up; I was frightened."

"There's a mutual explanation," said Kate, "and it's all over. Nap, do you like me as well as ever?"

"Oh yes; I have a heart large enough to love everybody."

"You have?" demanded Molly.

"I mean to be friendly with all."

"And that's right," said his mother.

"The heart is every thing," said Molly. "No matter what the form may be, whether handsome or homely; or the dress, whether costly or common; if the heart be true, it compensates for every other deficiency."

"Molly," said Nap, with enthusiasm, "your heart is as true as steel. I thought differently once," he added in a low tone.

"Why?"

"Because you wouldn't answer me affirmatively when I desired to know—you remember—and I attributed your hesitation to"——

"What?" she asked in a half-whisper, seeing Jack and Kate enjoying an interesting tête-à-tête in the opposite corner, while Mrs. Wax was bustling about in quest of preserved fruits and currant wine.

"My poverty."

"*Our* poverty, and our youth. We were too poor and too young to settle such serious affairs, and so we are still. But we may laugh over our old sports, and enjoy ourselves."

"Day after to-morrow I must leave you."

"Day after to-morrow?" Neither Kate nor Molly had been informed that the young men were merely passing on their way to the East, and had achieved decided success in Missouri. "And where are you going, Nap?"

"To Philadelphia and New York, to purchase goods. Molly, now or"——

"Never?"

"It may be so. Unless it is to get a wife, it will be quite impossible for me to visit Kentucky on my return to Missouri. But," he continued, his heart wholly recaptured as he gazed at the handsome girl, "if you will go with me to Venice, I will surely come for you."

She promised to write him her determination. He might look for a letter soon after reaching Philadelphia. That was reasonable, and Nap was in high spirits. The image of Polly then faded from his mind, or assumed a repulsive shape. Such was the impressible nature of Mr. Wax.

And Jack ventured to make a similar proposition to Kate. But Kate's father had provided in his will that if his daughter married contrary to the wishes of her guardian before she arrived at the age of twenty-one, her fortune should all go to General Frost. And that was not all: the General, whom she sincerely esteemed, had her voluntary promise not to marry without his consent during her minority. She was then just twenty. There was one whole year to elapse before Jack's hopes could be realized. She felt quite certain that the General would not give his consent for her to wed young Handy, and he had her solemn promise not to marry during the period named. So there was nothing left them but patiently to await the fulfilment of the allotted time. But during the interval she resolved to convince her guardian that no other person could make an impression on her heart.

The sweetmeats furnished by the old lady having been partaken of with an appreciating appetite by the young people, the rest of the evening was spent in the narration of adventures: in Missouri, by the young men; in Kentucky, by the young ladies. And as the ladies were the last to speak, which is said to be not unfrequently the case, it was not to be wondered at that when the clock struck ten, Náp startled them all by a premonitory blast of his nasal trumpet. He, of course, apologized, and Jack assisted him. They had walked so far that day, had slept so little the night before, &c. &c. The girls only laughed the more heartily as the boys grew the more eloquent.

But the time had come for the young ladies to depart, and they arose for that purpose. It was but a few steps to General Frost's mansion, and thither Handy conducted Kate, while Molly was adjusting her shawl.

When Nap and Molly sallied out into the street, they were met by two men who paused in front of them. By the light of the moon they were recognised to be Molly's father and Mr. Augustus Smart, the young lawyer.

"Take my arm, Molly," said the former. "I don't approve of your going about of nights, or in the daytime either, with this idle vagabond."

"Idle vagabond, father!"

"You haven't looked at his clothes, Molly," said Smart. "I saw him on the common with a dirty dog in his arms."

"And you told it to my father!"

"I called to see you; you were away. Your father asked the news, and the return of Nap was all I had to tell him."

'Good-bye, Nap," said Molly, relinquishing our hero's arm, and obeying the command of her father.

"Good-bye, Molly," exclaimed Nap, in a tragical tone, having been hitherto speechless. "But, Mr. Brook," he continued, following them a few steps, "it's all a lie about my being a vagabond"——

"A lie, sir!" exclaimed Smart.

"I—I've got three thousand dollars, Mr. Brook," continued Nap, in a bolder voice, still following; "I've got them in drafts, sewed up in my drawers, and if you'll come to mother's in the morning, I'll show them to you. That's more than you have got yourself, or Mr. Smart's father either. Vagabond, indeed! I wore these old clothes purposely to try Molly's heart, and it's as true as steel. I'll put on better to-morrow, if they are to be had in the village for money, and then we'll see who's the finest gentleman, Mr. Augustus Smart or **Nap Wax**. I haven't told you all yet, Mr. Brook," said the excited **Nap**, still following, while the one addressed seemed to linger and listen. "I own a whole town, sir, with the exception of some lots I gave away."

"What town?" asked Brook.

"Venus!" cried Nap, unconscious of his mistake in his whirling perturbation; "and Colonel Benton says I am to be the 'Dodge of Venus!'"

"And Colonel Benton knows," said Smart, "you'll dodge any thing that kicks at you."

"But you won't dodge out of the way when kicked. I know Molly kicked you."

"I'll see you to-morrow!" said Smart, recollecting Nap's constitutional weakness. "Please accept my arm, Miss Molly," he continued, turning to the girl.

"Excuse me!" was heard by Nap, as he wheeled round and retraced his steps toward his mother's cottage. Soon he met Jack, to whom he related all that had occurred.

"Now, Nap," said Jack, after some little reflection, "you have an opportunity to distinguish yourself."

"How?"

"He said he would see you to-morrow?"

"He either said that, or else I would hear from him."

"Good; Nap, I know him to be a coward"——

"Are you sure? If I thought so, I'd give him a thrashing."

"Nonsense. You never were rational on the subject of fighting. But as he meddled in this matter, and slandered you to Molly's father I would not wait to hear from him."

"Would you go before he has time to come or send?"

"Listen to me, and take my advice. I never got you into a scrape in my life, but I have helped you out of difficulties."

"True, Jack, and I pledge myself to follow your instructions."

"Very well. Then, at early dawn, Smart must hear

from you. He must read your note in bed. I will bear it. You must demand satisfaction, and invite him to meet you with pistols on the common before breakfast."

"Why, Jack, blood might be spilt!"

"Not a drop. I'll engage that neither of you shall be injured. Nor shall you fight. He will not accept the challenge, I am sure. But if he should do so, rely upon me to prevent the meeting. You will have no use for pistols, and need not procure any."

"I hope he won't get any, either!" said Nap.

"I am certain he will not. Come into your mother's cottage and write what I shall dictate."

It was done, under the repeated assurances of Handy that nothing serious should grow out of it. The note was a peremptory demand to meet the writer at the time and place indicated.

Long before the sun had risen, Jack had penetrated the bedroom of Mr. Augustus Smart.

"By Jupiter, Jack, is it you?" exclaimed Smart, rising up in bed and extending his hand. "I knew you had arrived; but I did not expect you would be the first to call. I intended to go over to your mother's immediately after breakfast. Well, how have you been, old fellow? I am very glad to see you."

"I am very well; and my friend Nap is well also. He has changed much, however, since he left Kentucky."

"Is the tale about his having made money, true?"

"Every word of it. But that is not what I meant. You know he was once supposed to be constitutionally a coward."

"Oh yes. I've thrashed him many a time, when he might have whipped two of my weight if he had chosen. But he hasn't changed in that respect, has he?"

"He has. In Missouri, he practised with gun and pistol, first at a target. When he became a good shot, he tried his skill at *animate* objects. He shot one or two individuals in Missouri."

"The devil he did! What a change! I must let him alone, then. I did intend to call him to an account for an insinuation he made last night, which I didn't relish. But I'll not do it."

"He was fearful you would not."

"Fearful I would *not?*"

"Yes."

"I *will* not."

"Hence he determined to make a call upon you. He charged me to deliver this note."

Mr. Augustus Smart turned very pale as his eye ran over the brief epistle, and he trembled perceptibly.

"Handy!" said he, springing up, and endeavouring to put on his clothes, "do you know what he has written me? Just read it."

"He read it to me before he sealed it."

"Per--per--haps, then, you are his fr--friend?" said Smart, between his quivering teeth.

"I am. We were always friends. I hope, though, this matter may be attended by no fatal consequences. Of course you will be on the ground with your friend. Good morning."

"Stay! Don't go yet, Handy. I've got no friend. I don't believe I ever had one in my life! Won't *you* be my friend, too?"

"I cannot take the responsible position of being the friend of both on such an occasion."

"I mean a mediator. Can you not reconcile us? Can't a meeting be prevented?"

"Oh, certainly, in the usual way, you know."

"Tell me how?"

"I will."

Taking up a pen, Jack wrote a few lines on a sheet of paper he found upon the table.

"Sign this, Smart, and the whole matter will be amicably adjusted."

"I will!" cried Smart, after reading it hastily. "There! Now I hope it is all over."

"I hope so," said Jack, preparing to depart.

"You merely hope so?"

"I know so, so far as you are concerned. If he does not ratify what I have done, I shall take your place on the common. You may go to bed again and sleep in peace."

Smart did go to bed, but not to sleep, after such a spasm of excitement; and Jack proceeded briskly and gayly to Mrs. Wax's cottage.

"Have you seen him?" asked Nap.

"Oh yes. It's all settled."

"Settled? What do you mean? You know it was agreed there should be no fighting. I won't fight. It's against the law—its against my conscience, and"——

"It goes against the grain!"

"Yes. I'll not fight, Jack; and I hope you haven't settled it that we shall meet."

"Suppose you fire with powder only."

"'Twon't do. I won't risk it. He might slip in a piece of lead."

"But what can you do if he accepts the challenge, and demands a meeting?"

"Back out. I'll do it!"

"What would Molly say?"

"If she cares any thing for me, she'll be glad of it. If she would have me shot, what better proof need one have that she is indifferent about my fate. Then why should I hesitate on her account? What's that?" added Nap, seeing the note in Jack's hand.

"It is his answer. Read it."

Nap did so. It was a full retraction and a complete apology. Nap rubbed his eyes and read it over again.

"Durn him!" cried he, "I've got him down as flat as a flounder! Jack, I thank you. I feel like a hero. I believe now it is always the best way to put on a 'stiff upper lip,' and act the 'dare-devil.' I'll do it hereafter.

Molly shall know all about this affair. I'm sure it will please her to have a brave sweetheart, and to learn that the persecuting Gus Smart has been cowed."

The Jew clothier was now sent for, and Nap was soon transformed from a vagabond into a dandy. From the crown of his head to the sole of his foot, the metamorphosis was complete. He likewise bought sundry articles of jewelry, and among them three or four rings for his fingers, the largest ones the Jew could furnish. He also purchased a quizzing-glass, which he suspended from a button-hole by a ribbon, in imitation of Colonel Benton, who was under the necessity of using a magnifier when reading small print.

Thus attired, our hero sallied forth and boldly presented himself at the house of Mr. Brook, and was instantly admitted by that gentleman. Mr. B. had learned from Handy that Nap had not exaggerated in regard to his fortune, and he now hastened to explain away his seemingly unfriendly treatment of the preceding evening. He attributed it all to the representations of Smart, whom he denounced as a slanderer, and as one deserving disgrace and punishment.

"He'll not meddle again!" said Nap, proudly. "I have settled with him, and hermetically closed his lips for the future."

"How?" asked Mr. Brook.

"What have you done?" cried Molly, fixing her large dark eyes on Nap in utter amazement.

"Read that!" said he.

It was done.

"Good!" said Mr. Brook. "That's the end of him. He must leave Kentucky after that. He can go to Oregon or California. I didn't think such courage was in you, Nap."

"You didn't demand satisfaction?" asked the incredulous Molly.

"I did. I challenged him to fight me with pistols! And that, too, on the common, before breakfast!"

Molly's astonishment was very great; and her father's admiration of Nap's conduct knew no bounds. He even intimated very distinctly, that henceforth his opposition to our hero's marriage with his daughter would cease. He then withdrew and left them together.

But the news of the challenge did not excite Molly's admiration. Nor did Nap's metamorphosis seem to please her much better. She was grave and taciturn, and the conversation ended without any further preliminaries of the match being settled.

Meantime, Mr. Brook hastened to circulate in the village the news of Nap's success in Missouri, as well as an account of his triumph over Smart. Nap was instantly a hero and a gentleman, and not without honour in his own country.

CHAPTER XIX.

General Frost lectures Kate on the blessings of celibacy, and the curses of democracy—Mr. Brook informs the General how Jack managed the affair of honour—The General approves his conduct—Nap sits in the porch of the inn, and acts the lion—Jack and Nap set out on their Eastern journey—The hack breaks down, and they linger on their old play-ground—A row in Bullock's orchard.

"KATE, if there is any thing in your nature I like above all the other qualities you possess, it is your fearless candour, your perfect honour. It shows the stock whence you derive your blood and name. How much better, how much braver, in you to be the first to tell me young Handy had returned, and that you were in his company last evening, than to wait for others to bring me the news!"

This of course was spoken by the old General, wrapped in his velvet gown, and sitting in the library of his spacious mansion, while Kate occupied a chair on the opposite side of the fire-place.

"I never have deceived you, sir, and I never will. I will do nothing which I am ashamed to avow."

"I know it, Kate. I know that very well. Else I would not trust you alone, to go and come when you please. You are a Frost—you will never forget that, Kate. It is a good name, and a good family. And it seems to me the strangest thing in the world that any one should be desirous of changing it. You cannot possibly get a better one. Don't give it up, Kate."

"Do you know any marriageable bachelor of the name of Frost, sir?"

"No, Kate, not one. But why do you ask?"

"Simply to find out whether you desire me to live and die an old maid."

"Live and die an old maid! Why, Kate, you are a mere girl yet. Old maid! You won't be one for twenty years to come. Pooh, child; don't think of marrying until you are thirty, at least. But why the deuce should you wish to marry at all?"

"I—I don't particularly desire it. But if one should be dying for me"——

"Let him die and be d——d!" roared the old General, furiously. "Dying for you! What business has any impertinent puppy to be dying for you? I didn't die for anybody, did I?"

"But have you been happy all your life? Didn't you fight Colonel —— because he"——

"Yes! But he destroyed the peace and life of—— No matter, Kate. You have no business to be raking up old matters. I shot the rascal, and that was enough. Just think how plain Mrs. Handy, a common housewife name, would sound beside Miss Kate Frost. How do you like the contrast?"

"Oh, you know, a rose by any other name would smell as sweet."

"That's poetry, which is nonsense. All poets are mad. Dying for love!"

"But suppose I should happen to be dying for a—a"——

"A fool! Why, then, the sooner you died the better."

"Suppose he was no fool; say he was young, handsome, brave, and chivalrous?"

"Then it couldn't be this counter-hopper Handy. Tradesmen are not that sort of people."

"In Europe, where you have travelled so much, they may not be. But remember that in this country it is the man, and not his occupation, which is considered. President Fillmore was a clothier, and Franklin a soap-boiler and printer. Roger Sherman was a shoemaker, and the governor of Tennessee is a tailor."

"They were exceptions to the rule. I maintain the rule itself exists, and will exist in this country as well as in others, unless human nature itself be changed. Democracy is the devil in disguise, and would turn the world upside down if it could. But its antics will soon betray it in all its deformity to the people, and then it will be demolished, as it was in France, or be compelled to run into the ocean and be drowned like the swine. It must go the whole hog. Here! I've just been reading a specimen of democracy in the Herald. Look at it, when you have leisure. The President or his villanous subordinates have just removed one of the C.'s from office, alleging as a cause the incumbent's ill-health. His disease was contracted from exposure in the service. His ancestors were distinguished centuries ago for meritorious conduct, and one of the family supplied General Washington with the greater portion of his wealth. They served their country before the Revolution and since, and yet the democracy would destroy them. On the same day this C. was removed—who has a large family unprovided for—was appointed"——

"Who?"

"Oh, you can't guess! You need not try. I'll tell

you. A—— S——, whose father was hung the other day. And the son confessed he had been a —— himself! That's your democracy?"

"But, my dear sir, the subject was not politics. It was matrimony."

"Matrimony! You pronounce it as familiarly as if you knew something of its nature."

"What do you know against it, sir? You were never married."

"No, thank heaven! And certainly never will be, unless I do it merely to bestow my fortune on some one to punish you. And then it shall be under a stipulation that my wife shall never come within my sight!"

"Ha! ha! ha! Oh, General, you are a woman-hater because you never had one to comfort you. Excuse me; some one is coming."

When Kate retired, Mr. Brook entered, and related what had transpired between Nap and young Smart. He had also learned that Jack had dictated the challenge, delivered it, and then wrote the retraction and apology. The General listened with interest, and manifested symptoms of approbation. As Brook was an humble admirer of his, and a great newsmonger, he had easy access to the old soldier, and he was now doing Jack a service, without intending it, and without being aware of it. For if he had thought that his narration was calculated to affect the young man's prospects, he would not have dared to utter a word in his behalf in the presence of his patron, whose opinions and caprices he never ventured to oppose.

Mr. Brook soon withdrew to tell the news to others. Although duelling was in direct violation of one of the statutes of the State, as it is in all the States, yet the enactment was necessarily suffered to remain a dead letter, since a majority of the community opposed the application of its penalties. And in this instance the rumour of a challenge only produced an agreeable excitement in the village. As long as the lawmakers are in the habit of going to war, and arraying nation against nation for the purpose of wholesale slaughter, growing out of some trivial dispute or point of etiquette—so long as the most skilful slayer of human beings and destroyer of the wealth of nations is applauded the most, and has the highest honours showered upon him, it is hardly to be supposed that individuals can be kept from hostile collision, where calumny has stained the innocent, or an unprovoked insult is offered the unoffending.

Such at least was the opinion of the brave old General. And whenever his eyes rested upon an eloquent denunciation of the duello in any of the gazettes, he was in the habit of exclaiming, This rascal would wish to have the power of inflicting irreparable injury without incurring the liability of being made to suffer for it. A dastardly coward! No doubt he has perpetrated more injuries than the mere breaking of an antagonist's arm, in a fair and honourable manner, with one's own person exposed to the aim of his adversary.

"That fellow must have a spirit of no low degree," soliloquized the General, a habit he was addicted to when pleased with any subject. "It was admirably conceived, and executed with gallant intrepidity. Some of the boy's ancestors must have had good blood in them, and it shows its quality in such acts as this. Blood is like the mountain torrent; sometimes it is hidden in its descent and supposed to be lost, and then, unexpectedly, bursts forth again and dazzles the eye of the beholder."

"What is that bright object, sir, which your thoughts seem to be dwelling upon?" asked Kate, who came in noiselessly and resumed her chair.

"Eh! Is that you, Kate?" asked the General, aroused from his abstraction and lifting his eyes to hers. "Did you hear me?"

"I could not avoid hearing you, sir. But you mentioned no name. You merely said 'that fellow.' Who it was you alluded to in terms of such high commendation, I am unable to conjecture."

"Oh, it was a young fellow of spirit; one who has performed an action worthy of the past generation. A right noble fellow."

"Then, perhaps, sir, he might please your ward also; and of course you could have no objection to him. May I know him, sir? I will promise to admire him for your sake."

"The deuce you will! Oh, no doubt of it. No doubt, no doubt. But I won't tell his name, for fear you will want to marry him."

"You know I am to marry no one without your consent"——

"For a whole year. But I shall want you longer. And yet if I don't tell you who this rascal is, your woman's wit will find it out."

"I'll guess, sir."

"Who do you suppose it was?"

"I don't know. You say you won't tell. Is that candid?"

"I will tell. I will be as candid as you are. It was"——

"Who?"

"This Jack **Handy**."

"I thought so!" said Kate, blushing deeply. "But what has he done?"

The General told her. Then she owned that his conduct did not please her so much at it did her guardian. She thought it was not well to be engaged in such affairs, either as principal or second. And the General said he had no doubt that by the time the rascal had won his consent, his wayward ward would be ready to reject him. She retorted by reminding him that it was no part of his authority to cause her to wed any one of his selection. Then the General, in a pretended rage, ordered his horse and rode into the country, as was his custom in fine weather.

About the same hour that the tall old General bestrode his noble steed, Nap sallied out from his mother's cottage, and moved toward the inn with the deliberate walk and contemplative air of Colonel Benton himself. He occupied a seat on the porch, rising every moment to shake hands with the passing people. Those who went by on the opposite side of the street he bowed to. And as all had by this time heard of his acquisitions in the West, and of his challenge that morning, much curiosity was manifested to see him, and to converse with him. As numbers saluted him, and accosted him with marked respect, it was natural for his susceptible mind to conceive the idea that he was the lion of the place; and so he strove to play the lion's part. His gestures and tones were in exact imitation alternately of those of the great men whom he had marked on similar occasions. It was a happy hour for Nap; and as appearances always have their effect upon the imaginations of the weak and unreflecting, he really succeeded in convincing numbers that he was possessed of genius and had not hitherto been appreciated. But there were others who watched him at a distance, and made him the target for their shafts of ridicule. His dress and actions were almost ridiculous. But these envious wits had seized upon a portion of Mr. Brook's literal narration of the occurrence the night before, and made themselves merry at our hero's expense. They dubbed him " Dodge of Venus," and the appellation adhered to him.

The tide of public opinion, however, ran too strongly in favour of Nap to be arrested or diverted from its course by the jeering and depreciating "outsiders," who might be envious of his good fortune. When the people ceased to come forward and shake his hand, he sat down and conversed freely with those who formed a circle round him. The tales of far-western habits and scenes never wearied them; and Nap, like his great prototype, interlarded his narrations with many profound, and sometimes **rather startling** reflections, **which were** swallowed **by the** gaping multitude. And when the conversation flagged, or when the industrious **listeners** departed to their shops, Nap's happiness **did not cease.** He scanned his new habiliments with amiable satisfaction. His chain, his glittering rings, and even his polished boots, so different from the old **ones,** gladdened his eyes, and elicited his unfeigned admiration. His feet, however, were twelve inches **long, and proportionally** broad, without **the usual curvatures; and his hands,** like Sir Walter Scott's, (only **Sir Walter never admired his,)** were of huge dimensions, **red,** and with an unsmooth exterior. It was not, however, the uncouth proportions of his members **that arrested his gaze:** it was the glittering sparkle of the rings, and the glossy surface **of** the varnish. **The enormous size of his** hands and **feet** was not at all strange or annoying to him—he had long been in the habit of seeing them without emotion, and seeing them, too, among others quite **as** huge and unsightly.

Nap sometimes thought if Molly had married somebody else during his absence, or had openly contemned him **in** his recent humble attire, **that** his triumph might have been still more complete. He knew that **his** pride, high **as it then was, would have** been more blissfully exalted, and he would have inflicted **a** most consummate retaliation on the venality of her gossiping father. But when he considered the handsome manner **in which she had eulogized** the properties of **true and** faithful hearts, **in** contrast with **riches and** the shallow adornments of the person, he thought **he could** not have the resolution to perpetrate any species of hauteur toward the father, which might also inflict a wound upon the daughter. **Nevertheless,** without being conscious of it himself, Molly **had a rival now,** ever-present—his **new-born** vanity. It must be owned that, without constitutional meanness, or premeditated infidelity, our hero began to admire himself almost, if not quite as much, as his early love. Supereminently impressible himself, and, like the chameleon, taking the hue of the objects that interested him, he presumed that he was now creating an immense sensation in the community of C——; while he failed to consider the utter insignificance and worthlessness of any such effect produced by such a cause.

Yet, evincing his delight by a condescending smile, he towered in his own estimation far above his unambitious friend and fellow-traveller. And when the day arrived for their departure, and the ceremony of leave-taking was over, the best hack that Mr. R——, the landlord of the inn, could procure, drove up to Mrs. Wax's cottage gate. Jack was decidedly in favour of returning on foot to the point where they were to take the stage. But Nap would not listen to it. His days of humiliation were over. Henceforth he was to be a star of the first magnitude. His fond mother, in the blindness of her affection, approved of all he did, and rejoiced in the rising importance of her son. And so did Mr. Brook, exulting in the magnificence of his future son-in-law. Molly regarded his display differently. She saw that the flashing brilliance with which he was surrounding himself might blind his vision to her more substantial charms. Handy was silent and grave. He had just terminated a tender but clandestine interview with Kate, whose guardian was absent on his daily ride into the country.

As they drove up the hill, slowly departing from the village, Nap folded his arms on his breast and surveyed the handsome cushions of the carriage. It was the first time he had ever enjoyed the luxury of riding in a hack. This coalesced gratefully with the grandeur of his ideas. In silent meditation, for Jack too had a subject amply sufficient to occupy his thoughts, they proceeded several miles, when, a wheel striking against a rock, the hindmost axletree was broken in twain.

"The boat is sunk, Nap," said Jack, as they sank down between the wheels; "but luckily there is no danger of drowning this time."

"Hello! Stop, driver!" cried Nap, roused from his prolonged reverie, and once more under the influence of his old apprehensions of injury to his corpulent person. "Let me get out!" he continued. And when he did get out, the driver assured him that the horses had not moved a step after the carriage broke down. He said that they were not of the running-off breed, and were always ready to stop when any thing was the matter.

Fortunately, the accident occurred within hearing of the ring of a smith's anvil, and the accommodating Vulcan was in readiness to put aside all other work and repair the injury.

While the axletree was being welded, the young men strolled into the silent wood, where they had often rambled in early boyhood.

There, for the first time, at parting, Nap yielded to the influence of a crowd of solemn memories that rushed upon nis mind. The present faded away, and he was in the past. Silently he and Jack stood arm in arm, and gazed at the enchanting scene. It had been the play-ground of them both, where Kate and Molly had often enlivened the hour and partaken of their sports. If the boys had changed, and the girls had become stately women, there had been no alteration of the scene where they had played. The hawthorn, the beech, and the maple were still there on the margin of the peaceful stream. The grape-vine, suspended from the tallest tree, yet hung in its old place The rays of golden sunlight, struggling through the young leaves above, illuminated the profound solitude of the place precisely as they had done in former days, when they exhilarated the hearts of the guileless children. The half-decayed trunk of a fallen oak, the moss-grown rock projecting from the earth, and the old marks carved upon the rind of the beech, remained precisely as they had left them. And if none of these mementos had changed, how was it possible for the young men to avoid becoming boys again in fancy? Years enough had not rolled over their heads to produce forgetfulness; a sufficient number of the harsh vicissitudes of the world had not yet cicatrized them into callousness; and hence the healing fountains were stirred within them, and grateful tears gushed forth and trickled down their cheeks.

"Nap," said Jack, "our happiest days were passed within this lofty arbour. Such blissful moments will never return. We can only remember them, and grieve that we were forced to relinquish them. Happy must be the lot of those who are not compelled by fortune to abandon the cherished scenes and innocent companions of their childhood."

"Jack," said Nap, applying his handkerchief to his eyes, "I have a mind not to abandon them. I've never been so happy since I left home as I was before."

Awakened to a consciousness of duty, the duty of the man, in contradistinction to the impulses of the child, which now wholly possessed his companion, Jack yielded, in the reaction of his spirits, to a hilarious fit of laughter.

"Why, Nap," said he, "we could never appreciate the enchantments of such scenes as these, if they were not revisited after long separations. We enjoy them because we have been absent from them. If we had remained here, we should have grown weary of them."

"I don't think so. I don't feel so. And I am almost determined to turn back and remain with my mother and Molly the rest of my days. I wonder what a few acres of land here, including this spot, would cost?"

"This is in the centre of a large farm, every acre of which is worth a hundred dollars. It would require all your money, and would then be unproductive. Nonsense, Nap. Make a large fortune, and then come back and buy the whole county!"

"I will! I can do it! I have already made more money than any one supposed I could in a lifetime. Who can tell how far the tide will lead me? I will follow it on to fortune." Nap had read Shakspeare in Missouri during the long rainy days and dreary nights.

"That's right, Nap. It is as the great poet says. Put your trust in him, and never mind what malicious tongues in C—— choose to say of you."

"Jack, what have you heard them say? I thought they were all praising me."

"Then you were mistaken. No one who meets with success is praised by envious rivals. They attribute your good fortune to the old hackneyed adage, 'A fool for luck.' But you must bear in mind that any one is a fool who would not be lucky."

"They are a pack of idle fools, Jack, and I am glad to leave them! Let us go to the shop and hurry up the blacksmith."

They did so; but yet it was far in the afternoon before the injury was repaired.

Night overtook our travellers before they reached the point where they expected to find the mail-coach in readiness to convey them to the Ohio river. And as there was an inn on the roadside, from whence arose the savoury fumes of fried ham and eggs, the driver declared they would have to sojourn there until morning. He said his master never permitted the horses and carriage to travel in the night, unless there was a special bargain made to that effect. Of course there had been no special agreement of that kind on the present occasion, and therefore he paused at the porch of the inn.

Our young men yielded the more readily to this, inasmuch as they were both well acquainted with the landlord, a jolly old publican by the name of Bullock. They had known him before their emigration to Missouri, and they had refreshed themselves at his house a few days before, when going to C—— on foot.

"Censarn it, Nap," said Bullock, "I didn't know you in all them gewgaws. The other day I told the old ooman I didn't think you'd made out very well in Missouri; and she said she always thought you'd come back worse off than you went."

"You should not always judge from appearances, Mr. Bullock," said Nap, smiling condescendingly.

"That mought do for other folks. No doubt, other people oughtn't. But we innkeepers always look at the clothes and other fixins about a stranger before we kill the chickens. Money is scarce, and bacon's high."

"In our case you need have no apprehensions," said Jack, who felt the pangs of a keen appetite.

"Oh, I'm always bound to take in old acquaintances. I meant strangers. And many times, strangers, when they come to pay the bill, find they've lost their money."

"But we haven't lost ours, Mr. Bullock," said Nap, jingling some gold coins in his hand.

"I know that. But if you had, as I said before, any thing in my house would be at your sarvice. But I've had great losses lately."

"What losses?"

"They steal my chickens and turkeys out of the apple-trees. The old ooman conceits that it's our own niggers does it, and to-night I'm going to make 'em wrap up in their buffalo-robes and watch in the orchard. If another turkey or chicken is missing, they are to be cowhided, by their own consent; and if they catch anybody there, they are to cowhide him. That's the bargain. They think the rogues are white folks."

"But suppose an owl or an opossum should catch a fowl to-night?"

"Oh, they must keep their eyes skinned. But as a nigger can't keep awake, I think they'll catch the hide in the morning. Though I wouldn't advise any of you to go into the orchard, if you have any occasion to travel to night, without letting me know it, and having me along with you."

Nap and Jack promised not to go in that direction ı they should walk out.

They had an excellent supper, and some fine cider, and afterward retired well satisfied to bed—Nap sitting up until Jack fell asleep.

About midnight the young men were awakened by the distressful cries of some one in the orchard. The orchard was near the house, and the tree under which the scene of violence occurred was near the window of the room occupied by the travellers.

"Stop! stop, I say!" cried one, under the lash, the blows being distinctly heard by our young merchants.

"Gin it to him, Pompey! Giv him Jesse!" said one of the negroes. This was heartily responded to by the shrill whistle of the cowhide as it descended upon the back of their captive.

"Now you gin him some, Sambo!" said the other.

"Oh, you infarnal rascals! Don't you know me? Stop, I say!" This was answered by blows more violent than ever. "Murder!" cried the sufferer. "You'll kill me. Don't you know *me?* I'm"——

"Stop his mouth, Pompey," cried Sambo, "or he'll tell a lie to git off."

Pompey lashed him again.

"Oh! You'll skin me alive! Stop, I say! I'm your master! I'm John Bullock, your owner!"

"Now dat's a lie!" said Sambo. "Massa John told us to cowhide anybody we catched out here."

"I'm your master, I say!"

"Dat's a lie, I say," continued Sambo. "Massa John Bullock's a gen'leman. He's not prowling 'bout dis time o' night arter his own chickens; and he gin us liberty to cowhide any white man we catched in dis orchard. Lay on some more, Pompey. Hah! hah! He tell us he's Massa Bullock! when Massa John's been in bed and 'sleep dese four hours."

"Stop, I say!" cried the desperate victim. "If you hit me again, I'll sell you both!"

"Sell us? Lor' a'mighty! Dat is like Massa John's

voice!" cried Sambo. "Bless us! Is you Massa John, sure nuff?"

"Yes I am, you infarnal scoundrels! I came out here to see if you were watching well, and you've cowhided me half to death."

"Lor' a'mighty, Massa John, why didn't you tell us you was comin'? Den we'd a-knowed it was you. We beg your pardon, Massa! You tole us to whip any white man we cotched in de orchard."

"I did, boys; that's a fact. And if you didn't know me, I won't punish you for what you've done. But you ought to have known me."

"De moon ain't shining, Massa John. It's so dark we can't know nobody. We won't tell de neighbours what's happened, Massa John. Missus can cure you; she's got some salve made of elderberries, and we knows it's good."

When Bullock re-entered the house, Nap and Jack could hear the low laughter of the negroes, and easily understood from their remarks that they knew well enough who it was they were cowhiding. But the affair was kept secret. Bullock was afraid to sell the negroes, knowing that if he did so they would make known the cause of it, and then his neighbours would laugh at him all his life. And the negroes were afraid to divulge the secret while they belonged to him, aware that if they did so, he would certainly sell them to be revenged. But Nap and Jack, auditors and witnesses of the transaction, were not compelled to suppress it. And from them the anecdote has been derived.

CHAPTER XX.

Nap meets with Miss D——, and is fascinated—Discussion on fame—Parson H—— shocked—Mr. F—— argues with the parson on wine—A brief dispute between two reverend gentlemen—Nap converses with Miss D——:. Rich shopkeepers and authors—Nap has a notion of becoming an actor.

In due time our young gentlemen arrived at the Ohio river, and embarked on the steamboat Editor, for Pittsburgh.

When they sat down to dinner, Nap's eyes rested upon a lady opposite at the table, of surpassing personal charms, and of such intellectual endowments that, although he had so recently parted with Molly, they did not fail to make a very great impression on his susceptible heart. So sudden and complete was his fascination, that the dinner remained almost untasted, notwithstanding he had owned to a voracious appetite but a few minutes before. The lady was Miss D——, whom Nap had once seen decked in the habiliments of. the princely house of Capulet, and whose personation of the character of the lovely Juliet had ever after dwelt in his memory as the vision of a reality, rather than a mere counterfeit presentment. He now feasted his eyes, while neglecting his plate. He luxuriated upon her musical words, and every tone thrilled through his heart. Her very ideas were contagious; and he would have defended with his life—if he had been at all capable of voluntarily putting it in peril—any position she assumed, or argument she advanced. She was conversing with Mr. F——, an actor of unrivalled popularity. The subject was one which has engaged the attention of critics, moralists, and political economists for centuries, and has never yet been solved to the satisfaction of those interested in it, viz. the reason why one is not immediately appreciated in one's own country, and why so many obstacles are to be encountered by the author, the actor, the orator, the editor, the artist, &c.

The lady seemed disposed to attribute the reluctance of one's countrymen to acknowledge the claims of native genius, to an original trait of our nature, to which reference had been made by the Saviour himself, when he said that a prophet was not without honour except in his own country.

This was followed by a startling crash, occasioned by a gentleman at Nap's elbow, who had petulantly dashed down his knife and fork into his plate, and then leaning back in his chair, seemed to be half convulsed with rage.

"My friends!" cried he, "are you not aware of the blasphemy of using the name of our Saviour in such a discussion as this? Do not be guilty of such profanity, I beseech you, as to use his sacred name, and the authority of his words, in a conversation on the merits of actors, artists, &c."

This of course produced a sensation, and Nap, like the rest, scanned the face of the speaker, who happened to be no other than Parson ——, from Missouri, and who had been so unjustly suspected of snoring by the steward on the Martha Jewett.

"Sir," said Mr. F., with one of his majestic motions of the hand, "Christ denounced all the evils of the earth, and enumerated the perpetrators of them. The hypocrite, the adulterer, the murderer, the thief, and even the lawyer; but not the actor."

"I did not know there were any theatres in his time," said the parson.

"But there were very many; there were not less than a dozen in Asia Minor, when the Saviour himself rebuked the usurers and the hypocritical Pharisees. There was one in Jerusalem, where he taught daily in the temple. They were scattered over Greece and in Rome, hundreds of years before the Christian era, and not once do we find them denounced by the Divine teacher."

Parson —— spasmodically drew a Testament from his pocket, with a determination to find some passage which might admit of an interpretation condemnatory of theatrical representations.

Mr. F. then proceeded to dilate upon the nature of the obstacles usually to be encountered by the young aspirant for histrionic or literary fame. He attributed them to foreign influence and European enmity to our republican institutions. British managers had possession of most of our theatres, and British theatrical critics pronounced judgment upon the merits of our actors. Mr. F. was a thorough Democrat, and desired to see his country purged of such pernicious influences.

Miss D. then spoke, and Nap gazed and listened as if under the influence of some potent enchantment. She complimented Mr. F. upon having surmounted all the obstacles he had described, and felicitated herself upon having overcome many of them, and on being inspired with an indomitable resolution bravely to encounter any others that might be interposed. She then took up the cudgels in behalf of native authors and artists. With ample preparation, and unwearying perseverance, they might succeed here as well as in other countries. The weak in all nations complained of unjust treatment, while the strong everywhere succeeded, if endowed with genius, energy, and patience. But displays of greatness could not be readily appreciated at home, among one's friends and kindred, until fully contrasted with specimens from abroad. The child that attains a gigantic stature, does it so imperceptibly that his parents and brothers are not amazed at his proportions, until his surpassing height is compared with the altitude of others of similar pretensions.

Nap swelled with importance. He was not exceedingly tall, but he was very fat, and might yet some day shoot up a head and shoulders above his contemporaries. Handy observed the animation of his companion with interest. He saw that his impressible heart was yielding to a new image, and he was rather pleased when the reverend Mr. —— arose from the table with a Testament in his hand, and beckoned them both away.

Nap, however, if he had not spoken much with his tongue, had been so eloquent with his eyes, as to attract the attention of the party opposite. And, when in the act of rising, he was thrown into an ecstatic convulsion by the polite and condescending notice of Miss D. Before withdrawing from the table, she indicated by a nod her pleasure that he should fill his glass from the Hock bottle standing between them, and drink with the rest to the success of genius throughout the world. He did so; and if his tongue was mute, his eyes said plainly that he conceived his fair monitress to be the most adorable of that fortunate class then living in the universe.

Soon after he followed Jack and the preacher to the forward part of the cabin, where divers parties had preceded them, engaged in various animated discussions.

"My young friends," said the parson, seriously, "are you aware that the persons sitting at the table are *actors*?"

"One is an actor," said Jack.

"And the other an actress," said Nap, "and a glorious one."

"A what? Is it possible that respectable people can be found to sanction their profession?"

"Why not? Christ did not condemn it."

"But he condemned all manner of lasciviousness. Did I not see you drinking wine with the actress?"

"I don't know whether you saw me or not," said Nap; "but I certainly drank with her."

"And did not Christ drink wine at the wedding?" asked Jack, who knew that Parson —— was a most zealous advocate of total abstinence.

"It is not said that he drank it."

"But it is said he made it. He converted the water into wine."

"It was a miracle, my young friends, to show his power and his divinity, and could not have been intended to sanction the drinking of it."

"I think differently," said Mr. F., who followed the company to the social hall, and felt justified in participating in the conversation, inasmuch as the reverend gentleman had himself set the example of interposing during the discussion at the table.

"Upon what grounds, sir?" demanded the parson.

"Upon the ground that if it was not his purpose the wine should be swallowed, or if he had not sanctioned the drinking of it, he would have converted wine into water, rather than water into wine."

"That's a mere sophism. No one will deny that the use of intoxicating liquors is productive of incalculable evil."

"No," said Mr. F., "that is not to be denied; or rather, the abuse of them."

"Then if the vending of them be prohibited by law, they will cease to be made, and people will cease to abuse them, and not be abused by them."

"I doubt it. They will be made clandestinely, and surreptitiously used. Public sentiment will be stronger than law." This was said by young Handy, and Parson ———— was most indignant upon hearing him so express himself, for Jack had attended some of his lectures in Missouri, and had even contributed money in aid of the good cause.

"Public sentiment will make the law, sir! Hence your argument is absurd. You, yourself, sir, seemed to sanction the movement when at home!" The parson, naturally nervous, was now really quivering with excitement.

"I sanction such lectures as tend to demonstrate the immorality and misery flowing from a too free indulgence of the habit of drinking spirituous liquors. But the good effect I look for is the conviction of the minds of those addicted, or likely to become excessively addicted to the practice. With them, alone, is the responsibility, and not with the manufacturer or the vender of the article."

"Monstrous!" cried the parson.

"To prohibit the manufacture, or the vending of liquors, I conceive to be unconstitutional. It would abridge the rights of the citizen. And in regard to the public sentiment which shall cause such a law to be enacted, I believe it will subside like other temporary excitements. I regard the present enthusiasm on the subject but as an intemperate zeal, a species of intoxication, quite as likely to run into excesses, if continued much longer, and to produce as extravagant evils, as the one it professes to war against. Fanatics would make the laws, and religion, whose mission it is to conduct us to heaven, would soon be engrossed with the politics of the world, and employed in the business of overturning governments, and perhaps in the slaughter of offenders against temporal enactments, as well as against the laws of God."

"Monstrous!" repeated the parson, livid with ill-suppressed rage.

"Answer me this," said Mr. F. "When one of the followers of our Saviour drew his sword and cut off the ear of the servant of the high-priest, was the act sanctioned by him in whose behalf it was done?"

"No, sir, no! Jesus healed the wound, and rebuked the one who dealt the blow. But what has that to do with the proposed 'Prohibitory Law?'"

"Something, perhaps," said Mr. F., smiling. "The act was not approved, then. It was wrong. The sword had perpetrated a wrong. But the man only was reproved. It was not decreed that swords should not be made or vended. Millions have fallen by the sword in battle, and thousands have committed suicide with it, to the distress and injury of their families. Why not prohibit their use or even their abuse, by preventing the vending of them in time of peace. Yonder are men losing money at cards; why not prohibit the vending of cards? Thousands of evils seen around us every day, might just as well be assailed in the same manner. But then another Moses would be needed, invested with the awful power and authority of the original, and all human governments would have to be abolished."

"You are in error! You are in error!" said the parson.

"I think not," said Jack. "Since the days of miracles and prophets are over, and enlightened man is a free agent, with him alone rests the responsibility of doing wrong. Convince us it is wrong to drink ardent spirits, or to do any other evil thing, and persuade us to do right. That all will commend. But do not attempt coercion, or legal restraint, in matters with which we are only individually concerned, or which pertain to a future state of existence."

"Yes," said Nap, whose eyes had hitherto been directed toward Miss D., who was sitting at the other extremity of the saloon, "Render unto God the things which be God's, and unto Cæsar the things which be Cæsar's."

Mr. —— sprang up from his chair abruptly, and joined a white-neckerchiefed gentleman who sat silently a few paces apart, whom he supposed to be a clergyman, and one in all probability who would be likely to agree with him on the great subject of temperance.

But in a few minutes, the parson's voice was again heard in loud contention.

"Are you not a minister of God?" he asked.

"Yes; I am a bishop."

"And you will not forbid the use of wine?"

"I dare not."

"Then you cannot be worthy of the office."

"That is a matter of opinion. I care not what your opinion may be."

"But you condemn crime and immorality, don't you?"

"Oh yes. I am on my way to the East now, to prosecute one whom I have charged with such offences."

"And I am going to summon a synod to try one of our ministers for using in his church the tunes of negro minstrels adapted to hymns."

Literally true, every word. Both were armed for the contest; and they separated mutually resolved to punish and degrade their reverend opponents.

Meantime, Nap, who ceased to feel any interest in such bellicose subjects, embraced the first opportunity of drawing as near as possible to Miss D. And while his eyes rested upon her, at a respectful distance, he neglected no means in his power to attract her attention. His glossy boots were thrust out, and his jewelled fingers protruded, unmindful himself of the enormous size and uncouth shape of his feet, and the rough exterior and large dimensions of his monstrous hands. But he had quite an ingenuous and not unhandsome face, with an exuberant head of dark hair. And as it had by some means become rumoured—which Jack attributed to the humurous propensity of Mr. J. H., a Santa Fe merchant—that Nap was very rich, being the proprietor of a whole town in the West, the young man received many flattering attentions from the officers of the boat, and from many of the passengers.

In process of time, Nap ventured to address a few timid words to Miss D., and he was very agreeably surprised to find that she did not decline the conversation. Then he was desperately involved. Although she spoke only on the topics in agitation in her immediate circle, and expressed no sentiments different from what Molly herself might have done, yet Nap thought her voice and manner so superior to those of any lady he had hitherto had the good fortune to meet with, that in the exhilaration of the moment, he felt an almost irresistible inclination to lay his heart at her feet, if such a thing were at all practicable.

Nap had read Shakspeare in the solitudes of the Western wilderness; and having a retentive memory, he excited the interest of the gifted lady by repeating the passages which had affected him the most. Thus the student of nature found a subject not unworthy of her attention. **Success in her profession** depended in some measure upon the impressions she produced on the minds of just such specimens of humanity as the one before her. Hence she **was curious to** ascertain which actions and expressions of the poet's characters produced the deepest and most lasting emotions in the breasts of the class represented by our susceptible hero. She was, however, diverted to find him something of an enigma, and an admirer of the rather unstable gentleman of Verona, Sir Proteus.

But the music of her voice and the freedom of her manner, an eccentricity often the accompaniment of genius, completely enchanted poor Nap. He undoubtedly had been her captive, if she had chosen to put forth her hand and take him. During the first ebullition of his unbounded admiration, other attachments were completely forgotten. But we must do him the justice to say that he was not designedly oblivious of pre-existing engagements, nor was he capable of premeditatedly violating their obligations. He was only the slave of impulse, and liable to be swept **away by** the **last** violent inclination **that** impelled him. And although **he** was quite **prepared** at any moment to acknowledge the right, unfortunately he was too often incapable of resisting the wrong.

In the present instance, however, he was in no danger of committing an abandonment of either his first or second love; for Miss D. never dreamed that his palpable admiration of her had been elicited by the charms of her person. She merely supposed he was one of the "troops of friends" **who delighted** to do her honour as a public character, and **to** swell **the** plaudits that greeted her ears on every side in her professional career.

But Jack, **who** watched him narrowly, knew better. He saw that a revolution in Nap's purposes was being formed;

and that if the excitement under which he laboured should be prolonged, the mercantile days of his friend were numbered. Already he manifested a repugnance to converse on matters of business; and had several times hinted that it was a mere sacrifice of life to pass one's days in the obscurity of the Western wilds.

"What could you do in the East, Nap?" asked Jack, one night, when his companion was sighing in his berth at the prospect of parting with the being he was now worshipping, and lamenting the cruel fate which had cast his lot on the slimy banks of the distant Missouri.

"I might do as well as others. Others have gone from the West into the great cities and succeeded; why might not I do the same? Why should I not have my name repeated in the newspapers as well as others? Living in obscurity, who knows there is such a being as N. B. Wax in existence, except his limited circle of friends?"

"Oh, are you getting ambitious, Nap? Do you suppose one is more happy having his name before the public, a mark for praise or censure, as he may or may not be successful, or as the caprices of his judges may lead them to decide, than he who runs a prosperous career in private life, with no one to condemn, and ever contented with the approbation of his own conscience?"

"I suppose the first to be the happiest, even if the critics assail him. The last may live in peace; but when he dies he will leave no trace behind. His name will be forgotten by the children of his neighbours, and his own grandchildren will not mention it. Miss D. was telling me of a poor author, whose name is in the catalogues of all the public libraries, and whose volumes are distributed by tens of thousands over the land. His name, as a moral teacher, will be uttered by admiring millions for many generations to come, perhaps for centuries. But he is poor. He was compelled to sell his copyrights, and now enjoys but a small share of the profits derived from his published works; and yet she says he is happy. He dwells in the neighbourhood of a dyer, a chemist, and a dealer in linseys, who have made fortunes and built fine houses. She says they avert their eyes when they meet him. He does not come up to their standard of respectability. He is a tenant; they live in their own houses. He rides in an omnibus; they in their own carriages. They visit one another, and others like themselves with large incomes; but have no intercourse with him. Oh, you should have seen her lowering brow, her flashing eye, and quivering lip, as she denounced them. She said the fame they coveted was like that of the butterfly; while that which would reward the author she assimilated to the permanent brilliance of a star. People would gaze upon it for ever. When the ignoble dust of the proud cockney shopkeepers shall be mingled with its kindred earth, said she, their grandchildren will regret not being enabled to say that those who acquired fortunes for them had likewise merited the esteem and enjoyed the friendship of that same poor neglected author."

"Would you be an author, Nap?"

"No; not exactly. I cannot write. It seems to me I never can learn to punctuate. My letters are single paragraphs, I am told, and different subjects are sure to be run into one sentence. I make no capital letters, no periods, nothing but nonsense. That is exactly what the editors of the Post and Courier said when I offered them contributions. It was in the notice to correspondents. But I might improve."

"If you are not a genius, what can you do to become famous?"

"I might be an actor."

"The deuce!"

"I have been thinking of it seriously."

"What character would you like to personate?"

"I would like to be Romeo to Miss D.'s Juliet. But that I know is impossible; for I heard her say that all Romeos should be tall and slim."

"And you are fat. How would Falstaff do?"

"Not at all. I despise the character. I have **no low** humour in me. Mine is a dream of romance."

"**Yes**; and the sooner you awake to the reality of the absurdity, the better for you."

"I have spoken to Mr. F. on the subject. But he **is** not to let Miss D. know that I have any such purpose."

"What did he say? Did he advise you to become **a** player?"

"**No.** He introduced **me to Mr. S.**, who is studying **a** part in which to make his debut. He says Mr. S. has some familiarity with the stage, some education, and a passion for theatrical representations. If he succeeds, then, in time, I may follow, if my desire for that sort of distinction continues unabated. I am to witness Mr. S.'**s** first appearance on any stage, the night after we get to the **city.**"

Jack fell asleep. Nap did not **now** disturb him with his **snore. The poor fellow only turned over** and over and sighed. Sometimes he groaned, but was not heard by any **one** to snore. He must have snored, however, **if** he slept at all. Probably he had a few snatches of slumber when every one else was steeped in repose during the still hours of the night. But if he did, he must have been personating the lover in his dreams, for his perturbed brain was racked by no other theme.

In short, he was a changed being under the influence of the potent spell which had been cast upon him. He even grew slightly pale, and was becoming taciturn on all subjects **but one.** He seemed to be continually plunged in a **reverie, no doubt in fancy** enjoying the acclamations of a **worshipping multitude.** They sat in **a** fine coach, Miss D. and himself—in **his** imagination—the **cynosure** of **all eyes,** a **dual** constellation in a firmanent of **his own** creation.

Handy was much concerned for **his friend.** He **feared** he would go mad. **His** mind was already much deranged. So he exerted **himself to counteract** the effects of his idiosyncrasy. And when they landed at Pittsburg, and Nap had taken a last longing look at the retreating form of his divinity, Jack made a desperate effort to lead his friend's thoughts into a business channel. They had some purchases to make at this place, such as iron, nails, cast-iron pots, ovens, dog irons, spun yarn, &c.

It was laughable to see the aversion expressed in Nap's ingenuous face, when Jack read over the memorandum of articles usually bought in Pittsburg. But as he had come to buy, he could not refuse to purchase. Jack, however, transacted most of his business for him, having merely a passive concurrence on Nap's part, and with no manifestation of interest in the operation. Nap even calculated the amount of his funds carelessly, when paying for the goods, and did not examine his bills to see if they had been properly receipted. The merchandise was shipped, however, without delay for St. Louis, with instructions to the consignee to forward it by the first boat going up the Missouri river.

The impatience of Nap to leave Pittsburg was not unnatural. To say nothing of his anxiety to behold those "angelic features" once more, the dark cloud which hung suspended over the city, began to produce a very sombre effect on his feelings, and the coal-dust spoiled his shirts, of which he had not now a superabundance in a fitting condition to wear. Besides, he was beginning to cough violently, and hinted to his friend that he feared he was going into a decline. Jack merely replied that then he would be enabled to "look" the part of Romeo better. He had no fear of the consumption.

CHAPTER XXI.

The young men arrive in Philadelphia—Nap admires a chambermaid—They visit the theatre, and Nap is cured—Business maxims—Nap and Jack make some purchases.

IN due time our young men arrived in Philadelphia. It was late in the **afternoon** when they descended from the coach in front of a fashionable hotel, where they intended to sojourn during their stay in that city. They were conducted to their room by a white servant, while three **or** four mulattoes brought up the rear, bearing their trunk, (they still had but one between them,) their small carpet-bags, and their overcoats. Each one demanded and obtained a shilling.

Nap shaved himself, leaving bushy mustaches; then **scrubbed and** scoured **his** hands, neck, and face, and put on **his** last clean **shirt**. During this operation the chambermaid came in, and asked if he wanted any washing done. Of course he did. He would have had any thing done to accommodate her. She was handsome and neatly dressed, and Jack hoped a new impression was about to be made on his susceptible and impulsive friend. Doubtless Nap would have fallen in love with her, if he had not been on the eve of again beholding the enchanting Miss D., who had so recently monopolized all his thoughts. As it was, he could not avoid being amiable and condescending. But **when he uttered** the first familiar expression, the girl vanished. She was afraid of **the** strong Western men, and **was an** honest poor girl, soliciting a job for her indigen**t** mother.

The young men had not been long engaged in the agreeable process of renovating their persons, before the cards of their city acquaintances, who had visited Missouri, began **to come** in. **Even** the names of others, whom they did not recollect, were likewise sent up, accompanied by lithographed circulars and printed catalogues of the infinite variety of articles they kept for sale.

This was fortunate. Handy magnified the importance of such polite attentions, and Nap pricked up his ears while his friend dwelt upon the favourable auspices attending their first visit to the city. Doubtless their names were already known to the "merchant princes," the men of wealth, of character, and of influence; and all were quite ready to establish business relations with them, and probably some of them might introduce them into the very best society. This was exceedingly agreeable to Nap. He was much gratified at the prospect, and at the prompt manner in which the news of their arrival had spread over the city. He would indeed have been in ecstasies, had he not been previously fascinated with ideas of a different nature. As it was, the distinctions which Jack portrayed were appreciated; and Nap honestly confessed his regret that nature had not gifted him with a mind contented to achieve triumphs in the mercantile line.

After supper, the young men visited the theatre. They took seats in the orchestra-box, that they might have a good opportunity to view the actors more distinctly than they could from a more distant part of the house.

The house was crowded in every part. Large posters, announcing the debut of Mr. S., who had undertaken to perform an important part in a familiar tragedy, in conjunction with Miss D., whose appearance on any stage never failed to attract large audiences, had filled the frequenters of the house with eager curiosity, and they mustered in great numbers on the present occasion.

When the curtain arose, Miss D., as usual, was received with rapturous applause, Nap being more boisterous in his prolonged plaudits than any one else. When the confusion abated, and the lady approached the front of the stage, our hero did not doubt that he would receive from her a brief particular recognition. But he was mistaken. She did not deign to cast a glance upon him, and he winced under the disappointment. However, he cheered with the rest at the end of her periods, and awaited the appearance of Mr. S., upon whose success or failure depended his own fate in the profession. Mr. S. was a stage-struck, romantic youth, who had absconded from his family. His father was a wealthy planter, and one of the F"s.

Nevertheless, when Mr. S. appeared, and the applause which kindly greeted him had subsided, he found himself bereft of two indispensable qualifications of an actor, viz. a voice, and a knowledge of his part. Following his father's hounds, his voice could be heard a mile distant; and in his own chamber, with the key turned on the inside, he could stand up before a mirror and repeat every word of his part. He had done it twenty times. But now he stood speechless and petrified. After a long pause, he was again encouraged to proceed by a smart clapping of hands. Then followed a few hisses. The prompter repeated the word for the tenth time, and at length S. caught at it and ran off a sentence or two very rapidly, but in so feeble a voice that no one could hear what he was saying. Then the one to whom these words were addressed replied in louder tones than usual, and thus frightened the debutant the more by the contrast. And so he mumbled his sentences less distinctly than ever, and his attempts at gesture were quite as ridiculous as any thing else.

At the end of the scene, poor S. was saluted with a a wreath of cabbage-leaves, and a thundergust of hootings and hisses. Once more he ventured to appear; but again his heart failed him. At the end of the act, the boys called for him. They demanded that he should appear before the curtain to gratify their pleasure. Then it was that S. evinced some degree of independence. He told the manager he would —— first! The manager said it was necessary, else they would not be appeased. S. said he didn't care whether they were appeased or not. Such a reply the manager had never before heard from an actor. He deemed himself absolute—an autocrat of all the mimic Russias, and Denmarks, and Englands—and he would not put up with it.

"I will not have such a reply, sir!" said he, stamping his managerial foot.

"Very well; throw it away then. I will not take it back."

"You shall, sir!"

"Take care! Don't menace me! I may be thrown off my guard by your gas-light and painted scenery; but, sir, if you approach another step nearer, you will find me no timid actor in a real tragedy." S. drew the sword he wore, and really seemed to be prepared for the conflict. The manager, personating one of the characters of the play, likewise had a sword. But he did not draw it. Suddenly he discovered danger in the eye of the mortified and desperate young debutant from the South, and turned away from him. S. immediately donned his own clothes and left the theatre, while the manager had to make his explanations to the audience, and have another person to play the part, who certainly failed to produce so great a sensation in the subsequent acts as S. had done in the first one.

Mr. F., who was incognito in the pit, whispered to Nap that this was the twentieth debut he had witnessed of a somewhat similar termination, and that his would be the twenty-first, if he persisted in making the attempt.

Nap heard him, but was incapable of reply. He was convinced now that he could never be a successful player, and he despaired of winning a smile from Miss D., as a slight reward for his enthusiastic applause. By degrees his plaudits grew less loud and frequent. And when the green curtain fell, he arose to depart.

"Jack," said he, "I'm awake now, and sober. Why didn't you whisper my *right name*, for the time being, in my ear?

"What name was that?"

"Christopher Sly. I have been a fool. But I am glad I have not lost my money. Yonder are the boys we saw in Missouri. We have been sitting with our backs toward them, and they couldn't know us. Let us join them, and learn the price of linseys. Nap's a merchant again."

Handy felt an inclination to applaud this determination publicly, but suppressed it. They then directed their steps toward their Eastern friends, Nap exacting a promise from Jack never to divulge the tale of his "love and madness."

The greetings that followed were hearty and sincere. Uncle Billy, Joe T., John P., Sam C., M. J., &c. &c. &c., were all in the lobby, between the acts, and were surrounded by their Western constituents. But as our young merchants were in the city for the first time, they were entitled to, and did receive, some extra attentions. And it was well for the novices that they were taken in charge by gentlemen of standing and respectability, either partners in or representatives of houses in the highest repute —houses which might always be safely relied on, and which could boast their customers of more than thirty years standing.

But if the old and respectable houses might be relied on to deal in a proper manner with all their customers, never exacting a larger profit than was just and reasonable under the circumstances, the young gentlemen from the country, on their first visit to the city, could not themselves be always depended upon to buy of them as freely as they ought. They were intercepted in many ways, and prevented from doing what they designed. Sociable themselves, strangers had no difficulty in making their acquaintance; polite, they could not avoid appreciating a kindness; credulous, they believed many of the monstrous tales whispered in their ears about superior goods, and excessively low prices; and being urged to "make a beginning," they often purchased largely where they should not have bought at all—and bought nothing, where they should have purchased every thing. Such had been the case with very many novices, who repented it as they grew older and obtained experience.

It was not so with Wax and young Handy, in Philadelphia. The brother of the latter had written his friends to have them in their special keeping until their memorandum-books were checked off; and as the young men naturally confided in those they had known the longest, it was not difficult to comply with Joseph's wishes.

The first day was spent by our young gentlemen in "looking around," and calling upon their acquaintances. Their drafts were deposited at Messrs. R. & Co.'s, which had been the head-quarters of the country merchants in the section of the country they came from, almost "from time immemorial." And the chief of the establishment, as was his usual custom with very young merchants, took an early opportunity to give Nap and Jack some good advice. He told them very frankly that they would not be able to know whether goods were really cheap or dear by looking at them. It would take them a month to become familiar with the market, and as much longer to become calm and self-possessed amid the strange sights and confused noises of the city. A proper selection of houses to buy in was more important than a mere selection of styles. Every house knew the kind of goods they wanted, and if they confined their operations to the right sort of houses, they would not be permitted to go wrong. Every jobber, desirous of making customers and retaining them, wished those who purchased his goods to prosper with them. They were deeply interested in the success of their customers. For if the country merchant failed in business, of course the city merchant would be the sufferer. If he succeeded, the city merchant shared his prosperity. They were identified in interests. Hence the young gentlemen could not go amiss if they confided in houses of established reputation; and it would be better for them to be entirely governed by the advice of the experienced members of such houses, as to qualities and prices, than to **rely** upon their own judgment. Of course, it would be necessary for the purchasers to exercise their taste and discretion in regard to patterns, colours, textures, &c., choosing those which they might deem **to** be the **best** adapted to their localities. But their safest policy would be to put as **much** responsibility as possible on the jobbers. They would not regret it when they got home **and** opened their goods. **On the other** hand, if they took all the responsibility themselves, relying altogether upon their own judgments, the jobbers would naturally seek to make the most they could out of them, and **would be** justifiable in **doing so**. But **in such** a contest he said the jobbers would **have** an **immense advantage, and** advised them **not** to enter the lists against them. The safest way would be to **rely** upon their promises, **and** believe their statements, and they **would not be likely** to deceive them. And if they did, they would **be** accountable, and would have **to** indemnify **them**. He concluded by saying, "**There**, boys, I've delivered my speech. Think of it, and act as you **please.** Any goods you want of us, Uncle Billy will sell **you.** He knows what you want, and you know him."

Both **Nap and Jack** drew forth their memorandum-books, **and** purchased a considerable portion of their staple dry-goods immediately afterward. In the afternoon they monopolized **the attention of** their friend Joe T. They implicitly **believed whatever** he told them, and they acted wisely. He was perfectly familiar with the kind of goods adapted to the wants of their customers, and offered no other. William **S. and Mr. F. attested** their cheapness, and **the young men knew** the prices they would bring in Missouri. So **their** goods in Joe **T.**'s line were soon bought; **and the** operations of a few hours amounted to thousands of dollars.

Pretty much the same thing occurred at "Sam's" **house,** at C. C. & Co.'s, and at Jno. P.'s. In the hardware line, they never dreamed of looking farther than S. & S.'s, the legitimate successors in one of the oldest houses in the city. And it was very much the same in the hat line. They **had** scarcely ever heard of any other than the old house **in** Third street. Nor could they have been induced to look into any other house in Marshall J.'s line than his.

Thus in a week they had nearly completed their purchases, and had bought judiciously, because they dealt **with the** right sort of men. And if it had not been for the stock Jack was to lay in for Joseph, they might have been ready to set out **on** their return home about the tenth day after their arrival.

Generally, **a** moderate stock, it is supposed by experienced merchants, **may** be purchased within **a** week; and a very small assortment it is always best to order by mail, provided the country merchant is **in good** credit **and** fortunate in the selection of his houses. **Such a selection,** it can never be repeated too often, **is** of infinitely greater importance, than any advantage a "smart buyer" may suppose himself capable of achieving by running about **from** house **to house, and city** to city, **in** pursuit of cheap **goods.** All the good houses in the different cities pay **about the same prices for** their goods; **and any** of them will sell, without **much** urging, **at a moderate advance.** None of them **seek to** obtain the **large** profits which some of **their** credulous **customers** are **led to believe. A fair** per cent.,—and **it is** generally a small **one,—is all they** desire **or** strive to obtain. They do **not expect to realize large** profits, and generally they are **not disappointed. If** a house in **the city with a** capital of a **hundred** thousand dollars can sell the amount of three hundred thousand at **from six to** eight per cent. **advance, it** is considered a good business. In the West, that amount of capital invested in **ten stores,** if well managed, **might produce a** gross profit **of fifty thousand dollars.**

But the idea that one merchant in the city possesses material advantages over his neighbours in getting up his stock, or that merchandise is decidedly cheaper in one Eastern city than another, is ridiculously absurd. Prices are like flowing waters, and will reach a common level in all the markets near to each other. If the New York jobber can buy goods lower from the agents in Philadelphia than from similar agents in his own city, of course he will do so. And the Philadelphian is likewise sure to go to the commission house which sells on the best terms, whether it be in Boston, New York, Baltimore, or at home. So the country merchant, when he hears that goods are from fifteen to twenty-five per cent. lower in one city than another, will do well to reflect a little before he relies implicitly on the truth of the statement. If such were really so, the intelligent jobbers who were undersold would hasten away and buy them themselves. And so with auctions. If goods were to be had advantageously under the hammer, the jobbers would be the bidders. They may *seem* to be low sometimes; but it is the part of wisdom to know the article will answer the purpose for which it is bought. The distant buyer cannot conveniently be indemnified for imperfections discovered a month after the purchase, and when the article is a thousand miles away.

Such is the information derived from good sources, and which may be useful to the young country merchant, doing a limited amount of business. Without such information is credited and acted upon at the beginning of his career, the inexperienced countryman may blunder through two or three seasons before he is undeceived in regard to the amount of his talents and the extent of his sagacity. After paying dearly for the whistle, and when he is bound to own that he did not know more than those who had preceded him—in short, when he acknowledges his ignorance—then he is beginning to learn something of the mysteries of the profession, and may with caution and economy, make a fortune. And unless he is willing to learn—instead of assuming to know more than anybody else in matters of which he is necessarily ignorant—it would be much better for him to remain at home and order his goods by letter. If he orders from houses of good standing, he will get his stock quite as cheaply as if he bought it in person; but even if he pays five per cent. more, provided he wants only a few thousand dollars' worth, still it would be best to do so, on the score of economy. His personal expenses, if he visits the East from any of the distant States, will be equivalent to the extra per cent., not to mention the value of his time when at home, and the sacrifices **always** incurred **in** consequence **of his** absence.

CHAPTER XXII.

Nap makes some wonderful discoveries in the city—The mercantile agency also makes a discovery—A Mr. Pike is attracted from New York—Nap goes with him and operates on **a** large scale—Returns **to** Philadelphia, **and** has his eyes opened.

NAP had ceased to purchase. His memorandum-book was "ticked off." His goods, about five thousand dollars' worth in all, were shipped, and scudding by railroad and steamboat on their way to Venice. He only awaited the motions of Jack, now buying for Joseph, who had stipulated to defray his expenses during his absence, and to keep Benjamin at Troy until his return.

Although Nap spent with Jack much of the time in the various establishments where he was making his purchases, and where both of them had become familiar with the principals and the clerks, yet he had ample leisure to run about the city and see the lions and elephants. His first annoyance was swollen feet and aching **corns. Larger** boots than the ones he wore could not be obtained; and he was not willing to cut holes in them, as some one suggested. Every morning they shone like ebony mirrors, and were in such admirable contrast to the old foxy pair he had been in the habit of wearing at home, that he was willing to bear the infliction rather than be deprived of the pleasure. Unfortunately, no one but himself was aware of the contrast, and he failed to see that every one around him wore polished boots, and much better shaped ones than his own.

We doubt if it would be better always to see ourselves as others see us. When Nap enjoyed the felicity of exposing his polished boots on the railing of the balcony at his hotel; displayed the gold and jewelled rings on his enormous fingers, and stroked his dark bushy mustaches with an almost ineffable appreciation of his beauty and imposing appearance—what would have been his feelings if he had looked upon himself with the eyes of a majority of those whose attention he attracted? Some mentally called him a fool; others an ass, country booby, and village snob. His large feet proved he had been a foot-passenger in the journey of life; his monstrous hands indicated that he had been habituated to vile manual labour; his heavy chain proved his vulgarity, because such had been out of fashion a whole year; his clothes came from a slop-shop; he wore his shirt-collar down, when it should be up; he held his quizzing-glass in the wrong hand; he leaned back in his chair, always a sign of ill-breeding; he wore a black-satin vest, in fashion five years before; he cleaned his finger-nails and picked his teeth in public; he *chewed tobacco!* Such were the thoughts of the beaux and belles, the fops and hotel-waiters, who beheld our hero. And would it have been better for him to have beheld himself with their eyes? Why, the poor fellow might have committed suicide!

Nap, however, had explored the principal streets and looked into some of the alleys. Every morning, when he called at the Messrs. R. & Co.'s counting-room for letters, he made it a practice to study the map of the city. One morning he bent over the chart so long, and seemed to be so deeply abstracted, that Mr. R. placed his hand on his shoulder, and in a half-jocular, half-familiar manner, said—

"Well, young man, haven't you mastered your lesson yet? Let me assist you. What is it you wish to find?"

"I want to solve some mysteries, which have been puzzling my brain for two days."

"Mysteries? There are no mysteries here."

"No mysteries!" said P. M——r, from Tennessee—the office being full of merchants from Missouri, Kentucky, and Tennessee. "I venture to say the young man will deny that. You must not probe his secrets. He may be endeavouring to trace the route of some of his nocturnal wanderings."

"No," said Nap, innocently, "I have not yet wandered much alone after night. I have been warned against it. The only time I cruised at all in an obscure street was on Sunday night, and then"——

"Ahem! Never mind—never mind," said the other.

"You were in my company," continued Nap, amid much laughter. Nap felt exalted. He looked triumphant, and an Irish beggar-woman coming in, he gave her a quarter of a dollar, and she curtseyed to him, for she had just been dismissed at the next door with a copper.

"Then," said Mr. M., who had laughed heartily with the rest, "you are studying the map, perhaps, for the purpose of making the next cruise by yourself."

Nap had no rejoinder for this retort. He simply denied it, and declared very seriously that it was another matter altogether he wished to elucidate, and until he succeeded in doing so, he could not be sure of the sanity of his mind. This announcement attracted the attention of all who were present. And Nap, finding himself thus noticed, proceeded to declare that he sometimes believed the **maker** of the chart must be a madman, and that many other characters in the East partook of the same lunacy, or else his own head was turned.

His audience, whose curiosity was now much excited, demanded the reason why he supposed so.

"The other night," said he, "I stepped into a room and saw a man walking with his feet up against the ceiling and his head downward. *His* head was turned. So much for *him*. The next day, I called at the telegraph-office precisely at **ten** o'clock, A. M., and wrote a despatch for St. Louis. After paying for it, I asked the operator when he thought Mr. Morrison would receive it. He said about a quarter before ten. 'In the evening?' I remarked. 'No, sir,' said he; 'in the morning.' 'To-morrow morning, you mean,' said I. 'No, sir!' said he; 'this morning.' And gentlemen"——

Here Nap was interrupted by explosions of laughter.

"You may laugh, gentlemen," he continued, quite red in **the face,** but **hang me if** I ain't telling the truth. And when the operator repeated the assertion, a very respectable old gentleman, who stood by, said it was **true.** Then the president of the company, a big, fat man, and a newspaper publisher, I am told, came forward and offered to explain the matter. I knew it was impossible. I said I would not hear a madman explain such an absurdity. They **might** as well attempt to make me believe the sun don't set **in** the **evening** as such nonsense as that."

"They were right," said Mr. R., after the uproarious laughter subsided. "I could explain it to you myself. And I could also convince you that the sun don't set in the evening."

"If *you* say so, it is so," replied Nap, "and I am deranged. But **that is** not what I am studying the map for. Don't the Schuylkill river empty **into** the Delaware below the city?"

"Yes," answered **several.**

"**And when one stands** at the **foot of** Market street

and faces the East, is not the source of the Delaware river on his left hand and its mouth on the right?"

"Oh yes," said they.

"You are all quite sure of it? The left hand points up the river, and the right down?"

"Quite sure. You are perfectly right," said Mr. R.

"Then durn me if you ain't perfectly wrong, or else the world's turned topsy-turvy! For I'll take my oath that two mornings in succession, I have walked down to the river, and have seen the current running at least five miles an hour *up stream!*"

A convulsive burst of laughter followed.

"Gentlemen," said Nap, gravely, "if you will go with me now, and do not find it as I say, you may pitch me into the river. I thought I would say nothing about it for a day or two. But the papers are silent on the subject. Perhaps no one has informed the reporters of the occurrence. It may be an earthquake at sea, or a sink in the mountains"——

Here the deafening peals distracted him.

"Gentlemen!" said he, "do you doubt my word?"

"No!" said Mr. McD——ll, of Louisville, an enterprising merchant, and sometimes a wag, "I do not doubt your word, nor will any gentleman doubt it. It is a most strange and mysterious phenomenon. Gentlemen," he continued gravely, looking around significantly, "let us not mention the affair to any one, until we behold the awful spectacle ourselves. Let me see," he added, looking into an almanac; "I have an engagement at ten o'clock. At eleven, let us meet at this place and go in a body down to the river with Nap. Let us agree to this, and promise not to name the wonderful occurrence to any one until we return from the wharf."

They agreed to do as he requested, and Nap seemed gratified that his veracity was about to be so signally vindicated. Jack would have interposed, if he had not been withheld by Mr. G., of Kentucky, who whispered that if the joke were permitted to go on, the lesson might be serviceable to Nap, in demonstrating the important fact that the young gentlemen from the country, so wise in their own conceit, are not always the best qualified to make curious discoveries in a city.

At the hour appointed, some twenty merchants from the West and South might have been seen going in procession toward the river. Mr. G. and Jack Handy were in the van, while Nap was kept in the rear. They marched down through the long market-houses, and attracted much attention. Such a number of Western buyers never yet moved in a body in Market street, without producing a sensation. They were joined by the salesmen from the right and the left at every opening between the stalls. These gentlemen had too keen a vision not to distinguish our party among the boarding-house keepers, the butchers, and vegetable women. They were so well practised that a solitary merchant, in a large crowd, could be singled out at a glance, and taken on the wing at a snap-shot. All who joined the procession of course were invited to accompany it; and soon its numbers swelled to such an extent as to attract the attention of the police and the little boys. Something extraordinary must be going on down at the river, and every one felt a curiosity to see what it was.

When the head of the procession reached the wharf, a double file was formed, and Nap advanced through the centre. He walked boldly forward with an expression of triumph on his features. He stood upon the extreme platform while the water flowed at his feet. But now it flowed the other way. It was running down stream. Several times during the long pause that ensued, Nap took out his handkerchief and rubbed his eyes. He then scrutinized the faces of his friends.

"What's the matter, Nap?" asked Jack; "you are pale."

"God knows, Jack! I declare to you most solemnly

that I saw it flowing the other way, in the opposite direction, and up stream."

"I don't doubt it," said McD.

"But I do myself, now," said Nap, after another fit of abstraction. "I must have dreamed it. I saw it in my sleep."

"What is it?" asked a policeman.

"What's up?" asked a runaway London apprentice.

"What's the row?" demanded a Schuylkill ranger.

"Gentlemen," said Mac, seriously, to the crowd of outsiders, "we are from the West, and have just come down here to look at the Delaware river."

"Just to look at the river?" cried several.

"Yes. It's a very fine stream, isn't it? It's broader, and no doubt deeper than our Ohio."

"Sold!" "Humbugged!" cried many voices, and an immediate dispersion took place amid loud laughter. No one inquired further about it. Many acquainted with Mac, supposed the whole affair was merely one of his pleasantries; and of course they had no desire to acknowledge themselves the victims.

But poor Nap, as ignorant of the theory of the tides as he had been of the personal appearance of a monkey, seized Jack's arm and effected his escape. He saw from the countenances of his friends that he was doomed to be reminded of the utter groundlessness of his solemn asseveration. Jack intended to call at Messrs. L. G. & Co.'s, where they bought their books, and procure a work on the tides, for Nap's special benefit, but forgot to do so. And four or five hours afterward, Nap, who had wandered away from him, returned with a most excited countenance.

"What's the matter now, Nap?"

"Jack, I've been down there again. The current's running up stream now! Come with me; I'll show it to you!"

"Nonsense, Nap!" said Jack, grown weary of the matter. He then explained the subject, as well as the mystery of the seeming annihilation of time and space at the telegraph office.

For several days, Nap kept pretty closely to his hotel, and resisted, as well as he was able, the importunities of new city acquaintances to buy more goods. It was in vain he assured the young salesmen, and even the principals of very good houses, that he had already bought and shipped as many goods as he intended to send home when he left Missouri. The amount of the bill, they declared, was not the object; and the houses that seemed so pertinaciously to solicit his custom, desired merely to have his name on their books, with a view to future operations.

The increasing attentions which Nap received, at length affected his mind. He began to think that he must be the most popular country merchant then in the city. And he could only attribute this gratifying result to superior qualities of intellect or developments of person.

But the secret of it was, that Mr. J. H., the Santa Fe merchant who travelled with him up the Ohio river, had assured one of the attachés of the mercantile agency that Nap had not only an ample capital invested in his business, but was the owner, with the exception of a few lots, of the entire town of Venice, the capital of ———— county. And likewise, just at that time, appeared a new Gazetteer, containing the name of his town, and of the county of which it was the capital. The number of inhabitants in Venice was omitted; but the county was described as one of immense resources, and the town as being advantageously located.

The mercantile agency therefore booked Nap as being A. I. No. 1. And, in addition, Mr. ——, who had been to New York and Boston, had represented the founder of the American Venice as one who might be worth perhaps a half million of dollars at some future time.

Hence it was that Nap received so many kind attentions, while young Handy was neglected, in comparison, by the many individuals to whom he had not hitherto been introduced. Not only were cards and circulars showered upon **our hero**, by the business men of Philadelphia; but letters came by the score from New York and Boston, with pressing invitations **for** him to visit those cities before returning home.

A young gentleman, by the name of Pike, **was sent** over from New York, expressly to make his acquaintance, and to induce him if possible to accompany him back, and establish business relations with the great house he **represented**.

This was **too** flattering an instance of personal kindness for the benevolent heart of Nap to resist. And finding his efforts to induce Jack to bear him company unavailing, he determined to accept **Mr. Pike's** invitation, and spend a few days in the great metropolis.

He **was** in the finest spirits the day he was to **go to New York. He had just** received **a letter** from **Molly.** She did not, of course, say she **would accede to his request** and marry him on his return from the city; but she addressed him a few lines because she had promised to do so, and she could do no less than inform him of her continued good health, and of the good health of all those he might have an interest in at C——. Then she hoped his health **was** good; and she presumed he would enjoy his visit to the city very much. Finally, she warned him against the temptations of her **own sex**, knowing his susceptibility to new impressions, particularly at *first sight*. Then after a brief "Yours, &c.," her name followed. **Nap could see no intimation** that his suit had been granted **in such a letter as that.** There was nothing in it new or interesting; **nothing** worth the postage, which, however, had been paid **by the** fair writer. But there was a brief postscript, viz. "We shall expect to see you again on your way back to Missouri."

Now, as Nap had distinctly stated that it was his pur**pose to** return to Missouri without passing through Kentucky, **unless** Molly would consent to marry him, it was impossible for him to interpret the final line otherwise than as an acceptance of his offer. Hence his fine spirits. He had not as yet distributed his money, pro rata, as he intended, among those of whom he had purchased his goods. The only expenditures he had as yet made were for his board, and to pay the premium of insurance on his goods. And now he determined to postpone his disbursements until he returned. Uncle Billy warned him that he would need some of his funds in the rival city. Nap supposed not. At least he would only carry with him the small sum of fifty dollars. If more should be required, he was to draw on the Messrs. R. & Co. for it.

During their ride through New Jersey, Mr. Pike was assiduous in his efforts to ingratiate himself in the confidence of his victim. So fine a bait did not often tempt a *Pike*. Mr. Pike was one of those salesmen who did not receive a stipulated salary. But he got more. He had two and a half per cent. on all the bills sold to customers of his introduction. If he could sell Nap ten thousand dollars' worth, his share would be two hundred and fifty dollars, a pretty good day's work. To that end all his talents were directed. He expatiated on the policy of any one having the means, and unlimited credit, overshadowing his competitors by the gigantic stature of his establishment. He had been in Missouri often. He had seen merchants selling year after year the pitiful amount of ten thousand dollars' worth of goods without diminution or increase. Then one bolder than the rest would double his purchases, and find that his sales increased in the same proportion. Large stocks attracted people from a distance; and when a new town, in a fine county lying along the river, took a timely start in the race of improvement, it was sure to go ahead. All the little villages in the interior went down, while it went up. No doubt Venice would soon be the great central trading-point for several counties. Small traders would go there to replenish their stocks, and wagons would roll in from a distance loaded with produce, and always return laden with goods. *He* was convinced that from fifty to seventy-five thousand dollars' worth of goods might be annually sold in Nap's town.

Nap was in a fitting frame of mind to listen to such suggestions. Several merchants in Boonville were selling more than the amount stated, and Boonville once was as insignificant a place as Venice. If he could increase the amount of his sales to forty or fifty thousand dollars, he might retire from business in a few years, and be a doctor, lawyer, or member of Congress.

Mr. Pike, pursuing the subject, and knowing that Nap was beginning to be annoyed in his county by several competitors within twenty miles of him, ventured to predict that if Mr. Wax would adopt the plan of the successful merchants before alluded to, that every semblance of competition would be swept away in six months. In the first place, one half of the petty establishments bought their goods in St. Louis, and paid twenty-five per cent. advance on Philadelphia prices; and the rest purchased in Philadelphia, paying at least fifteen per cent. advance on New York prices. He did not go beyond New York; that was the fountain-head.

Nap remarked he had been assured by the merchants in Philadelphia, that there could be no material difference in prices between the cities.

"You'd believe your eyes if you saw a difference, wouldn't you?"

"Oh yes," said Nap; "though I have lately seen some things which no one else seemed willing to credit."

"Well, I suppose you know what you paid for Allen's prints?"

"Yes, eleven cents. They have risen lately. The jobbers make only a half-cent a yard, for I saw the bills that came from Messrs. F. L. & Co., Allen's agents."

"And White Rock linseys?"

"Oh yes, I paid twenty-one cents. They cost twenty and a half. I saw the bills."

"Very well. Now we sell the same prints at ten cents, and the linseys at twenty."

"Then I shall buy some of you. But it is most astonishing that the merchants should make such misstatements. I never do it at home."

"Interest—self-interest; it leads one to the very devil!"

Mr. Pike did not deny that his house paid quite as much as the others for their prints and linseys. Nor did he deem it necessary to admit that he was in the habit, as many are in all the cities, of offering leading staples at less than cost, with an intention of piling the lost per cent. on "something else;" and which intention, in such cases, is almost invariably accomplished. Mr. Pike, at the same time, was conscious of having done such things, and of a deliberate purpose to repeat them upon Nap.

They put up at the Irving House. A crowd of two and a half per cent. salesmen immediately surrounded our hero. They were introduced by Mr. Pike, who said in all candour, that he was not only desirous of selling Mr. Wax all he could himself, but was likewise anxious for him to buy of his friends. This was quite true. And Mr. P. knew that by an "arrangement," he would be entitled to a share of the commission if Nap made a bill with any of the houses where he might be instrumental in introducing him.

It must not be supposed the house represented by Mr. Pike belonged to the better class of New York establishments. The men of business there are classed precisely as they are in other cities. But the house of Messrs. Block & Tackle, whose most energetic salesman was Mr. Pike, was a very large concern, and did, if Mr. Pike's veracity was not to be doubted, a business of a million a year. And yet a certain Wall-street broker could have testified that the partners commenced business only a few years previously, with the diminutive capital of $17,500. The houses of established reputation and of ample capital did no boring. They had no representatives authorized to thrust themselves upon strangers. Their salesmen were quite as polite and kind in their attentions to their customers, as gentlemen should be; and generally they *were* gentlemen. But when a stranger desired to transact business with them, they invariably required a satisfactory reference. They did not send to the "agency" to learn the standing of those with whom they had no acquaintance.

Nap was tempted, and yielded. So great had become the influence of his friend Pike, that he seemed to be wholly subject to his will. They had visited all the lions in company, and some of the lionesses and tigresses. They ate and drank and smoked together. Nap had been persuaded to clothe himself anew from head to foot, consulting exclusively his friend Pike's superior taste. He had even bought new rings and chains and a watch of Pike's selection: on the latter there was a margin for a commission of no less than twenty dollars. All of which were paid for by drafts on Messrs. R. & Co. The nameless luxuries were settled for by Pike. Nap was not permitted to defray (directly) any portion of the expense.

Even the complexion of our hero improved under such pampering, and his hands were beginning to grow tender and become smooth. It was with an inexpressible satisfaction that he now surveyed himself in his new and fashionable habiliments, standing before the magnificent mirrors of the Irving saloons. So great a change had not often been wrought in so short a period. And as he called to mind the time when he started out on his adventures with only the paltry sum of $500 in his pocket, he could not avoid contrasting his humble circumstances in the wilds of Missouri with his present lofty condition in the metropolis of America. Now servants flew hither and thither at his nod, and even anticipated his slightest desires. His clothes were brushed every hour in the day; his boots were always like mirrors; and he was put to sleep under the process of being shaved. He had a lofty and gorgeously furnished chamber to himself, containing a fountain of sparkling water that ran whenever he touched a plated tube; a flame of brilliant gaslight when he turned a screw; ice, soap, and snowy towels. His curtains were of silk and lace; his sofa and chairs were covered with plush, and Brussels carpet was under his feet. His bed was of down, and his pillow-slips were ruffled and perfumed. Whether or not he still snored in his sleep he had no opportunity of knowing, for no one dared to disturb him, or ventured to intimate that they had been disturbed by him. Surely such accommodations as these were in marked contrast to those he had been accustomed to in his own humble abode on the dreary banks of the "mad Missouri."

Nap, unmindful of the good advice he had received in Philadelphia, was now thoroughly convinced that the tide of his affairs was at the flood, which he resolved should be "taken" without delay. And Mr. Pike sold him goods, as he supposed, some ten or fifteen per cent. under the prices he had paid for similar articles. But there were only three or four descriptions of goods in the whole purchase upon which Nap could institute a comparison. He did not bring his invoices from Philadelphia; but as Allen's prints, White Rock linseys, and Laurel D brown muslins were lower at Messrs. Block & Tackle's store than in the Philadelphia houses, every thing else, in his opinion, must be proportionally cheap. And so he went to work and bought, he knew not how many goods, without his memorandum-book. He then visited the houses of Mr. Pike's friends, where other descriptions of goods were kept, and operated with them all very liberally.

Pike stimulated him all he could. He told him repeatedly that no money would be wanted, except an insignificant sum to pay the premium of insurance for the safe transportation of the goods, and they were all to be entered on the policy of Messrs. B. & T.

At length, and it was no long time either, Nap supposed he had made purchases enough. The goods were shipped and the invoices collected. Then our hero trembled. Upon summing up, he found that his New York bills amounted to $30,000! For these, without scarcely knowing what he was doing, for it would have been pusillanimous, after enjoying so great a display of magnificence, to let fall an expression of regret, or doubt of ability to meet his engagements, he signed notes payable in bank at St. Louis. He then drew on Messrs. R. & Co. for some $600 to pay for insuring the safe transmission of his New York goods to Venice.

Then they ceased to overwhelm him with kind attentions. They were sociable enough still, but not so pertinaciously vigilant in friendly offices as they had been. Other victims demanded their attention. This one had been "put through," and they had no further use for him until his bills should mature. Nap, obtuse as he was, perceived the change, and immediately returned to Philadelphia. He presented himself unexpectedly before Handy, in his room, where there happened to be assembled a number of Western acquaintances.

"Well, Nap," said Jack, "Uncle Billy was right. He predicted they would induce you to buy something or other in New York; and he tells me they have paid Messrs. B. & T. some $600 on your account."

"If he bought $600 worth of goods from that house," said Mr. S. from Arkansas, who was in the habit of dividing his purchases between the cities, "I'll bet two to one he paid fifty dollars more for them than the same would cost at other houses in the same street."

"How easily I might win your money," said Nap, smiling. "But you have lost enough already in not buying all your dry-goods there. I paid ten cents for Allen's prints, twenty cents for White Rock linseys, and seven and a quarter cents for Laurel D's."

"There! I told you so!" exclaimed S.

"You thought you were *buying*," said Mac, "but you have been regularly *sold*."

"How so? Have you bought them for less?"

"Oh no; I paid more. And they paid more. Hence I know they put the profit on other things."

"Did you buy any thing else, Nap?" asked Jack.

"Certainly, I went my 'pile' on such a table as that."

"Yes, and you 'went it blind,' or I'm a Dutchman!" said Mr. S. of Arkansas.

"And he'll be called, I'm afraid, when he'll have nothing worth showing," said Jack.

"Don't be uneasy, Jack," said Nap, still smiling; but he did not smile long.

Jack proceeded to inform him that his friends then present had assembled in his room for the purpose of discussing a matter in which he was deeply interested. In consequence of a rumour being spread over the city that Nap was the proprietor of a whole town in Missouri, they learned an impression had gone abroad that he possessed unlimited wealth, and hence he had been for a day or so the subject of conversation in mercantile circles. Knowing his means were limited, and that his credit might ultimately suffer from such representations, they had met together as common friends to consult with Handy upon the propriety of counteracting such a misapprehension in his absence.

"But, Nap," continued Jack, very seriously, "I have learned since tea that the mercantile agency has rectified the mistake to-day, and they have appended to the information they had previously received, that the town of Venice is in a marsh, and would not bring a thousand dollars at auction."

"And that would be no bad speculation," said Nap, "for the ground cost me only fifty."

This produced much laughter.

"I hope, Nap," said Jack, "you have not represented it differently, and then the matter will die away quietly. But if you had made extensive purchases while inducing the people to believe your town was very valuable, I don't know if they might not have prosecuted you for obtaining goods under false pretences."

"I have never said a word about the value of the town to any man, woman, or child!"

"I am glad to hear it. But it did seem to me that the borers pursued you with more vigilance than any of the rest of us. Have they not treated you very kindly?"

"Like a lord. I supposed all were treated so. I wasn't to blame. But"——

"But what, Nap?"

"I'm afraid I have bought too many goods."

"Your purchases here amounted to about five thousand dollars, which did not seem to be out of the way. The six hundred dollars worth bought in New York won't affect you materially."

"Six hundred dollars worth!" exclaimed Nap, drawing Messrs. Block & Tackle's invoice, consisting of seven large foolscap sheets, from his carpet-bag.

"Eighteen thousand dollars!" cried Jack, looking at the foot of the bill, and turning pale.

"Oh, that ain't all!" said Nap, drawing forth other invoices.

"And here's a silk house bill," continued Jack, "amounting to thirty-five hundred dollars! Why, Nap, your entire silk bill ought not to be over five hundred!"

"It's done now," said Nap.

"Yes, done for!" said Mr. G.

"I couldn't help it," said Nap; "they pressed me so much. But if they sold me every thing low enough, perhaps I can realize a profit and pay for them at maturity."

"Never!" said Handy.

A brief examination of the invoices soon satisfied the party that Nap had fallen into bad company. It was quite apparent that he had been charged most unchristian prices for nearly all the goods. The leading articles invoiced below the usual rate, did not amount to more than three per cent. of Messrs. B. & T.'s bill!

"I will sell them for cost and carriage," said Nap, "if I can't do better."

"It won't do!" said Jack. "I hope you didn't promise to pay for them under a year or eighteen months? Let me see how you closed the bills. Look! he has signed negotiable notes, payable in four and six months in bank!"

"Negotiable? What do you mean by that?" asked Nap, reading for the first time the receipts appended to the bills. As for the notes themselves, he did not read one of them at the time of signing.

"It means that they must be paid on the days of maturity, or be protested. And if protested, bankruptcy and ruin may follow immediately."

"Ha! You don't say so? And you think they won't wait on me, if I pay them interest?"

"Not if they think there is any danger of your breaking."

"But there will be no danger. I can make the money out of the goods. I promised to be punctual, though."

"I'm sorry for it, Nap. Mr. R., who has had forty years' experience in his transactions with Western men, advised me never to promise any thing positively and unconditionally. He says, not one in a thousand can and will comply strictly with a promise to pay a certain sum at a certain time. When a correspondent writes him he will remit two thousand dollars on the first day of October, it is a safe calculation to rely upon receiving twelve hundred about the middle of November. This is a Western trait, which we must acknowledge does exist. Now instead of being able to raise thirty thousand dollars in four and six months, I venture to say you cannot realize the fourth of it in twelve and eighteen."

"Then what am I to do?"

"You should have thought of all this before you ventured to engage in such gigantic operations. I do not know what to advise, unless it be to offer the goods in payment, acknowledging your inability to pay for them, and apologizing for being induced to buy them. That would convince all that your motives were not bad, though your judgment was certainly defective. To-morrow we will consult Mr. R., and confess all."

"I'll do whatever you advise, Jack. I begin to feel uncomfortable. You got me out of a scrape in Kentucky, and I hope you will be as successful here. But the goods are on the way home; they are on the lake by this time. I have been a great fool!"

"I will do all I can for you, Nap," said Handy; "but this is a more serious matter than the other. No doubt that fish of prey—what's his name?—Pike—was much to blame. He knew you were inexperienced and impulsive, and the temptation to prey upon such game was too strong to be resisted. But the goods might be stopped at Detroit or Chicago. Instructions could be transmitted by telegraph. They *must* be stopped, Nap. How will you be able to pay the freight and charges on such an enormous amount?"

"I couldn't raise the money. I never thought of that. What a fool! What a fool!"

The next day they held a consultation with Mr. R. and several other experienced merchants. They coincided with Handy, and the houses in New York were instantly telegraphed on the subject. They replied that it would be time enough to take back the goods when Nap's notes were protested; and in the mean time they would institute measures to secure themselves against loss. Thus Nap's Philadelphia creditors became interested in the result. And as it seemed that no satisfactory adjustment could be made with the New York houses, Nap proposed to sign any instrument of writing which might secure the Philadelphians against ultimate loss, and which should be deemed legal and honourable by his friends. It was done. And then poor Nap was threatened by the other creditors.

They wrote him that if he did not give them satisfactory security, they would prosecute him for obtaining goods under false pretences. He knew they could not prove a criminal intention, by truthful witnesses; but as the penalty was ignominious incarceration, if found guilty by false swearing or otherwise, he became dreadfully alarmed, and even proposed to abscond. This, of course, Jack would not listen to; for that would be, in the estimation of some, an evidence of guilt. The poor fellow declared he was the most miserable man in existence; and he certainly was not happy.

CHAPTER XXIII.

Nap falls into the hands of **Mr. De** Coy—He visits a "hell" out of curiosity—**He** wins—He **goes** again—He loses—Escapes—Nap is tempted to marry a rich old maid, but is mistaken—He resolves to apply for an office—Calls upon Colonel Benton, who gives him good counsel—Nap sees the President—He sees the Secretary, and gets a promise.

It was during this exacerbation of Nap's evil star, that a Mr. De Coy proposed one of those schemes by which many a fortune has changed hands. Mr. De Coy was a flashy gentleman, who had contrived to become acquainted with our hero about the time that rumour designated him as a rich man—the proprietor of a whole town. So polite was he on all occasions, so assiduous in his agreeable attentions, so deferential in his conversation, and so obliging in his trivial favours, that Nap's heart was completely won; and in a very brief space of time a friendship of the most unreserved description subsisted between them. Nap, however, had hitherto omitted to inform his fine friend of his distracting reverse of fortune and unpleasant prospects.

"Napoleon," said De Coy one evening, as they sat together on the balcony of the hotel, enjoying the fine cigars which the flashy gentleman had furnished, "why the devil do you go about from city to city buying goods?"

"Pike prevailed on me to do it. I am sorry enough for it now!" Nap supposed his friend had heard the news.

"I'm glad to hear you say so. I would not be a merchant. The drudgery must be a great bore. I hate any sort of business that keeps one from enjoying life at all times."

"I do too. But then it is necessary to make money before one can spend it. Enjoying life as you do here must require a very large fortune."

"Large fiddlestick! You have enough for half a dozen men. What do you think is the amount I spend per annum?"

"Oh, some five thousand a year, I suppose."

"Say ten."

"Then, if that is your income, your fortune must be some hundred and sixty or seventy thousand."

"Not that many cents."

"The deuce you say."

"I say it—and it is as I say."

"Then where does your spending-money come from?"

"From Dame Fortune's bank, which is open to all."

"I wish her ladyship would permit me to have access to her vaults just about this time," said Nap, with a sigh.

"No doubt she would. But then you don't stand in need of her aid. It is different with me. To-morrow I shall have use for a five hundred or so, and to-night I shall go to the bank and get it. Would you not like to see the operation?"

"Oh yes, if it be not a robbing operation. The banks, they say, are closed in the evening."

"Not those that supply me. The paying-tellers place

the funds in my hand in the presence of the proprietors, and before a score of witnesses."

"They cash your checks?"

"They cash my cards."

"Now I understand. They pay when you win. I'm told such banks in the city have large capitals."

"Very large. I shall break one of them some of these days."

"Nights, you mean. But do you always win?"

"Nearly always. A bold better generally gains. Will you go, and look on? There will be no necessity for you to play or bet."

"Yes!" said Nap, desperately.

It was not a long walk. Nor did they leave the fashionable street. The signal was responded to, and Nap was introduced into one of the most magnificent saloons he had ever beheld. Some fifteen or twenty well-dressed individuals were betting at different tables, in the gorgeously illuminated room, and heaps of glittering gold dazzled the eyes of our needy hero. He did not propose to bet, however. All his funds, with the exception of some fifty dollars, reserved to pay his travelling expenses back to Missouri, had been disbursed.

De Coy began with an eagle. It won. Both eagles were suffered to remain, and both won. With but little shifting, and but few losses, he continued to bet on several favourite cards, and did not withdraw any of his gains until they had accumulated to a considerable amount, and quite as much as he had proposed drawing from the bank on that occasion.

"Now," said he, deliberately taking possession of the money, "I'm at your service, Nap. Let me see," he continued, looking at his watch. "I have detained you just twenty minutes. I must apologize for consuming so much of your time. We will withdraw, if you please."

"No, I'm in no hurry. This is a very interesting sight."

"It is better than selling goods for a living."

"If one could always win, as you did. Why didn't you let the money remain? I observed that you would have won again, and doubled the whole amount."

"Oh, I left it for the next time. But if you desire to try your luck, I'll wait for you. No doubt you'll win; but if you lose, it will amuse you. The excitement is worth paying for."

"I believe I will follow in your footsteps. I have an eagle in my pocket."

Nap did follow in his footsteps, and even went beyond them. For in less than thirty minutes he had won a thousand dollars!

"De Coy," said he, his face flushed, and his forehead perspiring, "this will do for me, too, to-night. Fortune is kind to us. We are lucky dogs."

"Well, quit if you are tired. But let us refresh ourselves."

"I see them drinking wine over yonder. I am the largest winner, and must be your entertainer. What will you have?"

"You pay nothing here. No one pays. The bank that supplies us with gold, furnishes every thing else free of cost. Call for any thing you please, and it will appear."

It was as he said. They regaled themselves with divers costly luxuries, and no pay was demanded. Then, still adhering to his purpose, Nap retired to his hotel accompanied by De Coy, who repeatedly assured him that they might have easily won forty thousand dollars if they had persisted in playing the bold game. The *bold game* was the only way to win. Nap believed him, and they agreed to break the bank the next night.

The next morning, Jack found, at Messrs. R. & Co.'s office, a letter from Joseph, containing a supplemental order for goods. His business was increasing rapidly at Tyre, and it was deemed necessary to have more goods sent out than he originally intended. This would detain

Jack several days longer, and he now determined to visit New York himself, as much for the purpose of making the acquaintance of some of the merchants as to purchase goods. But instead of being introduced by the Pikes and Sharks of the trade, he procured letters of introduction from Mr. R., Mr. C., and Mr. T., to some of the best houses in the city. This service is always willingly performed by the merchants of high standing in any of the cities.

Nap was invited to accompany him; but he promptly declined it. He had had enough of New York. He hoped never to see the city again, and could wish never to hear it mentioned more. And so he remained at his hotel. But he was not happy with his late acquisition in his pocket, nor much cheered at the prospect of further gains. He felt, somehow, as if the money so easily obtained did not of right belong to him; but rather as if he had taken it unobserved from the counter of some bank.

De Coy adhered to him during the day, and strove to cheer him up when his spirits seemed to droop. And he intimated that when it was meditated to break a bank, one ought not only to brace his nerves to play boldly, but he should be furnished with a strong capital himself. These hints were thrown out when they were walking in the vicinity of Messrs. R. & Co.'s establishment, whither Nap was going to ascertain if any letters had come for him. Nap made no reply to De Coy's hint; perhaps he was thinking of other matters. De Coy would not enter the counting-room with him, but remained without upon some pretext or other, not doubting his victim would act upon his advice and replenish his finances.

In the counting-room, Nap had the mortification of meeting with Mr. Pike, who was there for the purpose, as he said, of making an "arrangement" with him. His salutation was cold. His smile was gone, and in its place was a menacing expression. Nap, for once in his life, met the threatening gaze without quailing. He was growing desperate, because he considered himself already ruined, and ruined by Mr. Pike.

Mr. Pike had consulted with Nap's creditors in Philadelphia, and of course they would not now come to any agreement for the especial accommodation of the houses he represented in New York. Their plan had been rejected. And Nap had voluntarily signed an instrument which would effectually guard them from loss. Mr. Pike desired Nap to return with him to New York, and have a conversation with his creditors there. But he had been too well advised to be caught in such a trap as that. If they intended to proceed against him as they had threatened, they must first exhibit some evidence of his criminal intentions. Until that were done, they had no power to molest him in Pennsylvania, where his friends and witnesses dwelt.

"Why the mischief didn't you tell me your humbug town was worth nothing?" asked Pike, when Nap refused to go with him to New York.

"I would have told you all about it, if you had asked me. I did not know that you were ignorant of the value of my property in Venice."

"What, then, did you suppose made me so anxious to sell you goods, if it were not that I believed you to be a man of capital?"

"I thought it was your friendship for me."

"Friendship for a stranger!"

"Why, you introduced yourself, and seemed to be as familiar as a brother."

"It is my business to sell all the goods I can to good men."

"Yes, and to get all you can from new men. You charged me ten per cent. too much for most of the merchandise."

"If you knew that, why did you buy?"

"I didn't know it at the time. I was a novice. But if

you didn't know I was good for my contracts, why did you sell me?"

"I thought I knew it, but was deceived."

"And I thought you were selling me goods at honest prices, but was cheated!"

"Something must be done, Mr. Wax; and it is not necessary to use reproachful language," said Pike, wincing under the retort.

"I shall do all in my power to pay my debts," said Nap.

"No doubt. And I have a plan which would satisfy all parties. Let one or two men be appointed to receive the proceeds of your sales, and distribute them pro rata among the creditors."

"And what shall I do?"

"Sell the goods."

"And let your agent receive the money?"

"Yes."

"I won't do it."

"But you must do something to satisfy us."

"It was upon your tempting representations that the goods were bought; and it was in consequence of your urgent solicitation that I bought so many. I did wrong ignorantly—you have not the same justification, for you knew such an amount of merchandise ought never to be taken to a country store. I shall do the best I can with the goods. I will sell them at a profit, if possible, and pay for them when my notes mature, if I can. That's all I will promise."

"That won't satisfy us."

"Then you may go to the devil! The goods are bought, shipped, and settled for. You were *very* eager, I thought, to have my signature to the notes. Well, I signed them. Now, as I am advised, you can have no demands against me until they mature, and the less you annoy me in the mean time, the better it will be for all parties. I intend to go home and divide the goods, sending portions of them to different points; and perhaps I will sell some of them at auction to realize money."

"We'll stop that! We'll get out an injunction," said Pike, in great excitement.

"You can't do it, sir!" said Mr. R., who had been a silent auditor. "You were to blame for selling him the goods under the circumstances; and if he sees proper to avail himself of the laws of his State, he can keep you from realizing any of the money for eighteen months. And rather than make any sacrifices, I would advise him to do so."

"I am informed," said Pike, with some humility, "that if he were to scatter the goods, and attempt to run them off, we can stop him."

"If you can prove a fraudulent purpose," said Mr. R. "But that you can never do in Missouri, where he is known to be an honest man. From the outrageous prices you charged him for many articles, it would be no difficult matter for him to prove fraud against you. We intend to send out a friend to invoice the goods he bought of you at the market rates, and that is all you will recover. You may send a man also, if you like."

"If he does, his friend had better get his life insured," said Colonel T., from the southern part of the State, who sat by. "If the folks in Missouri learn how you have treated Nap, and no doubt the news will be spread over several of the Western States in a few weeks, they might handle your man rather roughly."

"When the notes mature, if he is not able to pay," continued Pike, "we can take possession of the assets."

"You can do no such thing. You can't even get judgment, unless you reduce your demands to the standard of justice. And even then, by giving security, he may put you off a whole year."

"But can he give security?"

"He can, if it be necessary." Mr. R. was emphatic, and Mr. Pike withdrew, foiled and dispirited, and convinced that it was not always safe to deal unjustly even with Western novices.

Nap, finding no letters, returned to his hotel. On his way up Chestnut street, he was joined by his smiling friend, De Coy, who had never ceased to watch the door of Messrs. R. & Co.'s establishment. He was one of the most accomplished "strikers" or "barkers," as they are called, in the employ of the "hells;" but he likewise did not always realize the full extent of his expectations from the "green ones" he introduced into the jungle of the tigers.

If Nap had confided the occurrence of the night before to any of his friends, he would not have returned to the faro-bank. But the first wrong step taken is ever apt to be followed by others. Whichsoever way a man's face is turned, thitherward his walk is likely to be directed. And if he travel the road to ruin, every step brings him nearer to destruction. De Coy had warned him against breathing a syllable in regard to their operations until they had broken the bank. He said if their intentions were known, the bank might adopt measures to defeat their purpose, or other persons might forestall them and carry off the treasure.

At the appointed time they repaired to the gilded "hell," and were met with smiling faces by the demons. Every luxury for the palate which money could buy was spread before them; while paintings and prints, decorating the walls, contributed to stimulate the evil resolutions of the unwary beholders.

De Coy, as on the previous night, was the first to bet; and again he won, but not quite so uniformly as before. Once all his gains were swept away; but then he doubled his venture, and recovered them.

Nap's impatience to realize at least enough to pay his New York creditors could brook no longer delay. So he put down five hundred dollars on a single card, and won! He continued to win until his gains still on the table, and still hazarded, amounted to several thousand dollars. Then he paused, under the influence of a sudden impulse which prompted him to seize what he had won, and retire for ever from a place where his money was subject to the chances of fortune or the knavery of the dealer. His hesitation was marked, and probably his purpose was understood; and before he could put his intention in execution, an adverse card was turned up, and all his treasure on the table had vanished. He grew pale, and then almost blind. But recollecting how De Coy had retrieved his loss, he immediately put down all the money he had with him, having held a sum in reserve which he proposed taking away with him under any circumstances. He was not aware that such intentions are impracticable in such places. He ventured all. That was playing the bold game, and the bold game, as he had been instructed, was the one with which to break the bank. He lost it!

"Napoleon," said De Coy, "remember your name. That is a mere trifle. Don't be agitated. Do as I did. It is the way here. When you are in Rome, do as the Romans do."

"And when you are in Turkey, do as the turkeys do," said one of the spectators.

Nap had done it already, and was done for. He had lost his all, and stood rooted to the floor, staring in consternation at the witnesses of his ill luck, who were evidently prepared to see him launch out thousands.

"Why don't you bet—and bet largely?" asked De Coy.

"Will you lend me some money?" asked Nap.

"Lend you? Why you are not a loser."

"Only fifty dollars," said the banker.

"Fifty, besides what I won last night," said Nap.

"Well," continued De Coy, "What of that? Did you not bring other funds to bet?"

"No!"

"You didn't? But you have other funds to draw upon?"

"No!"

"You have a town, and unlimited credit."

"No. My town has only about a dozen inhabitants, and would not bring under the hammer as much money as I have lost to-night. I was taken in and led astray in New York. I'm a ruined man, and that's the reason I came here. I wanted to win money—I had none to lose."

"Is that true?" asked De Coy, confronting his victim with ill-suppressed rage, and looking him steadily in the eye.

"It is, upon my honour."

"I've spent more than fifty dollars of the bank's money on you, or on your account, which is the same thing. And so you are a humbug, are you?"

"I suppose so, if you thought me rich."

"The deuce! What do you propose doing now?"

"I don't know. I wish you would advise me. The bank scheme is a failure. Is there not something else you can suggest?"

"Yes. Follow me!"

Nap did so intuitively, and they entered a small room but dimly lighted and miserably furnished.

"Here," said De Coy, "is the last remedy; and I advise you to make use of it at once, and be relieved of your distress. It is an infallible specific, and has cured thousands."

"What am I to do with this?" asked Nap, staring at a pistol which De Coy thrust into his hand.

"Blow your brains out."

"I'll be hanged if I do!"

"No you won't. But you may be hanged if you don't. Fire away! I want to see you disposed of. I like to have the witnesses against me put themselves out of the way. Dead men tell no tales. Why don't you blow your brains out?"

"I'll be d———d if I do!"

"Of course you will."

"Then I shan't do it!"

"You shall! If you don't, I'll do it for you."

"No, sir! I'm a coward, I confess, when there seems to be a possibility of escaping danger. But when it comes to this, that I must either kill myself or my enemy, I find that I am cool and dangerous. If you but crook your finger, I'll blow *your* brains out. I'll tell my tale, and the sympathy of the public wil be on my side. So beware! They will not hang me for killing a gambler who confesses to have been a party to acts of suicide, and who threatens to kill me if I refuse to kill myself."

De Coy, if he did not regard the words of his victim, believed his looks; and they said Nap might execute his threat. He believed likewise that the act would have the approbation of the public; and being really a coward himself, he endeavoured to change his tone and laugh lightly, assuring our hero that it was all a joke.

"That may be," said Nap, "but I am not in the mood to enjoy it. Open that door in the rear, and proceed down the back way before me. I shall follow, and will not take my eyes away from you until we are in the street. Obey, or I fire. My nerves never were more steady in my life." This was true, and Nap was much surprised at his own coolness. The "striker" obeyed. Nap dismissed him at the door of the hotel, and then shut himself up in his room, a prey to his own reflections. He did not snore much that night. No position in his bed could induce refreshing slumber to visit his unquiet couch.

He tumbled about on his pillow, and groaned repeatedly in agony of spirit. He had been assured that his numerous purchases would ruin him, and he believed it. How was it possible for him to realize even cost for his goods, after paying the expenses of transportation, in the time stipulated? The prospect was cheerless. He felt convinced that exorbitant prices had been charged, and he was sure a great many costly articles had been added which he had not selected, and which were not adapted to the wants of his customers. On these, enormous sacrifices would have to be made. It was true, as Pike had been told, he might keep his creditors at bay some eighteen months, and in the mean time dispose of a portion of the stock at the usual prices; but then, ultimately, interest must be paid on all the notes from the day they matured.

Whichsoever way he launched his thoughts, the result was the same—unhappiness. And all because he had failed to remember and follow the advice of one whose experience during a long series of years was entitled to profound respect. Poor Nap even doubted whether Molly would keep her engagement with him, when she heard of his fatal imprudence, if she had not heard it already. He felt convinced that her father would not now consent to the match. And if Molly refused him, he could not be sure that Polly would take another's "leavings." Miserable man! He felt tempted to marry a pious old maid whose acquaintance he had made at the dinner-table of the hotel, and who was said to be rich. This was a pale and thin pattern of maidenly propriety, who boarded at the hotel, and almost invariably sat at the table with the gentlemen. She had become quite sociable with our hero; but her conversation was generally on religious subjects, or rather in condemnation of irreligious practices. Upon sitting down, she always bowed her head forward and mutely prayed, instead of briefly giving thanks—a practice much indulged in by the uninformed. But when there were no strangers to mark her, and but few persons sitting in her vicinity, she made short orisons. At a full table, and when many eyes were on her, she bowed very low, and remained long in silent prayer. She prayed thus, most innocently, and surely without being aware of it, to make an exhibition of her piety to the company present. If the One to whom her prayers were due remained unthought of, it was not to be supposed that any such disrespect was intended.

Miss Pucker and Nap had agreed very well on all the

subjects discussed between them. He had accompanied her to church twice, and she had intimated a hope that her Western friend might become a member of the denomination to which she belonged. Matters stood thus, when it occurred to our hero that in the event of his being rejected by both Molly and Polly—a thing, now that luck was against him, he thought by no means improbable— he might win the hand and fortune of Miss Pucker. Then he would bid adieu to the West, and to the drudgery of business pursuits.

Hence, after his night of troubles, he dressed with more care than usual, thinking he might meet the lady at the breakfast-table. He was not disappointed in his expectation. She was sitting before a plate opposite to his, with a newspaper in her hand, which she perused with such intensity as to be incapable of observing Nap's salutation. He bowed twice without making any impression on her, so absorbing was her abstraction. And when she placed the paper beside her plate, and completed a secret prayer of unusual prolongation, poor Nap, who supposed, perhaps, she had been praying for him, was doomed to meet with no better success. Her eyes were studiously averted in some other direction. She would not deign to bestow the slightest notice on him, until he addressed her by name. Then, without moving her thin lips, she handed him the paper. The secret was revealed. There was a paragraph giving an imperfect account of his operations in New York. His name was not mentioned, but his person was described.

"I suppose, Miss Pucker," said Nap, "you have been told who this refers to?"

She looked in another direction, and would not hear him. She had resolved to cut him, and she did it in a decided way, before the charitable company then present. In truth, she was a fortune-hunter herself, and had hoped to share Nap's reputed wealth.

Nap was deeply wounded, and the blood rushed into his

face. But a moment after, Miss **Pucker** was forgotten. Another idea had flashed across his mind. His eye had fallen upon a paragraph of news from **Washington,** in which it was stated that a land-office **was about to be** established in his **county, and** that **Colonel Benton had** proposed **Venice as the most eligible point for its location.** Nap at once resolved **to apply for the appointment of** receiver or register. He **thought there could be no** doubt **of his getting it. If the government placed** the office **in his town, he felt that he was entitled to** demand the **best situation in it. So he** hastened **into Market** street, **and procured** enough **money to defray his** expenses **to** Washington **and** back again **to** Philadelphia, where he **was to** remain until Handy returned **from** New York.

Upon reaching Washington **he** called immediately upon **Colonel Benton, who gave him a cordial reception. But** the statesman's **brow darkened somewhat ominously when Nap** explained the **object of his visit to the** federal **city.**

" **What claims have you ?**" asked **the Colonel.**

" **I'm a Whig, but**"——

" Being a Whig **might not prevent you from** getting **an** appointment under **this Democratic administration,** I suppose, since **so many others have succeeded;** but upon what grounds do **you apply,** aside **from being a** Whig?"

" I wouldn't **vote for** General Scott, **because I** thought some great statesman **of** long experience, such **as** Clay, Webster, **or** Fillmore, should have been **nominated. It is** true, **I didn't vote for the** other candidate either, **because I didn't like the '** heads or tails' game by which **he was** nominated. **But then my** example and influence **caused** other **Whigs to withhold their** votes from Scott, **and in that manner I** aided **to elect** Pierce."

" **Bah!** You don't **understand me yet.** What I mean by **claim or** ground **is not what you may** have done for the successful **candidate. He is now the** President. **The** election **is over; and of course** he has **forgotten to whom he is indebted for his** success. Such a **thing as gratitude** in politics was never heard of. That is not the ground upon which appointments are made."

"Then, Colonel, what is the inducement?"

"Inducement! That comes nearer the mark. That is a good word. Do **you** not conceive? He desires to be a candidate again. **Can you aid** him? If so—if you can convince him of it—your business is done: you will get the **appointment.** Remember that Presidents, and their Cabinet-ministers, are oblivious of the past. They reward services *to be* performed, or rather contract to **pay for** them; but they **rarely** settle **for** benefits voluntarily conferred, because, in such instances, there are no *quid pro quo* stipulations. **The** question with them is, *What good can he do us,* if we appoint him? **or** *What injury can he inflict,* if we disappoint him? Will you recollect this?"

"**Yes**; I can recollect it. **But I** don't see what good I can do the President hereafter."

"Who do you intend **to** vote for at the next Presidential election?"

"I intend to vote for you, Colonel. But when you are elected you mustn't be an abolitionist. **You** say there is **no** such thing as gratitude in politics; but hang me if there **isn't** such a thing in private life. You have always been **my friend**; and I haven't had very many in this world. **You** advised **me** to buy the land and lay off the town of Venice. **It** cost me some fifty dollars; and before I left home I could **have** sold the vacant lots for **a** thousand. Still I've been unfortunate." Nap then confided to him his unlucky speculation in merchandise, while the Colonel listened and wrote alternately.

"**You** have **been** unfortunate, **sir.** It **can do you no** harm to tell me of it. But be careful not to mention it to the President. **It would defeat your** application, sir, even supposing there was a possibility of your getting the appointment. One-half the fools who apply for assistance come with tales of misfortune, ill-health, or distress of some kind, and petition for office to relieve them. I never heard of such applicants being successful. What can invalids and paupers accomplish for presidential aspirants? Sir, they are dead cocks in the pit! They are of value only to the buzzards. No! the applicant who is undaunted, confident of his powers to enhance the pretensions of the President seeking a re-election, and who has the courage to menace the incumbent if he don't grant his request, is far more apt to succeed than the poverty-stricken beggar. Charity may be given from one's private purse; but there is no virtue in bestowing alms from the public treasury. Here, sir, I have written a brief application for you, and signed my name to it. Get all the Missourians in the city likewise to sign it, and then call upon the President in person. But no begging, sir—remember that."

Nap withdrew, knowing there were a great many others awaiting an audience in the antechamber of the great man. He found no difficulty in getting signatures, after the Colonel had signed his application. Neither did he meet with difficulty in finding access to the President. For when he rang at the door, and was told by the porter that it was Cabinet-day, and consequently no one could see the President, he replied boldly that he must and would see him, and that he bore a letter from Colonel Benton to him. The name of Colonel B. staggered the porter. Porters at the White House hear a great deal, if they have good ears. And what this one may have heard the President or those in his confidence say in relation to the importance of granting Colonel B.'s requests, or otherwise conciliating him, if possible, it would be difficult to conjecture. Nevertheless, after a brief hesitation, the door-keeper ran up stairs and whispered that there was a gentleman below with a letter from Colonel Benton. The effect was tremendous. The council was adjourned. A file of secretaries came out, brushing past Nap, and some of them apparently scowling at him. He looked them bravely in the face, remembering his instructions.

The Cabinet-ministers were followed by the porter, who said the President would see Mr. Wax immediately. Nap followed him up the broad stairs, and without pausing at any of the anterooms on the left, boldly entered the office of the chief executive officer of the United States. His hand was cordially shaken, and he was kindly invited to sit down in a commodious chair luxuriantly cushioned. The President himself took possession of one with a leathern bottom and a rickety frame. But General Jackson used to sit in it.

"You have a letter, I believe?" said the great functionary in a mild tone and with a sweet smile.

"Not exactly a letter, either," said Nap, taking the document from his hat, "but it is folded like one. Here it is, sir; and I hope it will be successful."

The President received it. Instantly he recognised the handwriting, and his attention was fixed. But an expression of disappointment spread over his face when he saw the nature of its contents.

"This is an application for an appointment," said he. "I presume you are the Mr. Wax?"

"Yes, sir; and I hope it will be convenient for you to appoint me."

"I must send you to the Secretary. He takes charge of all applications. Yours, you may be assured, backed as you are by men of such high standing, will receive due consideration."

"Thank you, sir. Will you please to tell me where I can find the Secretary? I am in a prodigious hurry, and must leave the city in a few hours, and return to Philadelphia."

"You will find him in the Treasury building. Any one will show you. But sit still with me a moment. Perhaps you can give me some information in relation to the condition of things in your State. I cannot understand how the parties are divided; but I see Whig Representatives coming here from Democratic districts."

"The Loco Focos," said Nap, "are divided into two parts—the Hards and the Softs. The Hards are the originals—all bullion and Benton men. The Softs are the paper-money or bank men, slightly tinctured with the old nullification. Sometimes they are called Rottens. But old Bullion is a host himself; and where one Loco Foco turns rotten, two Whigs grow hard."

"I must confess your elucidation does not make the matter quite plain to me. In New York we have Hards and Softs, but the significations are very different. There the Hards do not hold opinions assimilating with Colonel B.'s."

"Oh, they stole the names from him, but did not have the sense to comprehend his meaning. Every thing he originates is stolen by somebody. Texas was his thunder, but the Tylerites stole it. The great Pacific Railroad is his thunder, and they are trying to steal that too."

"He has his troubles. But why do you call the Democrats Loco Focos? The Whigs do that."

"I'm a Whig."

"You a Whig?"

"That is, I used to be."

"And you come here an applicant for office?"

"Certainly. You have members of your Cabinet who were Whigs; ministers abroad, comptrollers and auditors, collectors and postmasters. What difference does it make?"

"Oh, none, if you are a Democrat now. You voted for —Did you support Scott?"

"No, sir! I'm opposed to generals."

"But one was elected," said the President, smiling.

"Not much of a one. You had not been a military man all your life. I'll be candid. I didn't vote for you, either. I was neutral, and caused other Whigs to stay at home. I did not like the way in which you were nominated. It looked like the convention was selling the office to the highest bidder—and truly its members have been rewarded. But you had never been heard of as a candidate. Indeed, the nation had forgotten there was such a man living; perhaps a large majority never knew such a person ever existed. It was like a king dying without children, and being succeeded by some cousin from another country, who had never been looked upon as the heir apparent. I condemn all conventions, because they never nominate the men the people want to elect. They are sure to pass over the names of the great statesmen who have served the country all their lives. Excuse me, sir: I speak to you as I do to other people."

' Oh, certainly," said the President, rather dryly. "But who is your man for the next heat?"

"I won't lie. I am for Colonel Benton, first, last, and all the time. I owe him a debt of gratitude. He made Missouri. He has been known for three-quarters—no, one-quarter of a century, as the greatest senator on his side of the house. His name is blazoned all over the world, and his speeches in every document in the archives. We'll vote for him, and against all conventions. We Whigs needn't try to elect a Whig again"——

Here he was interrupted by a bow from the President, which he couldn't understand; so he sat still, and nodded back at him.

"Good morning, sir," said the President, bowing again and rising.

"Good day, sir," said Nap, bowing once more, and still sitting. "I suppose you have a great deal to attend to. Shall I wait here till you come back?" he added, seeing the President about to withdraw by a side door leading into another room.

"No," was the reply, and the next moment Nap was alone. After remaining thus for a minute or so, he arose and descended to the grounds. He wound his way, aided by such information as he could pick up in the streets, around to the Treasury building. After entering the premises, he wandered about a long time before he could find the **Secretary's** office, because the directions of the messengers and **clerks** were brief, and **sometimes** conflicting.

Arrived, at **last, at the** door of the important functionary, our hero again blundered upon the right means of obtaining instantaneous admission. He said to the doorkeeper that **he had a** letter from Colonel Benton to the Secretary. Although **this** sub-official person had just turned away high revenue functionaries, and even a Democratic Governor, yet he whispered to Nap that if he would stand there two seconds he should be admitted. He vanished and returned with a smile of success. Nap **was** ushered in abruptly, and invited to sit down.

The Secretary held out his hand to receive the letter he understood Nap was the bearer of. Nap gave him the application. He read it, and then frowned most darkly.

"Is this all? Why, sir, there are the B.'s, the S.'s, the J.'s—to say nothing of Dr. P., Colonel M., and some forty others, applying for the same office. They are all known—you have never been heard of before."

"Does that make any difference?" asked Nap.

"I think it ought."

"Why, sir, the President had never been heard of before he was nominated, and there were such men as Buchanan, Cass, and Benton applying. And you, sir, were never known very extensively before you got this appointment; and I've no doubt many distinguished characters were longing **for** the place."

"This is extraordinary language for one who is seeking favours."

"No, I don't ask it as a favour."

"Upon what plea then do you demand it?"

"Colonel Benton's recommendation, my popularity and influence in the State, and my interest at Venice."

"I will file your application, sir, with the rest."

"I would like to have an answer before I leave, if possible."

"**It is hardly** possible."

"To get the answer, or the appointment?"

"Either."

"And when Colonel Benton recommends me?"

"Colonel Benton is not omnipotent. His recommendations are not always successful."

"But I *must* have the office."

"Why must you?"

"Because I own the whole town, with the exception of a few lots; and if you don't appoint me, I won't let you put the office there at all!"

"That is a novel inducement, truly. Is not Venice the capital of the county?"

"Yes, sir; and I am absolute there. I have given the county a lot on which to build the court-house. At present they hold the court in Sam Marsh's barn."

"In a barn!"

"On the bank of a slough. Piles were driven down in the sand, and the barn was built on them. Underneath is a stable, where Sam keeps his Jack; and it would make you laugh to hear him bray sometimes when the judge is speaking. This year, I believe, Squire Nix intends to keep his stud there"——

"Stud?"

"Yes, Albany Black, the largest stallion in the State. There is a high sandbank near the barn, behind which the pole is kept, and there they can't be seen by the people coming to the store."

"Mr. Wax, where were you from originally?"

"Kentucky, sir!"

"Indeed! Well, sir, I am much engaged now. But hang me, if you shan't have the office, provided my influence can serve you."

"Why, the President sent me to you. All you have to do is to say the word."

"So he made you believe. But it is a Presidential appointment. You don't understand those matters. Rely upon my influence. Good day, sir."

"Farewell. I must go. I'll tell Colonel Benton you are worth a dozen penny presidents."

"Penny presidents?"

"Yes, or copper ones. I mean those made by tossing up a copper—heads or tails—those caught in the game of blindman's buff in the convention, who had never been heard of before."

"You mustn't speak that way, if you hope to be the register of the office."

"Oh, I only do it to you in confidence. Good-bye." Nap departed abruptly, without having felt or manifested any of the awe which office-seekers usually evince in the presence of the high functionaries to whom they are the humble petitioners.

He called upon Colonel Benton again, and related to him all that had occurred. The Colonel laughed very heartily at his literal narration, and told him it was by no means improbable the Secretary would keep his word, because the novelty of the application could not be easily forgotten. But he said nineteen in twenty of the promises of the bestowers of official patronage were sure to escape recollection. It had always been so, and would so continue

CHAPTER XXIV.

Nap and Jack return to Kentucky *via* Bullock's inn—A bridal-chamber prepared—Mr. Brook looks coldly—Molly has taken umbrage—A telegraphic despatch, and a change in Nap's fortune—Mr. Brook is reconciled to the match—But Molly won't relent—Kate grants an audience to Jack—They are joined by a third person—The General capitulates, on condition that Jack will never be a demagogue.

NAP and Jack met at the hotel in Philadelphia, both having returned thither on the same day. Handy exhibited the invoices of the goods he had bought in New

York, which compared very well with the Philadelphia purchases, and proved that Nap had paid exorbitant prices to the employers of Mr. Pike. They proved, likewise, that there were fair and honourable houses in the great metropolis as well as elsewhere.

Nap then confided to Jack his adventure in the "hell," and the result of his trip to Washington. He was now out of money; and as he did not like to draw on his friends in Market street for more, he borrowed of Jack.

The young gentlemen then hastened to complete their final arrangements, and the next day they were in the cars rattling westward. No incident of importance occurred on the way, until they landed in Kentucky, and put up at Mr. Bullock's inn.

Handy had been persuaded to accompany his friend to Kentucky and see him married. He had received no letter from Kate, nor other intimation that his own happiness might be promoted by the visit, save in the meeting of his mother and friends. But he was willing to felicitate Nap on the joyful realization of his hopes, and bide his own time, truly faithful to the end, and as patiently as possible.

"Good morning to your noses!" said Bullock, on recognising the young men. "I'm glad to see you back safe. I've hearn tell that young chaps don't often get away from Fillymaclink in as good health as when they enter it."

"We did," said Jack. "I am always well, and Nap is still fat, you see."

"I do see."

"I'm not quite as heavy as I was," said Nap. "My coat is not so tight, and I am paler."

"You're red enough yet, and big enough too. But didn't you say you wasn't coming this way again till next year?"

"I'll tell you a secret, Mr. Bullock," said Jack, whispering loudly in his ear. "Can you keep a secret?"

"I can. Sambo!" said he to his negro man, who was passing.

"Massa, d'you speak to dis one?"

"I did. Sambo, can I keep a secret?"

"To de day ob you deaf. Massa wouldn't tell ef his back 'oud bust open."

"Clear out, you rascal!" said his master.

"Well, Bullock, Nap has come back to get married. He intends to take Molly with him to Missouri. So you may look for us to-morrow evening, and have a bridal-chamber in readiness."

"I'll turn my old ooman out of the love-chamber. We always call it love-chamber since we slept there the first night after we were tied together. She shall hang up the fine curtains, and put two beds in it. I don't mean two separate beds, but one top t'other, so as to make it soft laying for Nap, who is fat and heavy. And I'll have a turkey, as well as ham and eggs; some eggnog, and, if you like, a shiveree"——

"No! none of that nonsense, Mr. Bullock, if you please," said Nap.

"I won't, then. But I always did like weddings. They are the only real frolics, because they last all your life. But sometimes they bring aching heads, too! Well, I'm glad you're going to get Molly. I always liked that gal, but her dady's a —— hog. I know now you're getting along in the world, Nap; if you weren't, old Brook wouldn't let you have her. I know him well!"

"That's not saying much for Nap's father-in-law," said Jack, laughing.

"I know 'tain't, but he must excuse it, for it's the truth. No matter; he ain't going to marry the old man. It's the gal he'll have to do with, and she's a plump one."

Nap was not very communicative. His thoughts were not felicitous, for he could not be sure that the change in his circumstances would not make a change in the sentiments of both the father and daughter.

The next day our young merchants arrived at C——, and were affectionately received by their mothers. After the shaving and boot-blacking were completed, which they performed themselves, they sought interviews with their respective mistresses.

Nap called at Mr. Brook's house without hesitation, for when he left C—— for the East, a few weeks before, he was on the best terms with the whole family. This time, however, he was not to be so cordially treated. For when Mr. Brook came to the door, he looked coldly, and even declined the proffered hand of his once chosen son-in-law.

"Why, what's the matter, sir?" stammered Nap.

"Come in, and I'll tell you. Our merchants heard strange things of you in Philadelphia," he continued, when they were seated in the parlour. "And since then, the things you did in New York have been published in the papers. Everybody says you are a ruined man; and some declare your conduct wasn't honest."

"It's a lie," said Nap.

"Oh, that may be—probably the last part is, because a man needn't be dishonest to ruin himself. But ain't you ruined?"

"I have got into a difficulty, sir; but some of my friends think I won't lose much by it. Yet, if I lose all I have made, so I give up every thing, the Philadelphia merchants have promised to let me have more goods. If they do, I can make a profit on them, and then get up in the world again. In Missouri, credit is as good as capital, when one has friends in the East who know him to be honest."

"That may be. But Molly don't marry you with my consent. She can do better, and she's a dunce if she don't."

Before Nap could frame a reply to this emphatic speech, Molly herself entered, and silently and rather coldly gave the tips of her fingers to him.

"No, Nap," said she, "you must return to Missouri without me. But I do not refuse you because you have been unfortunate; and I am ashamed, sir," she added, turning to her abashed parent, "that you should make such an excuse for withholding your consent."

"Then, Molly," cried Nap, "why won't you have me? If you say the word, we'll be married, anyhow."

"I will not say the word!"

"Good! I'll leave you to settle the rest!" said Mr Brook, departing to spread the news of Nap's rejection by his daughter.

"You will at least give me some reason for the change in your intentions."

"Oh yes!" said she, taking a letter from her pocket, which she placed in his hand. "I received that a few days ago. It was too late to write you again in Philadelphia, else I should have advised you not to come."

Nap stared, and his heart palpitated as he read. The letter was from Polly Hopkins. It was a direct inquiry whether Molly intended to marry Nap or not. Whether she loved him; and, if so, whether it was reciprocated. She said he had avowed his love for herself, and was quite willing to wed her; but she had heard of his attachment for Molly, and had declined acceding to his request, until he had seen his Kentucky sweetheart once more. Sufficient time had elapsed for him to have done so, and he had failed to notify her of the result. Therefore, and not to be kept any longer in suspense, she had taken the liberty of addressing a letter to Molly on the subject, and begged to be favoured with a reply by the return mail.

"Did you answer it?" asked Nap.

"I did; and I was as candid as herself. I told her of our agreement. But I also informed her that the communication she had made would be the cause of my non-compliance with the engagement. And I told her, moreover, that I never would marry you until I was convinced you were incapable of loving any one else."

"Ah, Molly! Won't you believe me, now? Won't

you take my word, when I declare that at this moment you are the only girl in the world I love?"

"Yes, I believe you. I will take your word that you love me only at the present moment, when you see no other. But I cannot believe that you are incapable of loving others. I will not believe that you will not love this Miss Hopkins more than any one else when you meet her again. Nap, it is your nature, and I can't say I blame you for it. I might make you faithful, if the knot were once tied. But I don't know it. It would be too great a risk to run. I will not try the experiment. Such is my decision, and it cannot be changed. Return to Missouri, and if you will not wholly relinquish the thought of some day obtaining my hand, agree to do penance a whole year, like the characters in 'Love's Labour's Lost.' Either abstain from loving others, or else marry the next one you do love, and think no more of me. But if at the end of twelve months you can produce satisfactory evidence that your heart is captive to me alone, and has not been enthralled by others during that period, I may perhaps listen to your suit—provided I am not married myself, or engaged to some one else."

"That isn't fair," said Nap.

"It may not be fair in your opinion; but it is final. I impose no restrictions upon myself, because I have not been faithless."

"But you would not have me before I went to Missouri."

"I know it; and I did right. One should be able to steer his own bark safely through the world before he undertakes to carry passengers on such a long voyage. You were inexperienced."

"But then you say I oughtn't to be blamed for what I can't help. I acknowledge I can't help admiring a pretty girl wherever I meet her. It is my nature."

"And suppose I could not avoid falling in love with every handsome man I met? Would you like that?"

"No, by Judy!"

"It might not be my fault, but my nature. But then one is not under the necessity of marrying a natural monstrosity. A hair-lipped or club-footed man is not to be blamed for his deformity; but neither is a girl to be censured for declining to make such blemishes her own. Farewell. I have been frank with you." She placed her slightly trembling hand in his, and turned away her face.

"Oh Molly! Don't leave me. I'll root out my very nature for you. I loved you when we were little children together. Only you. I love you now more than ever. Fortune may smile again."

"Nap, if all the gold in California were yours, my resolution would not be changed. But were your inconstant nature changed, I would take you without a dime in your pocket!" And then she vanished.

Nap strolled despondingly homeward. As he entered his mother's gate, Mr. Brook came out. He did not seem to observe him, and Mr. B. brushed past without speaking.

Mr. Brook had just informed Mrs. Wax of the news. She was the last in the village to hear of her son's misfortune. But she was the first to cheer him. She knew he was incapable of meditating a dishonourable action, and believed he would soon retrieve any loss consequent upon his imprudent purchases in New York. She was aware, however, that a change had taken place in the mind of Molly; but she did not attribute it to the pecuniary difficulty. She knew her better.

Nap told her every thing, and she said she could not blame Molly. She insisted that Molly was a good girl, and the proper one for her son to marry. But she was resolute, and he would have to abide her decision. She believed Molly to be sincerely attached to him; and if his mind could be once fixed, they might be very happy together. She therefore advised her son to be circumspect and patient for twelve months, and he would then be well rewarded.

Handy at that moment came in, bringing a letter and a telegraphic despatch for Nap, which he had found at the office.

"Which shall I open first, Jack?" asked Nap, really shivering with the apprehension that he was to hear more bad news. Every communication he had received of late, whether by telegraph or by mail, had been a source of annoyance to him.

"I think I would open the despatch first, as it probably contains the most important news. It may not be bad news, though, for the sender of it seems to have paid for its transmission. Perhaps, however, you had better pause, and prepare your nerves, which, if what Mr. Brook has been telling about town be true, must be in a shattered condition."

"It is true, Jack, and old Bullock's arrangements will be for nothing, unless you can persuade Kate to go Hanged if you don't blush!"

"Do I? But, Nap, I didn't think Molly was capable of acting in this manner."

"Oh, it isn't because he's been unfortunate," said Nap's mother, "but because he fell in love with that wild Polly, and wanted to marry her. She has written Molly a long letter."

"Nap, I thought Polly would get you into a scrape. Don't you remember what she threatened the day she met us in the prairie, when I had a chill after meeting the bloody Irishman? But I'm glad that Molly hasn't rejected you on account of the New York dif"——

"It's over! It's over! Huzza!" cried Nap, who had peeped into the despatch. Leaping up and upsetting chairs and tables, he danced over the floor, and continued to huzza with all his might, while holding the paper over his head.

"Nap! are you going mad?" cried his mother. "You have broken a flower-pot and upset a pan of milk!"

"What is it, Nap?" demanded Jack, following him.

"Sunk! Sunk! The boat's sunk in Lake Erie with all my New York goods on board!"

"Lord bless us! What a misfortune!" cried his mother, clasping her hands and looking upward. "Oh, my son, you seem to be born to bad luck!"

"Good luck, mother! Say good luck! Fortune smiles on me, mother!"

"Don't go mad, my poor boy!" cried Mrs. W., weeping bitter tears.

"Mother! won't you believe me? I say it's the best news I ever received in my life. It puts thousands in my pocket!"

"I can't understand that. The vessel is sunk with your goods on board."

"Yes. The despatch says a total loss."

"And yet you gain by it?"

"Certainly. The goods were insured in a strong office."

"Insured? Then won't the office lose?"

"That's not my look out. If they hadn't been sunk, the office would have got my six hundred dollars for nothing."

"It is true, Mrs. W.," said Jack Handy, reading the despatch, and evincing almost as much excitement as Nap.

The communication came from Mr. R., of Philadelphia. He stated that the proper course to pursue would be to send him a power of attorney to receive the money from the underwriters; that the goods had been shipped under a contract to deliver them at St. Louis; consequently, no expense had been incurred besides the premium of insurance. Moreover, they had, as usual, been insured for ten per cent. above the cost, which amounted to three thousand dollars. The six hundred dollars premium, when deducted, would still leave Nap the handsome sum of two thousand four hundred dollars profit. But that was not all. Mr. R. could obtain a discount of five per cent. on all the New York bills, which would be equivalent to one thousand five hundred dollars more, making for Nap, altogether, a clear gain of three thousand nine hundred dollars on his operations in New York.

No wonder the poor fellow felt relieved of the burden which had oppressed him; it was not strange that he danced about and huzzaed. He felt that he was out of the woods, and might exercise his lungs.

"Now for the letter!" said Nap. "I'm not afraid to open it, now. It's from Jim Rue; I know his hand. I wrote him that a letter would find me here about this time. I had just got Molly's letter in Philadelphia. I'm only sorry I told him I was to be married. No doubt Polly has been informed of it, and I shall get neither. The women don't seem to care half as much for money as we men."

He broke the seal and read the badly written epistle. None but he could read it; and it required patience even for him to understand the whole. Jim began by wishing him joy, which caused Nap to make a wry face. He then said "let her rip," and passed to other subjects. It seemed that many applications were made for lots after Nap's departure, and that Brother Keene had no sooner erected a building on his premises than he leased it to a Mr. Rhino, a Dutch Jew, who had put a stock of goods in it, which he sold at lower prices than Nap had been in the habit of doing. Thus he had competition next door to him. Jim likewise stated that some twenty new buildings had been erected, or were in the process of erection, since Nap had left Venice, and that there was much speculation going on in houses and lots. He had at the store, offers for more than twenty lots, amounting altogether to upward of two thousand dollars, which, of course, could neither be accepted nor declined until Nap returned. He said the whole of Nap's interest in the unimproved portions of the town would no doubt bring ten thousand dollars if sold under the hammer; and that a lawyer from St. Louis, who had been telegraphed from

New York, had spent several days at Sam Marsh's hotel, and was willing to offer nine thousand dollars, provided Nap would take his own notes given the house of B. & T. in payment. Jim further said that trade had been pretty fair until the "double-purple madder-dyed rascal of a Jew" opened his smuggled goods alongside of them. But his collections had been good, as well as cash sales, and hence he thought he would have money enough to pay freights and charges, unless a whole steamboat load of goods should be landed for them at one time. In a postscript he mentioned having seen Polly, who, he said, was not quite so "dare-devilish" as usual, when informed that Nap was to be married to Molly. "But," he concluded, "let her rip!"

Here again was cheering news for Nap. He could not keep still. He sat down first in one chair and then in another. He reclined on the settee for a few moments, and then leaped up and walked the floor, backward and forward, very briskly, as if urgently in pursuit of some object which could only be obtained by violent physical exertion.

Meantime, Jack Handy had withdrawn without being observed, so profound was Nap's abstraction.

"Mother!" said he, turning to his sedate parent, "I'm worth twenty thousand dollars. At least that. Perhaps double that. I will be worth a hundred thousand. I'll tear down this house"——

"You shan't do any such thing, Nap! Are you crazy?"

"Oh, I'll build you another. You shall have the best house in town! It shall be a palace."

"I don't want a palace. This old cottage suits me well enough. I love it, and the garden, and the yard. The rose-bushes, the grape-vines, and trees, and the green grass are my delight. I won't have any thing changed. I am happy enough, now; don't make me miserable, Nap, with any changes. Let well enough alone. There are changes enough in the world in spite of us. Don't let us make more than we can help."

"But I am rich, mother; and have no one else to bestow my wealth upon but you."

"I don't want it. I am content with the little I have. I have a house and sufficient victuals and clothes. Oh, I have seen rich folks in my day! And they had constant toil and care and vexation. And what was it all for? Just for their victuals and clothes. They did not eat a larger amount, nor wear more comfortable dresses than I did, and all my life I have been called poor. But I never envied them, for I knew I was as happy as the best of them. Now yonder comes a fool. It is Brook. Jack's been telling him the news."

"Let bygones be bygones, Nap," said Brook, coming in hastily. "It was only a mistake. Say it was a duty I owed my daughter—mere parental affection. If you love Molly, you won't blame me for endeavouring to promote her happiness. Won't you forget what passed betwixt us, Nap?"

"Oh yes. I forgive every thing. Think no more of it."

"Give me your hand! I wish you joy, my fine fellow! You are about the richest man in town, now; and, although I say it, who perhaps ought to be silent, yet it must be confessed by all, that you are going to get a girl who will make one of the finest wives the State of Kentucky ever produced."

"It is a pity it can't be as you wish," said Nap.

"Can't be as I wish? What! do you intend to abandon her? If you do, I'll sue you for breach of marriage contract!"

"That will not be necessary. I would marry her this hour, if she would have me."

"What! you think she won't have you—you who are worth, Jack says, more than ten thousand dollars?"

"I know she won't have me for a whole year. She said so—and what she says is so."

"That was when she thought you had nothing to make the pot boil. She'll think better of it."

"You don't know your own daughter, Mr. Brook," said Nap's mother. "She has the good sense and firm resolution of her mother."

"Would you call it good sense to put off such a match for twelve months?"

"I shall not call it any thing. I'll not make or meddle in any such affairs; and you had better follow my example. Let the young folks fix it to please themselves."

"She *shall* have him!"

"Will you tell her so?"

"Well, I wouldn't like to do so in those words. But I'll reason with her."

"And then she'll have the advantage of you."

"Come with me, Nap. You shall plead for yourself."

"No, sir. I have done that already. She might have relented if I had not heard of my good fortune, for she couldn't help pitying me. But now she'd turn her back on me in disdain. I know her well."

"Then I'll reason with her. I'll promise to give her the largest wedding she ever dreamt of."

"That will do no good. She despises such displays. We would have left town in twenty minutes after the ceremony was performed."

"Nap, suppose you threaten to sue her for breach of marriage contract?"

"Nonsense!"

"I'll go mad if you ain't married! My heart's fixed upon it!" Saying this, Mr. Brook ran off toward home.

"He's been half-witted all his life, and a worshipper of wealthy men. He thinks happiness consists in riches. He is a toady to General Frost, merely because he is rich. I believe he would flatter the Old Boy, if he carried money about him. Nap, if ever you do marry Molly, I advise you not to dwell under his roof."

"Molly is quite different from her father."

"I know that! She is a fine girl, and wou'l make any deserving man happy."

"Mother, I wish you would go and see her for me, while I write to Mr. R. If she puts it off a whole year, I'm fearful something will happen to prevent it altogether."

His mother did go to Mr. Brook's house, and had a long interview with Molly. But Molly could not be moved from her purpose. She read the letter from Nap's Missouri sweetheart to the old lady.

"He got that habit from his father," said Mrs. W., "and he can't help it to save his life. His father loved another when he proposed to me, and I put him off, too. But the longer I put him off, the more he fell in love with others. So I married him, and put an end to it. He never loved another afterward. He was cured. And so it will be with Nap; if you postpone it, he'll keep loving all the handsome girls he meets; but if you'll marry him, he'll be satisfied."

It did not avail. Molly adhered to her resolution. But she sent a kind word to Nap. She said she did not desire to be an obstacle in his way, if he preferred Polly, or any one else to her. But that it would be useless for him to suppose she could be induced to alter her determination.

During the progress of these events, Jack Handy had not neglected his own affairs. He had sought and obtained an interview with Kate. She had even received him in the General's library, the General himself being absent on one of his accustomed rides. Strange to say, after the first greetings, their conversation related chiefly to the affairs of Nap and Molly.

"He might have known she would be informed of his passion and proposition in Missouri; nothing of that kind ever was long concealed," said Kate, her clear blue eyes fixed upon Jack's face.

"Polly informed her by letter. She had it directly from the Missouri lady herself."

"I am glad of it. It served him right. What business

had he to be falling in love with any one else, when there was a girl in Kentucky to whom he had plighted his faith?"

"She had never promised to wed him; he did not know that Molly would wait for him, or indeed consent to wed him if he awaited the expiration of her time. Polly was handsome and seemed to be willing"——

"And the temptation was great!"

"Very. No wonder the poor distressed fellow could not resist it."

"Oh no; and I suppose all the distressed fellows find it difficult to resist such temptations. *You* must be sadly distressed when so long absent; and it may be presumed temptations are never wanting," said Kate, shrugging her alabaster shoulders.

"But, as yet, I have never yielded to any such temptations."

"How do I know that?"

"You don't know the contrary. No one has written you that I have acted as Nap did; you have no evidence of my transgression, or reason to charge me with any semblance of infidelity."

"But I have, sir!"

"You have?" asked Jack, looking her full in the face with the boldness of perfect innocency.

"Yes, I have. Your youth, your absence, the continued presence of young ladies, the"——

"There is nothing criminal or censurable in all that."

"But there is temptation. Confess, now, that you have been strongly tempted."

"I will confess that I am strongly tempted now, to—to snatch a kiss!"

"Have you never snatched them from others?"

"No, indeed!" said Jack, yielding to the temptation, which had not removed itself or resisted.

"Molly will not relent. I know she won't!" said Kate, without uttering a single reproving remark upon what had just occurred.

27

"I'm sorry for it. She would cure him effectually, and remove him beyond the reach of temptation hereafter. But she is implacable. There will be no wedding. And after he had engaged a bridal chamber, too!"

"Had he **engaged such a chamber?** Where? Describe it to me."

Jack repeated what had transpired at Bullock's inn, and Kate seemed to sympathize with the doomed **victim.**

"But there is more than one victim,. Kate!" said Jack. "What is it but mere caprice which withholds the greatest happiness I have dreamt of, hoped for, lived for ——"

"Are you quite certain the possession of the object you seek would be such happiness?"

"I **know it!** Oh, Kate, **why not seize the present** time"——

"And **not** disappoint old Bullock? **Ha! ha!** ha!"

"**Do not** laugh at me, **or treat the** subject lightly. I speak with an anxious and aching heart. Who knows, if we part now, whether we shall ever meet again? Disease, accident, death, may make it an eternal separation. The bursting of a boiler, **the** cholera, which is now in Missouri —but **no!** I would not expose *you* to it. You should be kept beyond the limits of its ravages"——

"**Jack,** don't frighten me!" Kate exclaimed, spasmodically, and quite pale. "Don't describe the dangers to which you will **be** exposed! You will run me mad, if you **do.** I have pledged my word to my guardian, as you are **aware, and** must keep it. **Were** I absolved, I would **go** with you. Your fate should **be** mine!"

"Would he not absolve you, if you were to plead with him? He is generous and noble. An aristocrat, he has in an eminent degree the attributes of true nobility. As Nap and I approached the village, we met him, and he surprised me by bowing and smiling as he cantered past."

"He saw you, then?" asked Kate, quickly, and somewhat startled.

"**Yes.** Why do you ask?"

"Because he may return sooner than I supposed he would; and he might think it cool impudence in me to introduce into his library one whose visits he has interdicted. Yet he admires you."

"Admires me?"

"He does, indeed, notwithstanding his haughty and repulsive looks. Sometimes of late, when I have been paying more attention to my flowers than usual, and withholding myself from his presence, he has come upon me, and scolded me for being pale, and thinking too much of some one then absent. At such times it is difficult for him to keep his countenance when indirectly attempting to detract from your merits. His features, whose language I have learned to understand perfectly, contradicted every word his tongue uttered. And most generally, for he can likewise read my thoughts, he has ended by admitting 'the fellow is good-looking enough; he has some spirit, too, and knows how to manage an affair of honour.' That was the comfort he felt bound to apply after the infliction."

"I have always revered the General, as a high-toned gentleman of the old Virginia school. I can appreciate his designs. And although they seem adverse to the consummation of my wishes, I know they are not the result of any disreputable motives. He simply deems me unworthy of you, as indeed I am, and as any man would be"——

"What do you mean, Jack? Have you the presumption to utter such words before my face, and then"——

"Seek your hand? It is true. What I have said is true. What I presume to seek is confessed. But without feeling any enmity for me, your guardian would have you wed some one of greater wealth, or more distinguished family, or more elevated position"——

"Enough, Jack!"

"Not merely for his own gratification, for he is generous and noble—but for your own welfare."

"My welfare! Should I not know what would most

conduce to it? What's that!" she exclaimed, hearing some one sneeze.

"Damn the snuff!" said the General, striding forth from a curtained recess, and walking deliberately toward the lovers, who stared in silent amazement.

"Sir!" said he to Jack, but at the same time kindly taking his hand, "you have stolen over my walls, as young Romeo did—and you have found a Juliet, quite as romantic and accommodating as the stage heroine. But then there is no feud between our houses. Take her!" He joined their hands, and turned away his face. They rushed into each other's arms.

"Stop that! No nonsense before me!" continued the General. "You are not married yet; you are only affianced. Sit down. Kate, what the devil can I do without you? I won't part with you! You shan't have her, sir! How dare you presume to rob an old man of his only comfort? And you, miss! What makes you so cold and cruel as to desire to leave me here alone to sicken and die without a nurse? I will not suffer long!" The General's eyes were moistened. Kate kissed his hands, and wound her arms around his neck. "I know you love me, Kate," he continued; "but I don't understand why you would kill me. I had the infernal gout all the time you were absent at school. But I thought the bishop's rules at the Hall would promote a habit of celibacy."

"We were plighted to each other, sir, before she was sent to St. Mary's Hall," said Jack.

"The deuce you were! Silence, sir! let her speak for herself!"

"It is true, sir."

"What an absurdity! The idea of children being faithful to their engagements!"

"You know, sir, one of your lessons has been that we should always scrupulously perform a promise, however trivial it may be."

"In business matters, miss! or in affairs of honour!"

"Our honour was involved, sir."

"Oh, of course. That was it. You were bound in honour to marry, and rob an old fool of his happiness. I have some fortune, sir; and I propose making it yours, if you will agree not to rob me entirely of my ward."

"I will settle my affairs in Missouri, sir, if you advise it, and then bring Kate back to your hospitable roof."

"Be it so! But I don't like the bringing Kate back!"

"You don't?" exclaimed Kate.

"No, Miss Pert! Because it implies that he will take you away."

"But we will soon return."

"The sooner the better, if you would see me alive. All the morning I have felt the gout coming. It may reach the stomach next time. Master Handy, I believe you have some good blood in your veins, or else I would see you at Jericho before you should have my Kate. Blood is like water under the earth. It may run out of view for generations, but can never be destroyed. I'll tell you an anecdote. The Duke of B——, who was childless, assembled all his tenants one day, and gave them a feast. He declared that his line, in a direct descent, would be extinct at his death, and he knew not who would be his successor. While speaking thus, his eyes fell upon a young man of lofty forehead and noble bearing. He turned to an old portrait in the gallery, which had been hanging there three hundred years, and was struck with the resemblance it bore to the young man's features. Others then observed it. Every one said the likeness was perfect. An investigation was instituted, and by the undoubted records of several parishes, it was ascertained that the young man was a lineal descendant of one of the Duke's ancestors, and the legitimate heir to the title and estates. And so he succeeded him. Thus, sir, whatever may be the vicissitudes of life, or the results of circumstances—no matter what may happen to be one's occupation—if he has good blood in his family, it will develop itself. It may be known by chivalrous acts, by lofty aspirations, and by the confidence it inspires in others. You have such blood, sir; else you would not have dared to aspire to the hand of my niece, nor would Kate have reciprocated your affection."

"No doubt of it, sir!" said Kate.

"You know nothing about it, you baggage! But, sir," he continued, addressing Jack, "before I yield my final consent, you must make me certain pledges."

"Name them, sir."

"First, if you ever turn politician, that you will scorn to be a demagogue."

"I will pledge myself to that."

"But you must learn from me what a demagogue is. I was elected Governor, without seeking the 'sweet voices' of the people; and might have been re-elected, if I had humbled myself to the demagogues and ignoramuses, which I scorned to do. I would advocate no measure I did not deem proper in itself and worthy the advocacy of a gentleman."

"Neither would I, sir."

"Then, sir, never be an advocate of the Maine Law—the main-spring of fanaticism—nor of the Public School project"——

"Is that a bad measure, sir?"

"It is unconstitutional. Education is a good thing, I grant. So is food, and so is clothing. We should bestow alms in charity. That is well enough, so it be voluntary. But who would submit to be taxed to buy bread and meat and clothing for all the idle paupers and improvident people in the country? And yet it would be quite as constitutional as the other clap-trap measure."

"It seems so, indeed."

"It is so. The demagogues will have public granaries next, as they did in Rome. Let them alone. They will get all power soon, and then they will quarrel over the spoils and cut their own throats, as they did in France.

Then a purification will ensue, and men of honour and intelligence will take the reins of government. But until that time arrives, the most respectable citizens will remain in obscurity. The post of honour now is in private life. Blackguards rule **the country, and no** decent man would associate with them."

Jack found no insurmountable difficulty in agreeing **to** the terms, and he had the felicity of espousing Kate **that very day.**

CHAPTER XXV.

The bridal party set out for Missouri, staying at Bullock's **inn the first** night—The steamboat Meteor blows up—Nap escapes.

"Where's Molly, Nap?" asked Bullock, as the party descended from the **carriage before** the inn.

"Don't mention her, I beg of you," said the disconsolate young **man.**

"Wouldn't have you? **Then** you must give security for your bill. I know Brook would have made her marry you **if you** had done **well** in the world. You must be out of money!"

Jack Handy informed the host that such was not the **case.** He then introduced Kate **as** his wife, and whispered that the decking of **the** bridal-chamber had not been for nothing.

"Good!" said Bullock. "**You're a clever** fellow. I'll tell **my** old ooman **to** fix every thing right. You shall have a nice lodging, and the best to eat the country affords. But I pity Nap!"

"See here, Mr. Bullock," said **Nap,** plucking him aside **when** Jack and Kate entered **the** inn, "I don't want you to be telling the folks **that I** engaged the bridal-chamber for **Molly** and myself, and was disappointed'

"It's too good a joke not to be told! I can't keep that a secret."

"If you don't, I won't keep your secret."

"What secret? The old ooman and me have no secrets now."

"Don't you remember the night Jack and I stayed here when we were on the way to Philadelphia?"

"Yes, I *do* remember it!" was the emphatic reply.

"And I don't think you'll ever forget it. Do you?"

"No. But what did you see or hear then?"

"One of the windows of the room I slept in was next to the orchard, you recollect?"

"So it was! Did you see or hear any thing?"

"Every thing?"

"The dickens you did!"

"Mum for mum, you know!"

"Mum's the word!"

"The negroes have never told it?'

"No, confound 'em!"

"Well, I shan't either, if you don't tell on me.'

"I'm dumb! Walk in. You shall pay no bill." And Bullock kept his word.

Nap snored but little, if any, that night, as he could not sleep until the day dawned, for brooding over his disappointment, and contrasting his lot with Jack's. But when he did fall into a slumber, he slept fast and snored loudly.

"What is that, Jack?" asked Kate, awaking just as the first streaks of morning could be discerned through the curtained window, and listening to the sounds in the next chamber.

"It is an organ that I have heard before," said Jack, springing up. "I will soon silence it. Sleep on; don't let it disturb you."

"But what sort of an organ is it? I never heard one like that before."

"A nasal organ. Poor Nap has just fallen asleep, and he always snores."

"Oh, is that all? Then let him alone. Don't disturb him on my account. I am sure it will not prevent me from sleeping now, since I know what it is."

Then Jack abandoned his purpose, and permitted Nap to remain unmolested.

Our bridal party were late at the breakfast-table, but they did justice to the viands. Bullock never once alluded to Nap's disappointment or disconsolate looks. But his "old ooman" could not refrain from some sly insinuations in the ear of Kate, who alone heard them, and reddened at them. Jack could only extort a promise from her to repeat them to him on some future occasion, which promise, it may be presumed, she did not fail to fulfil.

Before night, they arrived at a point on the Ohio river where there was lying at the wharf a steamboat bound for St. Louis. It was the old Meteor, a second-class boat, with inferior accommodations for passengers, and our party embarked on it with reluctance. But it might be several hours, and perhaps a whole day, before a better boat would arrive bound for the port to which they were travelling.

The Meteor, however, to their chagrin, had not been under way ten minutes before the Western Merchant, a fine new boat, hove in sight, and rounded to at the place whence they had embarked. It was a regular packet in the St. Louis trade, and no one doubted it would arrive at that port before the Meteor. Many openly expressed their opinions on the subject. The captain hearing such derogating surmises, resolved to do his utmost to prevent their realization. Hence the officers and crew not only put on more steam than usual, but worked with greater energy in the receiving and discharging of freight, wooding, &c. By this means the Western Merchant, which, with a moderate pressure of steam, would perhaps run eleven miles while the Meteor ran but ten, was kept behind all that day and the succeeding night. But it was apparent it could be no equal race, while one boat was strained incessantly to keep its distance ahead, and the other had not as yet made an effort to pass it. The Western Merchant might at any moment put an end to the contest by a little exertion, and it was not in the nature of any commander of a fine boat long to resist such a temptation.

Hitherto, nevertheless, the predictions of the Meteor's passengers had not been fulfilled, and a supposition began to prevail that the W. M. was not so swift a boat as the newspapers had represented it to be. Once or twice during the ensuing day the pursuing boat came in sight; but when the black columns of smoke arose from the Meteor's chimneys, which was invariably the case on such occasions, the W. M. fell back out of view again.

The race was the topic of conversation as long as the passengers were excited with the prospect of being beaten. Several of the travellers, sympathizing with the captain, were quite willing to run some hazard rather than have the boat on which they voyaged ignominiously passed under way. Others deprecated any violent efforts to prevent such an occurrence, and expressed their apprehensions of a catastrophe ensuing if they were not discontinued. Among those who condemned the officers for making such extraordinary exertions for the sake of maintaining a contest with a superior boat, or with any boat, were Nap and Jack. Nap was always alive to danger of any species. Jack seemed to be more particularly anxious for the safety of his dear Kate, for whom his love seemed to increase every hour. She only laughed at his fears, unconscious of the danger.

But one may become accustomed to danger itself; and perils, from familiarity, may cease to be exciting. It was so with our party; and they soon ceased to entertain any fears that they might be involved in a calamity.

Then it was observed by Jack and Kate that a change had come over the spirit of Nap. His jewelry, his gloves, and his fine clothes were discarded, and were succeeded by the plain apparel usually worn by capitalists. And he grew taciturn, seeming to be in the habit of thinking much more than he spoke. At first they supposed it to be melancholy, the accompaniment of a wounded heart; but presently they had convincing evidence that it was merely the pride of riches, the affected reserve and unassuming ostentation of one who had amassed a greater amount of wealth than most of those in pursuit of fortune with whom he mingled.

Yet Nap had learned more than one valuable lesson. He had tested the experiment of travellers wearing mean attire. It brought contempt from strangers and debarred him from the enjoyment of good entertainment. He learned that the world judges of one's merits very often by external appearances, and that the poor in purse do not receive much consideration from their fellow-creatures. He had likewise learned that too great a display of the evidences of wealth, sometimes subjects one to the approaches of sharpers. He had been the victim of De Coy. Therefore he adopted a medium course as the best policy. It was also an imitation of the apparel of some of the very wealthy men who had been pointed out to him in the East.

Yet Nap could not avoid betraying very great animation when the clerk of the boat required him, the second night after he had been on board, to surrender the upper berth of the state-room in which he had slept. Rich men, although they may be reserved and plainly dressed, generally think they are entitled to more privileges and greater consideration than others; and they feel, if they do not express, much indignation when others are in any manner exalted above them. By the merest accident, Nap had taken the upper berth, for he could have no especial partiality for it; but when the Hon. Mr. K. desired to have it, then he preferred it decidedly. He told the clerk that although Mr. K. might be an M. C., he doubted whether he was a richer man than himself. And when the clerk persisted in giving the berth to Mr. K., Nap said he would not sleep in the other. And he did not. He slept upon the floor, and snored so loudly that Mr. K. would most certainly have evacuated his quarters before the termination of the night, had he not been prevented from putting his design into execution by an unexpected occurrence.

There was not a single individual sitting or standing in the cabin. All had retired. It was after midnight. At such an hour, the officers having charge of the Western Merchant determined to pass ahead of the Meteor. To accomplish this, an extra pressure of steam was applied. On the Meteor the same means were resorted to to defeat the purpose. The consequence was an explosion of one of the Meteor's boilers. The rear end of it blew out and carried away several of the state-rooms in the gentlemen's cabin. Some three or four of the passengers were killed by the iron fragments which passed through the frail sides of the rooms, and as many by inhaling the scalding vapour which followed. There was a dull, stunning report—a crash, succeeded by screams and groans. The consternation that ensued among the surviving passengers, and particularly those in the ladies' cabin, where no injury had been sustained, made a scene not to be described. The steam which had filled the cabins was however soon dispersed or condensed, and no further injury was to be apprehended. Lights were brought in to ascertain the result. Jack Handy ran to the state-room which Nap had occupied. Upon opening the door he discovered his friend lying on his back, perfectly still, and—snoring! The explosion had not disturbed him. Mr. K. they likewise found lying in his berth, but quite dead. A piece of iron, weighing several pounds, had passed through the slight wooden partition and penetrated his temple.

"Awake, Nap! Arise!" shouted Jack.

"No; I'll sleep here, if I can't have my berth. I have funds in R. & Co.'s hands," said Nap, rubbing his eyes. The steam having expanded upward, the hot stratum did not affect those in the lower berths, much less the men lying on the floor ; hence Nap's ignorance of the "serious accident" which had occurred, and which had precipitated a number of human beings into eternity.

CHAPTER XXVI.

Our party taken on board the W. M.—Nap meets with Miss D. again, and wants to marry her—She rejects him kindly—A dissertation on authors—They arrive at St. Louis and find their goods—They likewise find true friends—Letters from Joseph Handy and Jim Rue—Nap arrives at Venice, and hardly knows his own town—Nap hopes to hear something about Polly, but won't inquire—his Jew competitor—Nap goes out to shoot snipe—Immense success.

THE passengers on board the "ill-fated" Meteor had been transferred to the Western Merchant, which now ploughed its way alone through the sparkling waters.

Nap of course had been much shocked at the spectacle he beheld on board the Meteor. Although unconscious of danger when the catastrophe occurred, the mere contemplation of the horrid death he had escaped, subsequently made him turn pale and tremble.

The morning succeeding the transfer of the passengers to the W. M., our hero, after a moderate breakfast, sat pale and alone on the guard behind the wheel-house. With his hand under his chin, and his elbow resting on the railing, he seemed to be reflecting on the vicissitudes of life, as he was wafted over the smooth surface of the Ohio. It was a calm, warm, cloudy day. Long he remained in this pensive attitude without being accosted by any one. After his thoughts had run their course, having been aroused from sleep and deprived of his accustomed rest the preceding night, his eyelids gradully drooped, and he would have fallen into a profound slumber, had he not snored so startlingly as to awaken himself. He was upon the eve of rising from his chair, to indulge his innocent propensity in his state-room, when he felt himself gently tapped on the shoulder. He turned his head slowly and gazed in silence, in astonishment, but in admiration. Miss D. stood before him. She looked like one of the Muses, and seemed to enjoy his surprise. She then gave him her hand in friendly greeting.

" Why," said she, "don't you exclaim—

> 'Angels and ministers of grace, defend us!
> Be thou a spirit of health, or goblin damn'd,
> Bring with thee airs from heaven, or blasts from hell,
> Be thy intents wicked or charitable,
> Thou comest in such a questionable shape,'—

and so on."

"'That I will speak to thee,'" added Nap, rising.

"Say on, but sit still, and I will sit beside you. Tell me your adventures since we parted," said she.

If Nap had been unmoved by the explosion of a boiler, he could not resist such charming condescension on the part of the actress. He felt as if he was in the presence of an old acquaintance, with whom he had been long upon terms of intimacy; and not only so, but she was, in his opinion, decidedly the most gifted and the most beautiful woman it had ever been his good fortune to converse with. And hence, whatever might have been his promises to Molly, whatever might have been his secret resolutions in reference to the habit of falling in love with every handsome girl he met, and which had in more than one instance subjected him to disappointment and mortification, he found himself now taken by surprise—caught napping—and he felt that he was quite ready to surrender his heart at discretion to the bright and beautiful being beside him. All his ills, as if by some magical process of sponging, were obliterated from his memory. Molly and Polly were both, for the time being, torn up by the roots from his breast and thrown overboard. Miss D. was the angel of his paradise; and, being in a fine humour, she smiled kindly on him, ever conscious of her own safety, but not always aware of the wounds she inflicted upon others.

Nap took up the thread of his narrative at the point of their separation in Philadelphia, and omitted none of his adventures from that day to the time of his meeting with Miss D., except a few nocturnal incidents which he was ashamed of.

"And so you are rich, now! I am rejoiced to hear it! And Molly would not have you? It is strange—most wonderful. She must indeed be an extraordinary girl, and worthy of being wooed and won."

"But I will not seek her any more. I would not, I am sure, if I thought"——

"She would not perform her promise," continued Miss D., half abstractedly, "because another had once made an impression on your heart. Was it really wise in her to act thus? They say such impressions are involuntarily received. And if you had never met with Polly, and had been wedded to Molly, what reason could she have to presume some other lady, superior in every way to herself, might not have made an impression on her husband after marriage? Every thing of that nature must depend upon the wife. Then, self-reliant, why did she not wed you?"

"She could not argue the case as ably as you do," said Nap; "but I should not be sorry she acted as she did, provided I might have only the slightest hope, the least encouragement"——

"And the other—what do you think will be her course?" continued Miss D., unheeding what Nap was saying, or wishing to say.

"I suppose she will put me off again, because I renewed my proposal to Molly. But if"——

"Then, between Polly and Molly, you are to have no wife. It is an anomaly. You are willing to marry either of them; either of them would marry you were the other away, or finally disposed of! It is a curious affair. An amusing comedy might be founded on it, if we had any real dramatists."

"But I will relinquish both. I will never see either of them again, if *you* will only have me. Myself, and all I possess, I offer for your acceptance."

"Mercy on me! No wonder neither of them will have you. Fate reserved you for me."

"Do you say so?"

"I said so. But I was precipitate. Yet I would not fear what other ladies could do to my husband. But I am already wedded."

"It ain't possible! You don't say so!" exclaimed Nap, rising.

"Sit down, and I will tell you. It is not to any man, but to all"——

"What?"

"I mean the praises of all. I am wedded to my profession. I must win the highest distinction, achieve the greatest triumph, in the line I have adopted. It might have been different before I embarked in the pursuit of fame"——

"But will you never marry a man?"

"I may. But it must be one capable of facilitating my progress to the nich I aspire to in the temple of fame."

"And might I not do it?"

"No. Let me be candid with you. Listen. Our affections should not be divided, else conflicts would ensue. You would love me too well, and I would be devoted only to my profession. I must have one in love with my fame more than with my person. One capable of sympathizing with me in my longings and my triumphs. One"——

"But could you not retire from the stage? I would have sufficient fortune"——

"To buy your wife a few useless diamonds, perhaps. Retire? No, sir! You know not the many sleepless nights through which I have feverishly tossed, the long days of toil through which I have struggled, and the almost insuperable difficulties I have painfully surmounted, to reach the eminence I now enjoy. To abandon the pursuit at this epoch in my life, would be like a relinquishment of my existence! I am just beginning to carve my name on the eternal cliffs. I will not scratch it out and substitute another's in its place. I will complete the inscription"——

"You can do it easily, and it will remain for ever!" cried Nap, blazing with enthusiasm.

"Not easily. No, not easily. The world supposes that the gift of genius bestowed by nature is the summum bonum. It is not so. Untiring energy, indomitable fortitude, the will to do, the power to bear, are indispensably necessary. They think it requires no exertion for me to pass triumphantly through my rôle! That it is nothing to bear the frowns of the envious and detracting of my own sex—to hear the awful denunciations of the clergy, who repeat the same words of the poet in the pulpit that I do on the stage—to be shut out from heaven, and shunned on earth"——

"I *seek* you! Who shuns you? Let any one dare to do it!" cried Nap, with extraordinary zeal and heroic emotion, the effect of the inspiration he had caught.

"These, then, are the sacrifices," continued the actress, unheeding the interruption, "which must be submitted to by those who would have their names repeated and achievements admired by future generations. And all the days of one's life, and all the faculties of one's mind, will alone suffice to win the prize. No disappointments must dishearten, no ill success deter the one embarked in the pursuit of fame from renewed attempts to win the admiration of mankind."

"I, too, will win immortal fame!" said Nap. "I will accompany you in the steep ascent!"

"Impossible! You know not what slight impediments may defeat one in the pursuit of his most cherished object'

Oh, the caprices of the public are infinite and ineradicable! Your form, the mere shape of your foot, the magnitude of your hand, would be sufficient to cause your condemnation."

Nap scanned his bulky chest, his enormous hands and feet, and felt that such remarks were unkind, even if well intended.

"But if I cannot be a celebrated actor, may I not become a successful author?"

"Have you a genius for poetry? a talent for prose? Have you ever written a play which was repeated in representation without the aid of influential friends? Have you published a work whose merits alone caused repeated editions to be issued, without concerting with the critics to have it simultaneously puffed at an enormous expense?"

"No, I never did. I have never written any thing for publication, except a few trifles which were not accepted. But I may have genius and talent nevertheless, which have remained hitherto undiscovered, like the gold of California."

"Have you read every thing within your reach?"

"I have. Shakspeare, Goldsmith, Tom Jones, Humphrey Clinker, and the St. Louis Republican."

"I mean thousands of volumes. Have you travelled over the world and beheld all the wonders of art and nature? Have you mingled with society, from princes down to robbers and cut-throats?"

"No, I have not!"

"Then you cannot be a successful author, unless your genius be of that extraordinary kind which supplies every deficiency of learning and experience by intuition. And, besides all I have enumerated, you should have a personal acquaintance with the literati of the country. You should be familiar with the manners, the habits of thought, the modes of dress, and all the peculiarities and infinite pettinesses of fashionable society in the cities. And then all your acquirements, all your labour may be in vain. Your book may be successful. But success itself has its miseries, and its fruits are not always reaped by the one who achieves it. The cupidity of some reckless publisher may rob you of your reward. He will steal your title, append it to some other work of which he may have defrauded another author, and by placing it in the hands of thousands, enrich himself, and deprive you of a well-earned distinction. Such things have been done in our own land as well as in others, while the indifferent millions have remained in profound ignorance of the injustice that has been perpetrated."

"I would sue the rascal."

"And what would you recover? A mere valueless judgment of the court—a verdict in your favour, but the damage still to be sustained by yourself. No. You were not born to achieve either literary or histrionic fame, or else there would have been some manifestations of your mission before this. You would have grappled with impossibilities, and although ever defeated, you would have still been planning new enterprises, for the very love of such desperate encounters, and not merely for the sake of indulging an idle passion for a poor fading object like myself. I said I would be candid with you. I have been."

"You have, indeed," said Nap.

"And will be. More than fifty young gentlemen like yourself, engaged in respectable and lucrative occupations, for which nature and their education qualified them, have made similar proposals to me, and have been tempted to embark in new and seemingly fascinating pursuits, for my sake, and for the gratification of their own romantic impulses. It is the evil of the age that men are deficient in stability, and are ever engaging in novel enterprises for which they possess not the first requisite. To all such my advice has been—Remain what you are—adhere to the pursuit you have adopted, and continue in it to the end. Success in any business will bring distinction, if that be your object; and success may certainly be won by perseverance. You can have no idea of the number of disappointed and degraded adventurers I have met with in the Eastern cities. Young men of education and family, in consequence of some defect in person or speech, or stricken with incurable embarrassment by a wanton hiss, remain poor, insignificant supernumeraries on the stage, at a salary of some three or four dollars per week—the frequenters of oyster-cellars, unnoticed in society, and avoided by their relatives! When, if they had steadily pursued some branch of business for which they were abundantly qualified, no doubt they might have achieved fortunes, enjoyed respectable positions in the community, and reaped the bliss of being the heads of happy families in domestic life. And so with many literary aspirants. After spending upon printers and paper-merchants the poor sum with which they first set out, and finding no adequate return in the accounts rendered by the publishers, they often become the dependent and pitiable attachés of the press—gleaners of scandal, fabricators of puffs, often of unworthy and pernicious subjects; or compilers for indigent or avaricious booksellers, the sycophants of great men, the parasites of popular but unintellectual singers and dancers, and the slaves of unlearned and unappreciating taskmasters! Would you be one of these?"

"Me? I'd see them all to the devil first!" said Nap, who had weighed every word that fell from the lips of the inspired monitress. "But I would not be a penniless adventurer. I have a fortune."

"How much money have you?"

"By the end of the year, I might raise more than twenty thousand dollars."

"That amount might suffice for a single year. You would be victimized at last. Schemes would be formed by those with whom you would associate, which would, sooner or later, deprive you of your fortune, and then you could never accumulate any more. I have known such instances One may be exceeding smart and successful at home, but extremely ignorant abroad. He may be a novice among those whose lives have been spent in acquiring the skill to win the fortunes of just such victims. Remember Pike and De Coy."

"Egad, neither of them injured me much!" said Nap, triumphantly.

"No; chance favoured you. But fortune is fickle. In a thousand instances of similar indulgences you would lose nine hundred and ninety-nine times. Your success in passing unscathed through their hands was not owing to any skill or wisdom of your own. It was the 'tide' in your 'affairs;' take it, and let it lead you 'on to fortune.' Such is my advice. Are you offended?"

"No, indeed! It is good advice, and I will follow it."

"Do so, and you will not regret it. And remember me kindly"——

"That I will! you are the greatest"——

"No flattery. But I would have your good opinion. You may serve me. One's fame is in the hands of the people. If they approve, partial critics may in vain vent their detraction. If they condemn, no system of puffing can long avail. When my name is mentioned in your presence by some one who may be actuated by splenetic prejudice"——

"I'll knock him down!" said Nap, doubling up his fist.

"No; I do not ask that. But simply say I was once a poor, unfriended American girl, striving to rise in her profession in spite of the combined efforts of the foreigners who monopolized the theatres of her native land. Say she succeeded—that she won both fame and fortune—that she was never a victim of the vices supposed to be inseparable from the profession she adopted. Simply speak of me thus, and I will thank you. Farewell."

"If I don't"—— here Nap's utterance failed him; and before he could recover from the choking sensation which oppressed him, Miss D. had vanished.

On the next day our party arrived at St. Louis. Nap and Jack found there the goods they had bought in Philadelphia, which Messrs. T. & Co. were about to send up the Missouri river. Those belonging to Nap, however, were held under advisement, inasmuch as the lawyer employed by Messrs. Block & Tackle, and who had been up to Venice for the purpose of purchasing Nap's real estate, was endeavouring to procure a writ of attachment with which to seize them. This both Mr. T., and Mr. Wm. M. M., the friend of the Handys, resisted, and had succeeded so far in preventing the seizure. None of them had been informed of the fact that the goods bought of Messrs. B. & T. were lost on board the North Star in Lake Erie. The loss of the vessel was known to all, but the names of the parties interested had not transpired.

"And now, Nap," said Mr. M., after relating what had been done, or rather attempted by the lawyer, "in the progress of this business, if you should require a reference to satisfy the judge, or even an endorser on any document to which you may affix your own signature, remember that I am your friend, and will take pleasure in serving you."

"Thank you! thank you!" exclaimed the grateful Nap; "but I have a document here which will quash the jack-lawyer's proceedings." He placed the despatch in Mr. M.'s hands.

"True! this will put an end to his application. I know Mr. R., and would venture my all upon the truth of his statement. Let me take this to the judge. Give yourself no further uneasiness about the matter; but consider it as finally disposed of."

This conversation took place on board the Western Merchant, a few minutes after she had landed at the wharf. Just above lay the Clendenin, a fine packet, which was to leave for the Missouri river that day. Jack and Kate took passage on the C., and Nap was to join them, provided his goods could be got on board before the time of starting.

Nap lost no time in calling upon Messrs. D. T. & Co. Already Mr. M. had been there with the information that the application for a writ of attachment had been dismissed; and then the goods were sent down to the Clendenin without further delay.

There was also a letter at the counting-room of Messrs. D. T. & Co., awaiting Nap's arrival, and one from Joseph Handy for Jack. Nap's was from the ever-faithful Jim, who crowded a superabundance of anathemas in his page on the "jack-lawyer," who had lately been hinting something about "security." Jim said he had sufficient funds not only to pay the freights, but was likewise enabled (as he did) to enclose a draft to Nap at St. Louis for five hundred dollars, which he had bought of a tobacco factor. "Buy groceries," said Jim, "and let 'em (the lawyers, perhaps) rip!"

Jack's letter, which Nap carried to him, was quite satisfactory also. The purchases his brother wished him to make were despatched in time for the boat. His brother congratulated Nap (supposing the young men would be together) on his marriage with Molly, and stated he had heard a rumour that morning of Polly Hopkins being married to a schoolmaster in the vicinity of Venice! Poor Nap reddened and paled alternately and in quick succession. He knew not what to say or do; and so he strode backward and forward and whistled. It was no sort of a tune. It merely inflated his cheeks and projected his eyes. Jack was too much occupied with his own thoughts to watch him narrowly. Joseph had not heard of his marriage with Kate, and he wondered how he would feel and look when he learned that Nap had met with disappointment, and he with unexpected success. He knew that Joseph would approve the match, for it was a good one in every respect. But he doubted whether his brother would cheerfully sanction his pledge to wind up his business and leave the State.

The young merchants succeeded in getting all their

goods on board before the boat started. Freights were not very abundant, and the captain generously delayed a few hours to accommodate his friends. Western steamboat captains are generally disposed thus to accommodate shippers; and **they have been** known to carry this sort of complaisance a whole day beyond the hour appointed for starting.

In due time, however, **for the** Clendenin was an **excellent** boat, Nap stepped ashore at Venice, and his goods were tumbled out after him. Although it was a fine bright morning, Nap could scarcely recognise his own town—the town he himself had founded. The sounds of hammers were heard in all directions. Trees had been felled, bushes cleared off, and houses were springing up on all the lots he had given away **or** sold. The court-house was almost completed, and had **cost the** county seven thousand dollars! Even Sam Marsh had erected an addition to his inn, and built another stable. More than half a dozen mechanics had **set** up their shops in **the place**; and Mr. Rhino, the Jew merchant, had built a wareroom on the rear of his lot. A spirit of speculation and improvement was rife, and there had been such an increase of population in **a few** months, that Nap declared he felt like a stranger, although standing on his own premises.

"**Let** 'em rip!" said Jim. "They'll make your fortune for **you**. But I wish that double-purple, madder-dyed Jew hadn't come here."

"Never mind him, Jim; we'll soon take the wind **out** of **his** sails," responded Nap, confidently.

"I don't know how we'll do it."

"He bought his goods in St. Louis, and paid **twenty** per cent. more for them than I did for mine."

"That makes no difference."

"It don't?"

"No, not a durned bit. **He** don't mark the cost on his goods. If **we** sell calico for twelve and a half cents a **yard**, he'll sell the same for a dime. That's his rule; his clerk told me so. No matter what his goods cost him, he's going to sell them lower than anybody else."

"He'll make no profit then."

"I don't know. May be he don't intend to pay for his goods."

"We'll see in a few months."

This conversation took place as they walked from the river toward the store, and while the wagoners were engaged in transporting the goods just landed to the ware-room. Nap was anxious to learn something specific in relation to Polly's wedding, but dreaded to inquire; and Jim's thoughts being launched in a different channel, he did not impart any information on the subject.

But as our poor unfortunate lover had regarded the rumour as well-founded, and had meditated on it, and had dreamt about it, as a "fixed fact," to quote Mr. Cushing, it was not impossible for him, considering his susceptibilities, to turn his heart's back on an old lover and look out for a new one. The new one, he thought, should be money; and for several days and nights the only images of women that crossed his imagination, whether sleeping or waking, were the forms of Molly and Polly, going in different directions, and both retiring from his presence, while there arose at his feet a most extraordinary "pile" of dollars.

All the first day after the arrival of the Clendenin, and much of the night, Nap and his faithful Jim were employed in wrenching off the tops of boxes and marking the new goods. During this operation, Nap was continually interrupted by the "welcomes back" and congratulations of his friends. Indeed, friend and foe seemed alike to press forward and seize his hand. A merchant is always popular when opening fresh goods, and a short absence from home is a great reconciler of differences in the West. If Nap had remained at Venice, some of his enemies would never have forgiven him; but now Jack Grove and Brother Keene were the first to shake his hand in token of a perfect reconciliation. Even Moses Rhino, the Jew merchant, and his next-door competitor, pressed forward and greeted him in a very friendly manner.

Nap bore all this as well as he could, although it seemed to him that he was the most popular man, Colonel Benton excepted, that ever crossed the slough. He absolutely strove to repress his vanity, for he had learned a few lessons during his absence. But now he was lord of almost all he surveyed, and it was quite impossible for him to avoid feeling something like a lord. Sometimes, indeed, he felt an inclination to be somewhat of a tyrant. He did not like the flags or signs hung out at the door of the Jew, and he would have compelled him, if it had been in his power, to change them. They were precisely similar to Nap's. If Jim put out a pennant of red flannel, or a streamer of blue calico, to let the travellers know they were passing through a town which had its store, Rhino did the same, only he displayed a few more yards of each. If Jim put on the box beside his door a frying-pan, Rhino had two on his. And this was not all. Rhino had the front of his store modelled and finished in exact imitation of Nap's, so that many persons from distant parts of the country fell unconsciously into the clutches of the Jew. He never undeceived them. On the contrary, when several one day asked, "Is this Mr. Wax's?" he replied, with a slight mental reservation, "Yesh, dish Mr. Wax's blace," and then sold them their goods.

Opposed, or undermined in this manner, there was reason in Jim's enmity, and there was danger that Nap's popularity might wane. Perhaps there is nothing so well calculated to injure a merchant's popularity as for his neighbour to undersell him. One's dearest friends, even one's own kindred, will leave their dollars on his competitors counter, if he gives the most "pork for a shilling." But Nap's equanimity could not be easily disturbed. His goods, his house, his town were all paid for, and he had advices from Mr. R., informing him that there remained in his hands a handsome sum of money, after paying all his debts, subject to his order. If the money should not be drawn out, six per cent. interest would be allowed him, as was the usual custom of the house.

And so, when Nap found himself idle, while his shelves were filled with new goods, and while Rhino's store was crowded with men and women, buying at low prices, he crossed his hands behind his back, as he had seen some capitalist do, and walked with deliberate step, proud eye, and triumphant lip, over his extensive grounds, now staked off in lots, many of which were worth fully $100 apiece, although half of them, from the effects of recent rains, and the level nature of the ground, were covered with water an inch or so in depth.

The slight inundation, and the high winds which prevailed in the spring, had brought upon the premises an immense quantity of snipe, while hundreds of wild ducks were heard quacking at the mouth of the slough, where there was a great depth of water. These arrivals did not fail to attract the notice of Nap. Ever since he had beheld Uncle Billy knocking down the birds on the wing, he had determined to become a good shot himself; and for this purpose he had bought a fine gun of Messrs. S. & S., for his own use, and had procured a book on sporting from Messrs. L., G. & Co., which he studied at intervals on the steamboats.

Thus armed and instructed, Nap strode by the inn toward the river.

"W–wh–where a–are yo–you go–going?" asked Sam Marsh, who stood near the stable, holding his jackass by the ear, and which was struggling to get away.

"To shoot some birds for dinner," said Nap.

"S–sn–sni–snipe?"·

"Yes. snipe. There are flocks of them on the flat lots near the mouth of the slough."

"I k–kn–know th–that. But they'll f–fl–fly b–be–before you can s–se–see 'em. I tri–tried it yes–yesterday with my o–ol–old m–mu–musket, but d–did–didn't get a s–sh–shot at 'em. I cou–couldn't s–se–see 'em in the g–gr–grass, but they s–sa–saw me and i–n–new. They s–sa–sail round and p–po–pounce down again out of r–re–ach. It's no u–us–use to t–tr–try 'em."

"How near did they fly to you?"

"S–so–sometimes I g–go–got in twenty s–st–steps of 'em before they f–fl–flew; but I c–c–cou–couldn't s–se–see any on the g–gr–ground, unless they were r–ru–running, and I knew I cou–could–couldn't k–ki–kill 'em no more that w–way th–than when they were fly–flying."

"Tell Mrs. Marsh I'll bring her birds enough for dinner. I intend to shoot them on the wing. Didn't you hear me practising a while ago?"

"I he–heard you s–sh–sooting. What did you k–ki–kill?"

"Nothing. But I hit the turnip Jim threw up for me. I'm a good shot on the wing—a snap shot, as they say. You'll see, provided they fly within forty yards of me." And Nap proceeded on his way, unheeding the incredulous looks of the innkeeper. He had not gone two hundred yards before the birds began to fly up. He was not quite in readiness to fire. He watched them well, however, and marked where they pitched upon the ground. He then approached in a stooping attitude, his gun cocked, and his fingers on the triggers. Presently a cloud of them arose. Perhaps there were several hundred in the flock. And as they were within the prescribed distance, Nap threw up his gun and fired both barrels. He was stunned by the rebound, and blinded by the smoke, for he had put in extra charges. When the atmosphere became clear, and he had recovered from the shock, he had the satisfaction of beholding several of the birds lying on the grass with their white bellies upward. What had become of the flock he did not know. He did not mark them. So, in accordance with a rule of Western gunners, which he happened to remember, he proceeded to recharge his gun before moving on again. This done, he stepped forward briskly to pick up his birds, resolving in his mind to boast of having killed them on the wing, which was literally true. But scarcely a tithe of his success had yet been revealed to him. As he proceeded, other dead birds met his astonished vision. They lay strewn over a space of ground in the direction he had fired for fifty yards: he picked up no less than twenty-seven, and among them there were six varieties, embracing from the smallest to the largest specimens.*

"That was a great shot!" soliloquized Nap, regarding the birds piled on the ground before him. He then tied them all by the necks with a string, having neglected to procure a game-bag, and drew near the mouth of the slough, where he had a shot at a large flock of ducks. He killed five, but was unable to get them, having neither dog nor boat.

"I'll send Sam for them," said he, charging his gun, and watching the death-struggles of his victims. Then turning his face homeward, he had not gone far before he encountered the flock of snipe again, and once more he ventured to discharge both barrels at them, notwithstanding his shoulder had been so severely punished before. This time he suffered very much, for he had previously been considerably bruised. He had not yet learned to charge his gun with the right proportions of powder and lead. Immediately after he fired, his ears were saluted with the cries of Sam Marsh's jackass, which brayed vociferously, and ran across the lot in the rear of the inn to where Sam was standing. Nap gathered up the snipe as he advanced, and found he had slaughtered almost as many as he did the first time.

"What's the matter with the jack?" he asked, as he drew near to Marsh, who was caressing the animal.

---

* The author killed fifteen, one morning, in Missouri, (but only one at a time,) and there were five different sizes among them.

"Ha–hanged if you haven't s–sh–shot him, N–N–Nap!"

"Shot him! I shot him?"

"Yes, d–durn him, and I'm g–gl–glad of it. I've cow–cowhided him, I've c–cl–clubbed him, and ne–never could '–le–learn him to co–come to me. B–but a few s–sh–shot in his r–ru–rump has done his b–bus–business. He's as g–gentle now as a s–sh–sheep."

"But I shot at the snipe, and killed about twenty. Here they are."

"Some of the s–sh–shot h–hi–hit him on the b–bu–butt. Don't you s–se–see the b–bl–blood?"

"I do so. I'm sorry for it, Sam. I didn't go to do it."

Sam told him not to mind it. They didn't go through his skin. It was as thick as a bull's hide. The shot only frightened him, as he couldn't understand how he had been punished. He couldn't see what hurt him, and that conquered him. Sam said if he had hit him with a bar of iron, he'd a–kicked up at him and run away; and ended by declaring the next time his jack wouldn't come to him, he'd get Nap to pepper him again.

Nap agreed to do it. And as he walked toward the store, he could not help reflecting that there was something like a fatality to dumb brutes connected with his sporting excursions, for he had shot two bitches and a jackass on such occasions. As he entered his own store, he saw several of his old customers coming out of the Jew's establishment, bearing the goods they had just been purchasing.

CHAPTER XXVII.

Nap's troubles with the Jew—Letter from Colonel Benton—Nap follows his advice—Showing how a man may make a fortune—Nap grows ambitious, and engages in a tobacco speculation, contrary to the counsel of his friend.

WEEKS passed by, and it was the same. The Jew did the business. It was in vain that Nap waited for him to exhaust his stock at the ruinously low prices he got for his goods; for no sooner did his shelves become empty than he replenished them. He either visited St. Louis every fortnight, or ordered new supplies from thence. He sold for cash alone, which he remitted every few days. His sales increased continually, and people came from a great distance to avail themselves of the unparalleled bargains he offered, while Nap would have scarcely sold any goods at all, if he had not held out the inducement of granting a long credit to solvent men. These, although convinced they paid, or were to pay him at least twenty-five per cent. more for their goods than the Jew would have demanded, continued to deal with him. But his business was small, while the Jew's cash operations amounted frequently to seven or eight hundred dollars per week.

Perhaps the greatest service that could have been done the Jew, was a remark made by Jim, and which was intended to injure him. It was a hint that he had backers or partners in St. Louis and the East, who smuggled the foreign goods he sold, and clandestinely sent away their domestic fabrics to defraud their creditors. If that were really so, thought the people, then Rhino could afford to sell them at a less price than anybody else, and consequently he was the man for their money. The question of morality they did not feel called upon to discuss. They stood in need of sundry articles of merchandise, and it was natural to procure them on the best possible terms.

But Nap was benefited in a way he could not have anticipated. The operations of Rhino attracted the attention of the country for many miles around, and increased the trade of the town beyond the calculations of every one. Houses were soon tenanted at a rent of two hundred dollars per annum, and lots were in greater demand than ever. Even Tom Hazel settled in Venice, and although he had joined the church subsequently to his spiritual exploit at the camp-meeting, he now opened a grocery or dram-shop in the town, in spite of the reproaches of Mr. Darling, who had likewise induced him to take the pledge of total abstinence. His first customer was the Rev. Jno. Smith, the blacksmith, who declared the brandy was to be swallowed as a medicine, he being subject to attacks of the ague and fever.

About this time Nap received a letter from Colonel Benton. It was a proud moment for him when he broke the seal. Several of his friends were with him, and all evinced a curiosity to know the subject of the communication. The Colonel informed him that the President had just sent his nomination to the Senate, as register of the land-office. He stated, however, that there was no probability of the office being a very lucrative one, and advised Nap not to accept it if it would be likely to withdraw his attention from more important matters. He had, at all events, been complimented by the tender of the office, and he need not be annoyed in hunting up security, and employing a clerk whose salary would amount to as much as the register's compensation, unless he desired it. The office would, at all events, be located at Venice, and Nap must reap the benefit of the increase of business and the rise of real estate.

"I won't have it!" said Nap. "I'll resign."

"No!" said several.

"I'm not qualified," continued Nap. "I've heard my friend E. M. S. describe the duties, and I know I'm not fit for the office. I'll write to the Colonel, and give him liberty to bestow it on some other friend of his, who knows all about the business. I thought I was ruined when I asked the President for it. Offices are only fit for ruined men, who are fit for nothing else. But Colonel Benton's the greatest man in America! Don't you think so, Sam?"

Marsh believed he was, with one or two exceptions; and so did Tom Hazel. The town itself had been spoken into existence by him; he had said, Let there be a town, and there was one; and it was doubtless owing to his exertions and influence that the office was to be located in Venice. The effect of this measure would be a large accession of guests at the inn, and an increase of business at the grocery.

And Nap, with whom the Colonel corresponded, was considered a great man, even if Rhino did sell goods lower than he. Nap could have been elected to the legislature in opposition to Colonel Hopkins. The people would have voted for him without distinction of party, if they did buy their goods of the Jew.

So great was the fame of Nap's speculation in real estate, that many other merchants endeavoured to follow his example. But most of them had put it off too long. They had not acted in accordance with the advice of the prescient statesman; on the contrary, a majority of them had been his bitter opponents. Among these were Joseph and Jack Handy. When they sought to buy lots in their respective towns, which were likewise increasing rapidly in population and trade, as all the towns in the Western States do continually, they found that the prices demanded by the owners were far above the figures they were prepared to offer. It was too late. But a man of penetration can at any time lay the foundation of an infallible fortune in Missouri, Nebraska, or in any of the new States. Let him go to some point where the settlements are few and far between. He need be at no loss in finding a rich soil. There is an abundance of it everywhere in the West. But let him acquire a correct idea of the features of the country, and then pause and consider which would be the most convenient and eligible location for a town, provided the lands were occupied by hardy and thrifty settlers. When that is found, let him make his purchase. He need not expend many hundred dollars. Then let him establish his store, and the population will come. They will come from a great distance, and he will not fail to sell his goods. It is an undeniable fact, that merchants in some of the older and more thickly populated counties of Missouri, do not at this day sell as many goods as the first traders in them did twenty years ago. But where there was one store then, there are twenty now. Yet it is the country merchants who found the towns. The store is the magazine of supplies, and a village is certain to grow up around it, if there has been a judicious selection of the location. When the store is established, next will follow the mechanics, and then the farmers will go thither from twenty, forty, sixty miles' distance. The lands rise in value in the vicinity. Population increases—is ever increasing —and, in a few years, the first investment of perhaps five hundred dollars will realize not less than five thousand, and probably fifty thousand. It has been known to reach a quarter of a million!

It was no wonder that Nap's ideas expanded with the astonishing rise in value of his real estate, and with the gorgeous prospects still before him. Most opportunely, the boat having his enormous purchases on board went to the bottom, thus making a wholesale transaction with the underwriters. If they had been delivered at Venice, Nap's speculation in real estate would hardly have saved him. Even the moderate amount of merchandise he had bought in Philadelphia seemed destined to remain on his hands. But inasmuch as his goods were paid for, the limited amount of his sales could not give him any painful uneasiness. But he was doomed to be much annoyed by Rhino, the Jew. This enterprising competitor, finding his system of "quick sales" answer his purpose, made a flying visit to the East, and bought some seven thousand dollars' worth of goods in two days, for which he paid one-half the money down, and the balance in a few weeks afterwards. Thus he was building up a character for promptitude both in the West and in the East; and he seemed to be contented with the prices he realized. And if he was satisfied to sell goods without a profit, of course the people were pleased to buy them.

Nap submitted to the necessity of the case. He was not compelled to sell at a sacrifice to raise money to pay his debts, or to build up a credit for ulterior purposes; and therefore he determined not to sell at all unless he got a fair profit. But he sold lots. In that business he could have no Jew competitor. The Jews in the West rarely have any real estate, until they have grown rich, when they preach honesty as the best policy.

Nap had a sale of fifty lots at public auction, which brought him four thousand eight hundred and fifty dollars. And he still owned upward of a hundred more. This was better than selling goods in competition with a Jew whose motto was, "Sell as high as possible—but sell, at all events." And Nap strode about over his premises with the important air of a capitalist. His hands were thrust under the skirts of his coat, and his growing corpulency projected in front.

So intent did our hero become upon the scheme of fortune-making, that for a long time no other object seemed to occupy his attention. He had not made any inquiries in regard to the particulars of Polly's marriage. He did not even ask any one the name of her husband, if indeed it was really true that she had a husband; and he had not heard the subject named by any of his acquaintances, which he thought was very strange. But he still dreamt of her, and thought of her sometimes with sadness. Yet he could not blame her, although he thought her conduct somewhat inconsistent with her character. He had certainly loved her, and would have married her before he had returned to Kentucky. And she had once intimated her willingness to wed him, provided he were honourably released from his engagement with Molly. And then to marry another without seeing him, or hearing what he had to say in explanation of his conduct, was an enigma which he could not solve. Such reflections as these often obtruded upon his mind. But he made successful efforts to replace them by others of a more pleasing character.

In imitation of Joseph Handy, Nap would seize his pen or pencil and cover a whole sheet of foolscap with figures. His calculations were on a gigantic scale. Mountains of wealth rose beyond every hill he ascended in the scale of fortune. An acquaintance residing at Venice, the agent of an Eastern capitalist, who had bought all the crops of tobacco in the county, had realized, the preceding year, some sixty thousand dollars profit! Nap was tempted to forestall him this year, and engage the crops for himself. He sat down and wrote to his friend R., in Philadelphia, on the subject, relating what had been accomplished by the agent, and intimating that within a week, by hard riding, he could secure all the tobacco then growing in the county.

His friend wrote him back substantially as follows:—In his opinion it would prove a bad investment. Nap knew nothing about the business. It was best for every one to stick to his trade; and it scarcely ever failed to be bad policy for a merchant to engage in any sort of speculation whatever, out of the legitimate operations of his business. In most instances—such as when they were owing for their goods—they had no right to do so. The money they expended for produce was not their own; it really belonged to their creditors. If they made fortunes on the capital thus used, they alone enjoyed the benefit of them. If they broke at it, their creditors sustained the loss, and that was manifestly unfair. In Nap's case, however, his capital was his own. His goods fortunately were paid for, and no one could share the risk with him. He had an undoubted right to engage in any kind of speculation. But it was the friendly advice of Mr. R. that he would forbear. Every one to his vocation. Nap had no experience in any other business but the selling of goods. The next year might be a disastrous one for the tobacco buyers; and he was inclined to think it would be, since it was to be inferred that inasmuch as the growing crop had not been already engaged, the speculators had reason to suppose there would be a material decline in the market.

Such was the counsel of Nap's prudent and experienced friend. But Nap, notwithstanding he had once bitterly regretted having failed to heed the advice of the same friend, and in exact accordance with the impulsive and precipitable nature of many of the young men in the West, did not await the reception of the counsel he solicited. He had already acted. The letter came too late, although it had been promptly despatched. And every tobacco-planter who had visited Venice, had already engaged his entire crop to Nap at a very high price. But as Nap had stipulated that but little if any of the purchase-money should be paid until some time after the delivery of the tobacco, he did not doubt his ability to ship it to St. Louis and get the proceeds of sales before the day of payment would arrive. It had been done by the agent alluded to. He had really paid for all the tobacco without using any of his principal's capital, and realized the splendid profit mentioned besides. Every hogshead had been sold in St. Louis immediately upon its arrival, for cash, and at a large advance.

CHAPTER XXVIII.

Nap resolves to buy Colonel Hopkins's tobacco—He meets Ben Handy, and learns news of Polly—He approaches the house circumspectly—Is joined by the Colonel, and they ride together to the house—The Colonel goes in pursuit of his bitch—Polly appears before Nap—She shows him a picture—He falls in love again.

THE time had arrived at last when Nap could no longer be kept in ignorance of the fate of Polly. It was necessary for him to see Colonel Hopkins, who was a tobacco-planter. The Colonel, unlike the rest, had not visited Venice, and it seemed to be an important point with the speculator to secure his crop.

Nap mounted his horse and rode over the county, beautifully variegated with grove and prairie, and was charmed with the bright colours and sweet odours of the millions of wild flowers. And now since his face was turned in that direction, his thoughts seemed to be almost entirely concentrated on Polly. He strove desperately to arrange some plan of behaviour in his mind, provided he should meet with her at her father's house. But he could not. Yet he felt convinced that Polly could not justly complain of being ill-used by him. She knew he was engaged to Molly long before he had met with her; and if he had become reconciled to his first love, surely there was no cause of offence in that. Polly herself had rejected or postponed him until he should have another interview with Molly. And if their vows had been renewed, why should Polly get into a passion and marry another man? Why did she write to Molly? Could she suppose that her communication would rupture the match, and that then her revenge would be complete by the bestowal of her hand upon some other suitor? Weak and silly girls might be capable of such conduct, but not Polly. She was emphatically a strong-minded girl, and never resorted to stratagems to wreak her vengeance. But why had she married? Nap could not conjecture why. Yet considering the thing as done and irrevocable, he strove to banish from his breast the painful emotions the contemplation of the matter always engendered. And to do this, he had to dwell upon his tobacco speculation. He calculated, for the thousandth time, the number of hogsheads his purchases would make, and how much the whole would cost him. Then supposing so many dollars would be cleared on each hogshead, it was easy to arrive at the sum total he would gain by the operation. And that there should be no mistake, no disappointment, in all his calculations he put the cost at home at the maximum, and the price in St. Louis at the minimum rates. The result was never less than twenty-five thousand dollars clear gain—provided there was no change in the market—just the salary of the President of the United States.

It was when Nap was plunged in such meditations as these, that he met unexpectedly with an old acquaintance, but a young man. It was Ben Handy. He, too, was in a deep study, calculating the number of thousands he would possess at the age of thirty, and as usual thinking solely of the dollars as an object of paramount importance. Indeed he seemed to have an aversion for the girls. He was supposing a case:—If, for instance, he should have one-half the profits of a concern, the sales of which amounted to some twenty-five thousand dollars per annum, the clear profits to five thousand dollars, how much would be his fortune at the end of a specified time? The solution could not be difficult. His personal expenses were put down at only one hundred and fifty dollars per annum, including board, clothes, and washing. Perhaps he allowed five dollars a year to be cured of the chills, to which he was occasionally subject.

The horses the young men were riding must have been asleep, or else engaged, like their riders, in most absorbing meditations, for their heads came violently in collision, and both were near being prostrated by the shock.

"Hello!" cried Nap.

"Hello, yourself!" responded Ben. "Nap, I was just going to Venice to see you. I wanted to know if you had any Missouri bank-paper that you would exchange for silver and gold. You are not remitting East, and the hard money will answer your purposes at home."

"Yes, I have some—a little," said Nap.

"How much?"

"About six thousand dollars. Would that little do you any good?"

"That little? What do you call much?"

"Wait till next spring, and I'll tell you!" said Nap, significantly.

"I don't know yet, Nap, how much paper I shall want. I'm on my way to Troy, to get all the funds Jack has on hand. I will call and see you on my return, and then we will make the exchange."

"Very well. I'll reserve the paper for you. See here, Ben," he continued, throwing his leg over the pommel of his saddle, and sitting sideways like a female, "can you tell me who Polly Hopkins married when I was in the East?"

"No, I can't. Nobody can. I'm just from there, where I stayed last night and collected some money from her father, which he had been owing for eighteen months. We had a squabble about the interest; but I made him pay it!"

"Then you saw Polly?"

"Of course I did. I couldn't help it."

"Did you see her husband?"

"Husband? I hope not! I believe she wanted to marry me."

"Marry *you?* How could she do that?"

"I don't know. I don't intend to let her try!"

"But Joseph wrote to Jack in St. Louis, that he had heard of her marriage."

"I know it. I heard Jack say so. But don't you know Joseph's way? Before he got done writing it, he thought of something else connected with the store, and then he slapped down the wrong name."

"The wrong name?"

"Yes. It was Mary Townly who was married, and not this Polly."

"And Polly ain't married?"

"Not that I know of. From her conduct to me, I should think she was still in the market."

"Ben, you are a woman-hater."

"Then, they'd better let me alone. I don't disturb them."

"Was the Colonel at home, Ben?"

"He was. But he was preparing to go on a long journey."

"Where to?"

"To St. Joseph. He had just heard of a bitch there resembling the one he lost last year, and he thinks she must be his animal. He swears he'll make some one sweat for having robbed him of his animal."

"Good-bye, Ben!" said Nap. "I must see him before he leaves home."

"Don't turn fool, Nap, and ask him for Polly," was the response.

Both put their horses into a brisk trot, and pursued their different directions.

When Nap arrived upon the old hunting-ground, through a portion of which the public road ran, he diverged in the direction of the bush where he had made such havoc with the grouse, and with the Colonel's pied bitch. There was a thick tuft of rank grass growing over the spot where the animal had fallen, but the skeleton remained, and some of the bleached bones were exposed. Nap descended from his horse, and piled a quantity of brushwood that lay in the vicinity over the remains. He had just completed this work, which caused him to appear, if not to feel, like one engaged in the attempt to conceal the evidences of a crime, when he beheld the Colonel himself approaching. He was riding rapidly over the prairie, followed by two or three negro men, likewise mounted on horses.

Nap hastily sprang upon his steed, and spurred away from the fatal spot; but he had not gone fifty yards before he was hailed by the Colonel and ordered to stop.

"Which way? Which way, Nap?" cried the Colonel.

"To your house, Colonel."

"Stop, then, a few minutes, and we'll go together. I'm going back as soon as I show my men where I want a new field to be enclosed and broken up. Here, boys," he continued, turning to his slaves, "the fence must run by yonder bush; beyond that, the land is wet. Remember it. Nap, what were you after, a while ago, under the bush?"

"Me?" exclaimed Nap, in great confusion, averting his face.

"Yes, you. I saw you dismount there."

"Oh, I've been troubled lately with a slight dysentery."

"And you covered it over with the bush. Well, I suppose the land can't get the cholera, if the people do. Brandy is the best remedy. Come, let us go to the house. Polly will cure you. She reads every thing, even the medical books of her grandfather, who was a famous physician. But why the deuce, Nap, haven't you been to see us since you returned from the cities? Too proud, eh? Oh, you're a rich man now! But Handy says you couldn't get the wife you courted. Ha! ha! ha! He says it was some of Polly's doings. I shouldn't wonder. She's a genius. If she was a man, she'd be another Missouri artist, like Bingham. He's to paint your town on election day. He'll have you in it, and me too, with my pot-belly. Perhaps Polly may be there. Daniel Thornton, Squire Nix, Adam Steele, Brother Keene, Mr. Darling, Sam Marsh, Jack Grove, Jackson Farnes, Tom Hazel, Jno. Smith, and my cider-man, Black Bob, will all be in it.

I've seen the first sketch of it, and it'll be a famous picture."

"Will he have the tavern and my store in it?"

"Oh yes, and it'll be better than an advertisement."

"But he mustn't paint the confounded Jew's store!"

"Why not? Oh, he'll put down every thing as it is, I'll warrant you. It'll be as natural as life itself. He has the genius to do it. But here we are. Jump down. Dick, take our horses, and rub them down. Put the saddle on mine in about an hour. I'm going to St. Joe after my bitch, and I'll cut the man's throat who deprived me of her!"

They entered the house. Nap's heart palpitated violently as he saw Polly's skirt vanishing from the room. The old lady, however, came forward and gave him a friendly greeting.

"Where's Polly?" demanded the Colonel.

"She just went out," said Mrs. Hopkins.

"Tell her to come here and make Nap some brandy medicine. He's got the dys"——

"Never mind, Colonel!" said Nap, quickly. "I feel quite well, now."

"Very well, then. But if you don't get sick, I doubt if you can see Polly. She don't like rich folks much. She's no worshipper of wealth, I assure you. So if you came to see her, I'd advise you to get sick."

"I came to see you, Colonel."

"Very well. I'm at your service."

"I want to buy your tobacco."

"I'm your man."

The bargain was soon struck. Nap gave him, or rather agreed to give him, fifty cents per hundred pounds more than he was to pay some of his neighbours. But this was to be kept a profound secret.

"And now, Colonel," said Nap, when his host was preparing to leave him, almost resolved to confess that he had killed his bitch accidentally, "you are not going all the way to St. Joe just to look for that old slut of yours!"

"I am! I'm determined to find out who took her away. I don't care so much for the bitch; but the rascal who stole her shall suffer for it!"

"But suppose no one stole her? Suppose she took sick and died."

"If she had, we'd have found her bones."

"But what if some one of your neighbours and friends had killed her accidentally?"

"If he had told me of it at the time, I should not have thought any more about it. But to conceal it this long, would make it another matter!"

"True! I hope you'll find her."

"I will, if she's upon the top of the earth!" Saying this, the Colonel mounted his horse and departed in quest of the lost animal. His family did not look for his return before the expiration of a week or ten days.

For more than an hour Nap sat conversing with Mrs. H., who was a highly intelligent lady, and famous for her knowledge of books, and particularly of the romances of Scott, which formed her principal source of happiness.

Just before dinner was announced, and when Nap was quite alone, Polly came in, tastefully dressed, and with a pleasant smile on her lip.

"Nap," said she, advancing to where he was, and giving him her hand, "didn't you want to see me?"

"Yes—certainly," he stammered, struck with her fine appearance, her tall, majestic stature, her perfect proportions, and her improved beauty.

"Then why didn't you say so?"

"Oh, I thought you would come in as you used to do."

"You've changed since I saw you last. And why should not I change also?"

"How have I changed?"

"You've become rich. I can't be familiar with rich men. They might say I was fortune-hunting; and that I could not bear. I'm too proud to play for money. I want a man. Why have you not been here before? I suppose you looked for me to go to Venice. You might have looked in vain! I never would have gone there until you got poor again. It was your duty to call on me."

"I heard you were married."

"So Jack Handy told me."

"And you never told me it was a mistake."

"Why should I? Were you not engaged to marry Molly Brook on your way back to Missouri? Did you inform me that the marriage was not consummated? I heard of your disappointment, however."

"Yes, you caused it!"

"Did I state any thing that was not true? Do you condemn me for writing that letter?"

"No, Polly. You told the truth. And now, since I see you again, and unmarried, I can't say I regret that Molly would not have me."

"Come, Nap, don't let us have a scene here before dinner. I've made up my mind what to do since you have been in the house. After dinner we will stroll down to the bank of the silver stream, and talk over some interesting matters. Walls have ears, and eyes too. The little negroes are peeping and listening now. Prepare yourself to hear my speeches. They will 'harrow up your soul,' as the poet says. I have a picture to show you, that will"——

"Birghams?"

"No. That is to be a great one, though. Mine will be for you alone. His is for the admiration of thousands, living and unborn. Come! Dinner is ready."

The strange girl then led our obedient hero to the table in the next room, and carved for him, while her mother heaped his plate with vegetables. He ate heartily, as usual, for he had an infallible appetite. But his eyes were constantly wandering toward Polly, whom he thought to be more beautiful that day than he had ever beheld her before. Between eating and gazing, he did not have an opportunity to say much, but he thought with great intensity. He was continually surmising what it was Polly intended to do, and what he might do under certain circumstances. He had recently resolved within his own mind that he would never again be carried away by his enthusiastic admiration, and that he would make no more precipitate offers of marriage; but wait until he had realized a large fortune, before entering finally into the inexorable bands of wedlock. And now, while masticating the rich food spread before him, and occasionally showing his faultless teeth, the remembrance of this resolution recurred to him, and several times while sitting at the table he determined, if possible, to carry it out.

After the repast was over, Polly boldly led the way toward the shining stream. The larks were singing on the green lawn, and wild flowers of all the varieties incident to the soil, climate, and season perfumed the air.

"Let us go to the hawthorn, Nap," said she. "The same that sheltered us once when solemn vows were uttered. I have converted it into an arbour, and often spend an hour there in utter solitude. It is my little world, where none intrude."

When she ceased speaking they stood before it. She had indeed tended it well. The vines had been symmetrically arranged, so as to form a perfect shade; and within was a rustic bench formed of willow boughs.

"Sit down, Nap," said she. He obeyed, and she sat down beside him. Polly wore a plain sun-bonnet, which she had thrown upon her head when leaving the house, and which now prevented Nap from seeing her features. Sitting close beside him, with her face slightly averted, it was impossible for him to see whether she was smiling or grave. Not knowing what to say, he said nothing, but awaited her developments almost with fear and trembling, and vainly conjecturing what she would do next.

"Now, Nap," she continued after a pause, "are you ready to see my picture?"

"Oh yes, I'll take a look at it, if you have no objection."

"Then glance your eye through this little window of our pavilion," said she, drawing his attention to an opening on her right. "You see yonder grove, and the undulating fields between. The sun is pouring his golden rays upon them. How calm and beautiful! Nearer, you see the snowy sheep, and the innocent lambs skipping about in playfulness. How fresh and purely green the meadow! All is bathed in golden sunlight, and no rude winds are howling past. How peaceful! You can just hear the gurgling ripples as the sparkling waters go dancing over their pebbled bed. See! A bass, when I was speaking of the beautiful stream, leaped above the surface, and his scales glittered dazzlingly in the sunlight. He, too, is jocund and happy. Hear the flutelike melody of the bluebirds! Poised upon their noiseless wings, they sing their young to sleep. Inhale the delicious perfume of the millions of blossoms around us; hear the concert of sweet sounds from hundreds of richly-plumaged birds; see the lovely landscape spreading out in harmony wherever the eye is turned; and then say if it be not a picture to make one's heart palpitate with happiness and love!"

"It is indeed, Polly. Why, you are a poetess! I am made very happy in beholding such a picture, and my heart is full of love. I did think I would hold my heart in check hereafter, and fix it upon my business speculations; but since I have seen you again, and heard your voice, and beheld your charming picture, I feel my resolution melting away, and know not what is to become of me. I'm afraid you wouldn't have me, Polly, if I were to propose again. I'm afraid"——

"Don't be afraid; I won't hurt you, Nap," she said quickly, and exhibiting just enough of her chin and nether lip for our hero to see that she was smiling.

"Once for all, then, Polly!" said he, spasmodically, and venturing to take her hand in his, "let us"——

"Don't be precipitate, Nap. You have not seen the whole

of my picture yet. Come with me along the bank of the stream." Still permitting him to hold her hand, they strolled beneath the row of hawthorns and willows. "How sweet the blossoms! and how purely white!" said she, plucking a small twig from a tree.

"White blossoms are emblems of weddings, are they not?" said Nap.

"Of innocence," said Polly, "and weddings are sometimes cruel and sinful. Hearts are sacrificed for gold. Nap, you must cease to grow rich. It will do you no good. It will make you a mere target for swindlers, but never happy, if my books are worthy of belief. If you grow rich, you will not be content to remain here. You will seek a denser and more refined society. And then, if it be in the city, you will meet with men far richer than yourself, and you will seem poor in comparison with them. That will make you unhappy."

"But I would have you with me to share my fortune and give me good advice."

"Never! I would not dwell a month in what is termed purely fashionable society for all the benefits a city life could confer. My mother, when young, spent just a month in one of the great cities. She says the fashions changed so fast she could not keep up with them. She had sent for the latest styles and patterns a month before she left home. But when she arrived in the city, every thing she had was out of date, and she was laughed at and ridiculed. And so with my father when he visited her there. He wore his shirt-collar up, when everybody else had turned them down ten days before. He wore square-toed boots a week after round toes had been adopted. He was termed a simple booby, and my mother a gawky country-girl. Thus it would be with you and I. You never could fall into the habits of thought and expression contracted by others born and bred in the city; nor could I ever act and dress to please the proud madams and impertinent misses. We would be insulted daily in the street, and thus be rendered very miserable. Strangers would stare at us if our dress, our gait, our limbs and complexions differed from the prescribed fashion; and our acquaintances even, I am told, would avoid a recognition of us in the public streets. What then should induce a country merchant, grown rich, and his country wife, if he has one, to push themselves into fashionable society?"

"I won't go into it!" exclaimed Nap. "I saw them looking at my big feet and hands, and whispering to one another, when I was in the city. I thought they were admiring my boots and praising my rings. But I soon found out that the gentlemen's servants wore quite as highly polished boots as mine; that the yellow barbers displayed more jewelry, and the apprentices finer clothes. The rascals who whispered must have been making fun of me. And as for my mustache and goatee, whenever I exhibited them on the balcony in front of the hotel, I was sure to see some rascal, after glancing at me, wrinkle up his nose as if he had smelt something very unpleasant."

"No, Nap, the city is not the place for happiness, unless one has been born and raised in it; and then I am told such an one is ever sighing for the country. But here, on the banks of this dancing stream, what *could* make one unhappy? Behold the golden rays of the setting sun streaming slantingly under the hawthorns. The tulips beside the silent path seem to spread their petals in quivering ecstasy, and the violets lift their fresh blossoms in meek adoration. The lark is trilling his last note high up in the blue vault. The flocks are slowly winding homeward, and the fowls are gathering under the trees nearest the house, where they may rest in security. In such a place as this, why could you not be happy all your days?"

"Oh, I could be, if you would only be happy with me. I know I could be contented to spend my life with you here!" Somehow or other, for he was unconscious of what he was doing at the time, Nap's arm had found its way around the waist of Polly; and it remained there as if she too was unaware of it, while they strode backward and forward, and spoke of rural felicity.

"But then would not Molly be unhappy? No one can be perfectly happy while causing unhappiness in others. Are you not still engaged to her?"

"I don't know that I am! She put me off another year; but I did not promise ever to be on again. I did not agree to the arrangement."

"But you could not help yourself," said Polly, laughing.

"Perhaps I can, though! There are other girls besides Molly"——

"If you abandon her, what will her father do? Jack has told me that he is anxious for the match."

"And that's true! I have received three letters from him already"——

"And how many from Molly?"

"Not one. But her father threatens to sue me for $20,000 damages, if I don't marry his daughter."

"And does that frighten you?"

"No. I wrote to Colonel Benton on the subject. He said in reply that Brook was a fool, and that if I had been ready and willing to marry Molly as I returned through Kentucky, and she declined it, I might, if inclined, consider myself absolved from any obligation to wed her at a future day."

"Colonel Benton is right! And Nap, I think your Molly carries her Kentucky pride a little too high. Perhaps she wishes you to acquire a little more polish. I don't think she is waiting, like her father, for greater riches."

"No; it is not wealth that sways her. But she dresses as nearly like the Eastern ladies as possible, and now sees a great many young lawyers and doctors, as her father confesses. They know French and Latin, and I don't. As Jim says, I'll 'let her rip!' Just say the word, Polly, and we'll"——here his utterance failed, but he pressed the laughing and unresisting girl more closely to his side.

"Nap!" said she, while he was all attention, "do you still snore?"

"Snore? I believe so! Don't laugh at me, Polly: but answer me!" said he, almost delirious with the thoughts and passions which agitated his mind and heart—the latter thumping audibly.

"Answer what question, Nap?"

"Will you have me, now!"

"Have you—and now? Nap, you have *me!* What do you mean by squeezing me so? Let me go! You never did that before. Let me go, I say!" she continued, making unavailing struggles.

"I can't! Upon my word I can't. Forgive me, Polly— but I can't, upon my word. My arm has grown there. Say yes, and let me have just one kiss"——

"Ha! ha! ha! And then I suppose your lips would grow there, too! But enough. Nap, you have held me long enough. Release me!" Her changed tone acted like magic. She was instantly obeyed. "And now, Nap, you shall have my answer. I will be yours when I can have all your affection. Don't interrupt me. Jack Handy told me you wrote to an experienced friend in the East for advice in regard to your huge tobacco speculation, and that you embarked in the ruinous business before receiving his reply. I know what his advice was. If you had awaited its arrival, and followed it, I would have married you this summer. But now your mind is to be absorbed with your gigantic speculation, and you could not be happy, or make me happy, with your thoughts so occupied. You will lose a great deal; I hope you may not be ruined. There are accounts of a decline of twenty-five per cent. But when it is over, you may come to me for consolation. And if you will then promise to relinquish the idea of ever making a great figure in the world, for which nature never designed you, and will promise to live with me all the days of your life in humble contentment"——

"But there must be something to live on!" said Nap.

"Oh yes; you may sell goods in a quiet way, or buy this farm, which is to be sold, and build a mill and found another town on it, if you lose Venice"——

"I will! But my tobacco speculation"——

He was interrupted by the excited voice of one of the Colonel's negro men who came running in from the new field, bearing in his arms the bleached bones of the bitch Nap had accidentally killed, and covered under the wild-cherry tree.

"Miss Polly! Miss Polly!" said Agrippa, "here's Juno! Here's her bones! I found 'em out dar under de wild-cherry tree. Som 'tarnel rascal shot her. Here's whar de bullets broke her ribs!"

"How do you know these are Juno's bones?" asked Polly.

"Dar's de bone ob her hind leg. Don't you see whar 'twas mended? You 'member 'twas broke once, whar de ole cow kicked her?"

"Oh misery! What shall I"—— exclaimed Nap, as the negro passed on with the bones.

"What's the matter, Nap?" asked Polly.

Nap made a full confession. And Polly seemed pleased that he had confided his secret to her. She told him to give himself no more uneasiness about the slaughtered animal. She would see Agrippa, and put a speech in his mouth that would satisfy her father and securely guard her lover against danger. And she told Nap, moreover, that if he would confide all his difficulties to her, of whatever nature, she would remove them also, or exert her wits to the utmost to do so. He promised to be guided by her in every thing, and was rewarded, as they drew near the house in the dusk of the evening, with the kiss he had petitioned for.

CHAPTER XXIX.

A mysterious rush of business—Jim goes on a secret mission to the planters—The rush continues—Mr. Brook writes again to Nap—The Jew grows melancholy, then desperate—Then exits—Nap has a fit of jealousy—He is found in the woods by Mr. Snorter—Another letter from Colonel Benton, who advises Nap to marry—Nap flirts with Sally Weighton—An oyster sermon—Polly surprises Nap—Mr. H. S. gets Nap out of his difficulties.

LATE as it was when Nap returned from his Elysian walk under the hawthorns, he mounted his horse and galloped off toward Venice, for the purpose of directing his faithful Jim to buy no more tobacco. What a change had been wrought in his ideas in a single day! He bestrode his horse in the morning with the conviction that he was about to realize a fortune from a single speculation; and he dismounted in the evening filled with apprehensions that he was doomed to lose the most, if not all, of his property! But then a vision of happiness had been revealed to him, which he thought would compensate him, if he could possess it, for all his losses, however extensive they might be.

A great change had likewise suddenly taken place in the business transactions at Venice, and Nap's goods had at last begun to move off. It appeared that a rumour had been secretly circulated in the country of a great pressure in the money-market having caused several extensive speculators in tobacco and pork to fail; and those commodities had in consequence suddenly fallen in price. So great was the decline, that the agents in Missouri were instructed to desist from buying any more tobacco from the planters unless purchases could be effected at a figure some twenty-five per cent. under the price Nap had been giving.

Hence it was conjectured that Nap would break down, and not be able to comply with his contracts. And this caused the very natural alarm of the planters who were in the secret, and hence the sudden run upon Nap's store. He was under no obligations to pay them before the expiration of the stipulated time; but he could not refuse to sell them any goods they might want. And now they crowded in upon him and ran up accounts with surprising liberality.

Jim met Nap with a broad grin of pleasure on his face. He had triumphed that day over the Jew, who had recently received a large accession to his stock, and now looked the impersonation of victory. The Jew, who stood in his door, and could not conjecture why it was that such an unexpected improvement should have taken place in his Christian rival's business, was the picture of chagrin and mortification. He was literally chap-fallen. The Jews generally show their feelings in their faces; and Jim had long been accustomed to behold Rhino's looks of exultation.

"Jim," said Nap, "we must buy"——

"Let 'em rip!" said Jim, waving his right arm triumphantly. "The richest men in the county have been in to-day, and I sold 'em a —— of a sight of goods! Rhino didn't sell 'em any thing!"

"That was all very well, Jim. But we must buy"——

"We can buy all the tobacco in the county. Mr. B. hasn't got a hogshead yet. And I believe we can sell all the goods hereafter. Let 'em rip!"

"I say, Jim, we must buy no more tobacco!"

"What?"

"We must buy no more tobacco. The price has gone down in Europe, and I shall lose like the mischief on that I have bought. I want you to get me off from as many engagements as possible. Agree to pay a moderate forfeit to each man that will give up his contract."

"I'll ride out to the bluffs to-morrow! I'll get you

off with some of 'em. Just let me manage it, and no questions."

"You couldn't do me a greater service, Jim. To say the truth, Jim, if they all hold me to the price I have agreed to pay, I'm afraid they'll swamp me!"

"I'll go to-night! Yonder comes Sam Marsh, and I'll hire his horse." He did so, and was soon galloping out in the prairie—such was his faithful devotion to Nap, whom he believed to be the greatest man in the State, or born to the greatest luck.

It was fortunate that Nap asked Jim no questions, for he could hardly have sanctioned the plan his lieutenant in business had conceived for getting him released from his contracts. Jim rode all night, and saw about a dozen of the largest planters who had not heard the news. He made plausible explanations to them why he could not remain till morning. It was necessary for him to reach some place a few miles distant without further delay, after giving his poor horse some corn, and taking a bite of something himself. But at every house he was asked the news. There was nothing to tell, he intimated, of public interest, except a prospect of an extraordinary rise in the price of tobacco. In the Eastern market, he said, it was quoted at twenty cents. He did not say it was a small lot of Jones's, from the celebrated James River plantation. This hint sufficed at several places. They offered him handsome fees to get them released from their contracts with Nap. Jim was generous, and would have no bonus. He said the planters were the best customers of the merchant, and it would not be fair for them to deliver their tobacco at a price below its value. And in virtue of his authority, being Nap's duly accredited agent, he signed releases. By such means, in less than forty-eight hours, contracts amounting altogether to some fifty thousand dollars' worth of "the weed" had been cancelled. And that service, together with the run of custom at the store, and the enormous profits charged, saved Nap from irretrievable ruin, as was quite apparent a few months afterward.

When Jim returned to Venice, he found Nap overwhelmed with business. The store was crammed with customers, while the Jew stood before his own door, "looking daggers" at each countryman or countrywoman who came forth from his rival's establishment burdened with merchandise. Each one of the planters who had been informed of the change in the tobacco market, and the probability of Nap's failure, had received the communication confidentially and under injunctions of inviolable secrecy. And as it was to their interest to keep the secret, it was done most faithfully. Hence when near neighbours met at the store on the same mission, and actuated by the same motive, each one supposed that he alone was doing the smartest action. Nap, of course, was ignorant of the motive which impelled them. Even their wives and daughters, who could not be intrusted with such a secret on any account whatever, exulted in the supposed newborn generosity on the part of their lords and parents. And as for the Jew, he seemed to be upon the eve of bursting with undissembled rage, while Jim, although he sympathized with Nap, was, otherwise, the happiest man in existence.

The run of custom which Nap's store had so unaccountably obtained, continued until his stock was completely broken. In the course of a few months, not one-half the articles asked for could be supplied; and Nap, now acting with the advice of Polly, declined ordering a new supply until the result of his tobacco speculation should be known. The idea of his going East for more goods until another matter had been consummated, was not at all to be thought of. And he was the more strengthened in this opinion, when the reverend Mr. Smith, the blacksmith of the town, and now the postmaster, placed in his hands a most indignant letter from Mr. Brook. Mr. B. abused him roundly for engaging in the tobacco speculation, which, he said, from the information he had received, would certainly leave him a beggar. He concluded by a most positive assertion that Molly should never be his wife. No daughter of his should ever marry any such a fool. Nap laughed heartily at this epistle; and Polly congratulated him on the termination of his fears of being sued for a breach of marriage contract.

Rhino, the Jew, became melancholy. He declared that the people would rather pay Nap a dollar than himself fifty cents for the same article. Never before had he been so completely frustrated in his calculations, and he had sold goods at more than one point in Missouri. He had a young clerk of his tribe, just imported from Germany, who was, or pretended to be, very ignorant of the English language; and when complaining to Marsh that the "beeble" wouldn't buy his "goots" any more, Sam told him it was owing to his clerk, who could not understand what was called for, or make himself understood.

"He's learnt de names of de money, and can tell dem de brice," said Rhino. But Rhino declared that when his man asked "von voman" a dollar for a shawl, she went to Nap's and paid two dollars for one precisely similar to it.

But Rhino had not played all his cards. Late one night, Nap and Jim were awakened by a tremendous kicking and thumping at the door, which was succeeded by a howling such as they had never before heard.

"See what that is, Jim," said Nap, without rising from his pallet of blankets on the counter. Jim drew a locofoco match from his pocket, where he always kept them, being an inveterate smoker, and lighted a candle. He then proceeded rather cautiously to open the door. No one was there. But sitting on the step next door, he beheld the clerk of Rhino, sobbing and howling in a most unaccountable manner. Jim asked what was the matter several times before he recollected that the boy could speak but few words in English. He thought his conduct most extraordinary, and approached him to see, if possible, wha had occurred. The cause was soon evident; a red glare in the rear of the store, and a cloud of suffocating smoke, saluted his eyes and nostrils upon pushing open the door.

"You double-purple rascal, what did you do that for?" cried Jim, tumbling the boy over. "What're you sitting out here for, when the store's on fire? Nap! Nap! Nap!" cried he, running to the other door.

"What's the matter, Jim?" cried Nap, springing up.

"Fire! fire! fire!" was Jim's only response. He ran over to Sam Marsh's tavern and pulled away at the bell, which had been hung before the door that day. This unusual sound at such an hour, soon aroused all the inhabitants of the town. Jim then ran back, losing one of his boots in a mudhole in the middle of the street.

"Run into *our* store, you infernal negroes, and carry out the goods!" This order was given to several colored men and women who emerged from a neighbouring kitchen, and being an order, it was promptly obeyed. But Nap was a host himself. He was a tower of strength. Barrels, boxes, and bales fled before him into the street. When the room was filled with the neighbours, he desisted from that operation, and confined himself to heaping loads upon the others. In less than ten minutes, two-thirds of his stock, reduced as it was, had been carried out, and piled in the middle of the street.

On the other hand, Rhino, who was soon upon the ground, never attempted to save any thing. He was fully insured. But, fortunately, Brother Keene, who had leased him the house, and had no insurance, ran in and smothered the fire with blankets. His hands were dreadfully burned, but his property was saved. And so was Nap's, which was separated from it only by a slight wooden partition.

Then began the process of carrying Nap's goods back again, and it required a much longer time to do it than it had taken to run them out. When this job was over, both Nap and Jim went into the Jew's store to see how the fire had occurred. It had originated in a corner remote from the stove, and equally as distant from the couch upon which the clerk slept. He could give no explanation. He merely declared that he had lain down and gone to sleep as usual, and at the customary hour.

"There's a double-purple madder-dyed rascal somewhere!" said Jim, after surveying the scene some time in silence.

The next day, Rhino had the damage assessed, which amounted to some two thousand dollars. Not one-fourth of that amount of goods had been burned; but the whole stock, and it was a pretty large one, had been considerably smoked. The company ultimately paid the damage.

And now began a resuscitation of business with the Jew. His damaged goods attracted customers, and he had a fine run of trade, selling, as he had always done, at any price he could get. Nap's stock grew more and more imperfect; and hence his sales diminished as those of the Jew increased. But Nap had enjoyed the satisfaction, if such a feeling were justifiable, of learning from Rhino's invoices, which had been produced after the fire, that his competitor was in the habit of paying from fifteen to twenty per cent. more than he had done for the most common staples. Hence he felt very sure that Rhino would not be likely to make a fortune from his profits at the prices he asked for his goods. But he was mistaken.

After "running off" his damaged goods, and reducing his stock as much as possible, during the month succeeding the fire, Rhino closed his door and made an assignment, as he said, for the benefit of his creditors. The assets amounted to about twelve thousand dollars, and the liabilities to thirty thousand. He had no money—for his creditors. A few days after, he was gone.

But two competitors came in his place; they were Christians, however, and Jim was satisfied, while Nap consoled himself with the reflection that the more business there was done in the place, and the greater the number of inhabitants, the more valuable would become his unimproved lots.

One of the new merchants, Mr. Jameson, was a bachelor, and a very polite one. During the two or three months succeeding his removal to Venice, he frequently rode out into the country, "electioneering," as he termed it; but his landlord, Sam Marsh, said it was to see the girls. Nap learned he had been at Colonel Hopkins's, and did not seem to relish his visits there. But one day, when Polly came to town in company with her mother, and rode by his store without stopping, and dismounted at Mr. Jameson's door, assisted by Mr. J. himself, Nap was seized with a fit of jealousy. It was the second time in his life that he had been afflicted with the passion, and it agitated his frame tremendously. Jim was standing beside him when the ladies trotted by, and could not avoid observing his change of countenance. Jim sympathized with him in every thing, and words were unnecessary, on the present occasion, to be informed of the condition of his principal's feelings.

"Let her rip!" said Jim, turning indignantly away, and retreating to the extremity of the room, where his cot still remained spread open as he had left it in the morning. But few customers came now to cull the remnants that remained, and country merchants are apt to grow negligent when they have but few visitors.

Nap had a habit, when greatly vexed, of prostrating himself violently with his face downward. This time he rushed back to where Jim was standing, and threw himself on the cot. It gave way under his weight, and came down with a mighty crash.

"Let it rip!" cried Jim. Nap neither spoke nor groaned. He remained perfectly silent and motionless. "What's the matter, Nap?" asked Jim, seeing he did not move. "Are you hurt?"

"Yes," was the laconic reply.

"Where?"

"Here!" said Nap, rolling over on his back, and placing his hand on his breast. Jim got a bottle of opodeldoc and drew the cork.

"Let me see, Nap," said he, unbuttoning the vest and shirt-bosom of his employer. "Let me rub some of this on it. If it's a cut from a splinter, or a bruise, it'll cure it. I don't see any wound. It must be bruised." He rubbed a quantity of the opodeldoc on the place supposed to be injured, before Nap could arrest his hand.

"The cot has not hurt me, Jim; but Polly has. It's my heart, Jim! I didn't think she was that sort of a girl! And I've been to see her every Sunday for the last six months!"

"Oh, she's just trying you. She wants to know if you can be jealous, that's all. She asked me, one day, if you ever got jealous. And when I said no, she said nobody could be much in love without being a little touched that way sometimes."

"But even if that's it, it is cruel in her!"

"May be she's going to call as she goes back."

"She ought to have stopped here first. Sam Marsh, and everybody else, will joke me at the dinner-table. They'll say Jameson has 'cut me out.' She oughtn't to have encouraged the fellow any at the start. He's forty years old"——

"And wears a wig!" said Jim, quickly.

"He does?"

"I'll swear to it! His head's as bald as an egg. Polly don't know that."

"I'll tell her! If I can't get a chance to tell her, Jim, you must do it."

Jim promised to do so, and to do it that day. Nap breathed a little easier, but he could not altogether control his violent palpitations. Sometimes he panted like a porpoise, and ever and anon ran to the door and peeped along the street toward Mr. J.'s store.

"There they are!" said he, in a whistling whisper.

"Are they coming here, Nap?" asked Jim, pushing the wreck of his cot under the counter.

"No! The d——l take his bald head! Jim, he's helping them on their horses. They won't come to see us. She shan't see me. Remember the bald head, Jim!" Having uttered this injunction, Nap rushed out, and turning to the right, dashed spasmodically along the road until he came to the giant trees beyond the limits of the town. Here he paused and got behind a large oak, from whence he could see if Jim hailed the party when they rode past the store. Soon he stooped convulsively, with his hands on his knees, his eyes enlarged, and his whole face denoting the interest he felt in what was going on. He saw them halt, and Jim step out toward them; but he strove in vain to hear what was said and the manner of it. Presently Polly and her mother rode on again. Nap retreated hastily a few paces farther from the road, to another large tree. He heard the hoofs of the horses playing on the dry road, there having been no rain for nearly two months. Then hearty laughter, ringing from the fair throat of his affianced charmer, struck upon his ears. It rang through the woods like the tones of a bell on a calm frosty morning. Oh! what could she be laughing about! mentally asked poor Nap, his knees shaking together as violently as they had ever done during a fit of the ague. When they drew near, he saw Polly lean forward, and almost prostrate herself on the neck of her horse, from the exhausting effects of her cachinnatory exercises. Her mother, too, was red in the face from recent merriment. Then they whipped forward rapidly and were soon out of sight and hearing.

Nap flung himself down on his face, and kicked up his heels in agony. He doubled up his fists and thrust them out frantically on each side of his head. He was found in that condition by the Rev. Mr. Snorter, the great gun of the camp-meetings, who was to preach that night in the court-house. His horse had been frightened by the motion of Nap's feet, which attracted his eyes in that direction.

As soon as he saw who it was he dismounted. Not doubting that Nap was under spiritual influence, the well-meaning parson prostrated himself on his knees beside the young man. "O good Lord," said he, "give him power to struggle manfully! Forgive his many sins, and grant him salva"——

Nap sprang up on his haunches and interrupted him. He stared at the reverend gentleman wildly, as he would have done at some beast of prey, until he comprehended his meaning.

"My dear young brother," said Snorter, "I thought you were wrastling with the Sperit; and so I felt bound to help you. I never forget any of our convarts. You came once within our holy altar—it was at the camp-meeting in —————— county."

"I haven't much faith in camp-meetings," said Nap, sullenly, and by no means pleased with the reminiscence.

"You haven't? May the good Lord have marcy on your soul! What was the matter with you?"

"Oh, I was afraid of having a chill, and drank too much brandy," said Nap, rising to his feet, and retracing his steps toward his store, while the parson walked beside him, exhorting him all the way to turn from his wickedness.

"Did you tell her, Jim?" asked Nap, springing into the store, and unceremoniously abandoning Snorter to his fate.

"Durned if I didn't!" said Jim.

"And what did she say?"

'She almost split her face open laughing."

"Did she say nothing at all?"

"She couldn't for a long time. But when she got her speech back, she asked for you."

"What did you say?"

"I said you had left town just a few minutes before."

"What did she say to that?"

"She said she wanted to see you; and that she has some news from Kentucky."

"I know what that is. Molly's married to Augustus Smart. And now I've got only one string to my bow. That's the reason she went to J.'s store first. Did she say any thing else?"

"Yes; just as she rode off, she said, Jim, watch Nap; don't let him hang himself in the woods with a grape-vine. Then she laughed like a wildcat all along the road as far as I could hear her."

Nap's incubus, the green-eyed monster, was removed for the time being by the entrance of the Rev. John Smith, blacksmith and postmaster. He bore a letter, the superscription of which was in the well-known hand of Colonel Benton. It was in reply to a letter written him by Nap, at the solicitation of Polly. Polly, it appears, had really become impatient for the expiration of the time allotted Nap to put his house in order for matrimony, notwithstanding her seeming flirtation with Mr. J.; and she had advised him to compromise with the tobacco-planters who had not yet released him from his contracts. She then requested him to write to Colonel Benton on the subject, and get his opinion as to the best plan of his extricating himself from his dilemma.

The letter began with a highly wrought eulogy of Polly Hopkins, for Nap had told him the whole tale; and it ended by advising him to settle with the planters without delay, and on the best terms they would grant—as any terms they might grant would be better than going to law. The expenses of lawsuits alone would ruin him. If he employed a lawyer at all, let it be for the purpose of getting him out of the scrape, and at all hazards to keep out of the courts. And as soon as his difficulties were over, the Colonel advised him to marry Polly Hopkins without delay, and always to take her advice before embarking in new speculations.

"Jim!" said Nap—Mr. Smith, the blacksmith, postmaster, and preacher having withdrawn—"how can I marry her, if she goes to bucking up to this baldheaded J.?"

"She's just doing it to try you. You'd soon cure her of that trick, if you would make a dead set at Sally Weighton during this protracted meeting, which begins to-night. Polly will be here every day, certain."

Nap thought he would try it, and was comforted. He then sat down and wrote to Mr. Switzler, at Brunswick, to come to Venice and negotiate him out of his tobacco troubles. He did this, because he understood some of the planters had determined to write to the same place and engage the services of Messrs. S—— and A——, who were at the same time the assignees of Rhino and the lawyers employed by his creditors to prosecute their claims.

The next day, sure enough, Nap was seen gallanting Sally Weighton to the court-house. And he ogled her a great deal during the singing of the hymns, and while Mr. Snorter was ranting from the text of the austere man and the ten talents. Mr. S. was originally from the Eastern Shore of Maryland, near the Chesapeake Bay, and he handled his text in a most unique manner. He pronounced *austere* OYSTER, and converted the lord of great wealth into an OYSTERMAN! "My dear brethren," said he, "you are not all, I reckon, familiar with the oystering business. They go out in large canoes, and with long-handled tongs pull up the wild oysters from the bottom of the bay, in shallow places, when the tide is at ebb. They get 'em up sometimes in great lumps as big as a half-bushel basket. These lumps are made of hundreds of oysters sticking together. They break 'em apart, and fill the canoes with 'em. And then they row up the creeks and scatter 'em in the beds staked out in the water near the house. They plant 'em there to keep the negroes from stealing 'em. If anybody goes after 'em in the night, the dogs at the house will be sure to bark at 'em and give warning. My dear friends, the next season some of these beds yield an increase of tenfold, some of five, some of two, and some of nothing. If they are sown in places where the tide leaves 'em too long, they die, or the coons eat 'em. It all depends on the servant intrusted by the owner or lord of the soil, just as it was with the oysterman who intrusted the talents with his servants. The talents were the same as oysters, and no doubt the oysterman had received them for a load of oysters. But the oysterman was not honest himself. He gathered where he had not sown, and I don't think he ought to have punished his servants."

In this manner Mr. Snorter edified his hearers; and before the subject was exhausted, he had risen to a high pitch of enthusiasm, and got some of the congregation, and Mrs. Fennel in particular, so greatly excited, that there was considerable shouting and moaning at the end of the sermon.

Polly, who was present, and whose presence had not been observed by Nap, for she occupied an obscure seat against the wall, watched her plighted lord with serious concern. She knew all about the impressibility of his nature, and did not believe Sally, demure and pious as she pretended to be, was any too good to take advantage of his complying disposition. Sally had a pretty foot and ankle, and she displayed them; she had a fine bust and handsome shoulders, and they were exhibited. These things were all apparent to Polly, who of course was initiated into the mystery of the best manner of playing off such innocent attractions, and so she determined to cut the matter short, before it had time to grow into formidable dimensions.

Therefore, when the congregation was dispersing at dinner-time, and when Nap was about to offer his left arm to Sally, he felt a smart slap on his right shoulder. Turning, he was confronted by the serious brow of Polly He turned pale, and then blushed deeply. His feelings were indescribable, but his back was turned upon Sally, who went out alone with her vail down and concealing a projecting nether lip.

Nap and Polly remained until everybody else had left the house.

"What do you mean, Nap?" asked Polly.

"Mean?"

"Yes. What do you mean by running after Sally Weighton?"

"What do *you* mean by running after Mr. J.?"

"Oh, was that it?" she exclaimed, laughing. "Nothing at all. I hope you don't suppose I could fall in love with a bald-headed man?"

"I don't know. Sam Marsh says they are the d——l after the women!"

"Indeed! But how did you happen to fall in with that cunning girl? Did she invite you to go with her to church?"

"No. It was an idea I got from Jim!"

"I thought so! Tell Jim I'll pull his ears for him, if he don't attend to his own business, and let other people's affairs alone. Don't fool after that girl any more, Nap, and I'll promise not to fall in love with Mr. J."

All was amicably adjusted before they left the house; and as they proceeded lovingly together toward the tavern where they were to dine, Nap related what had been written him by Colonel Benton, and particularly the conclusion of the letter. Polly thought the Colonel's advice very good, and promised to name the happy day, as soon as Hamilton S. had settled matters with the planters, so that Nap could dismiss the troubles his precipitate speculation had brought upon his mind, and henceforth attend to his legitimate business, and love his wife as all good husbands should do.

In the course of a few weeks, Mr. Switzler had seen all the planters with whom Nap had made contracts. After having a "talk" with each one of them, and representing the utter impossibility of Nap's compliance with his engagements, and the probability of his bankruptcy if required to receive the tobacco, and which might then prove a losing business to all the parties, he appointed a day for them to meet at the court-house for the purpose of effecting a compromise on some equitable basis. Having prepared them thus to entertain the proposition previously concerted, he returned to town, and made a handsome drawing of Nap's unsold lots. The price, at a "fair valuation," was marked in red ink on each lot, and the whole number amounted to so large a sum, that if Nap could have realized it, and had not been tempted to speculate out of the line of his business, it would have been sufficient for him to retire with.

When the planters were assembled in the court-house on the day appointed for the meeting, Switzler arose and made a most eloquent speech to them. He dilated on the important service his friend had rendered his county, in founding a town and bringing merchandise into the neighbourhood. He had obviated the necessity of the farmers going a great distance for their goods, and his improvements at the county landing had increased the value of the lands, and caused the agents of capitalists to settle in their midst, thus making a market at their doors. In this manner he painted the character of his client, and touched the sympathies of his auditory. He then laid before them his proposition. Each one was to put down on paper the sum which he supposed would indemnify him for the reduced price he might be under the necessity of taking for his tobacco from the agents of the capitalists. This was done immediately, for pens, ink, and paper had been placed before them on the long table. The amount, when summed up, was very considerable.

"Now, gentlemen," said Mr. S., unrolling his chart, "here is Nap's property. He gives up all to you, fairly and honourably. The lots are numbered and valued by disinterested men. You can either draw lots for the first choice, or I will put them up to the highest bidder, with the understanding that no lot is to be knocked down at a less price than the valuation placed upon it in red ink."

The latter plan was agreed to, and the bidding was soon very spirited. Jim stimulated the generous planters with an abundance of good brandy, and most of the lots brought from ten to twenty per cent. more than the valuation.

And so Nap had paid the penalty of his rash speculation, and had only about twenty lots left besides the one on which his store had been built. But he still had some money in the hands of his Eastern friend; about one thousand five hundred dollars' worth of **goods in** his store; and nearly one thousand two hundred dollars **in notes and** book accounts, after deducting the **bills of the planters, which** had been taken into account in the settlement at the court-house. Thus he was no better off, though by no means a bankrupt, than he might have been, if he had done nothing from the beginning but reaped the usual profits of his business. His successful speculation in lots had only induced a second speculation which was not so fortunate, and which swallowed up most of the gains of the first one, for he had advanced considerable sums on some of the crops. But his credit was saved, and he was **not likely** to embark **in** any new projects which might result disastrously.

Joseph Handy had been the most successful of **any of** the young merchants who left C———, in Kentucky, without capital, and sought their fortunes in the wilds of Missouri. Although enterprising, and his ideas ever on the wing in **quest** of dollars, yet he never ventured far in the field of speculation. He pursued his proper business very steadily, being thoroughly conversant with it, and made every thing else **subservient to his** legitimate occupation. **No wild scheme,** promising incredible results, could ever tempt him to wander from the beaten **path.** The system of realizing fair profits, and consolidating such accumulations with his capital, while the expenses of his family **were** inconsiderable, soon produced the effect he desired. His business increased in volume **every** year, like the snowball in its revolutions; and the amount of his annual sales, originally some ten or twelve thousand dollars, now reached to fifty thousand, and might in a few years be more than double that sum; while his net profits could not be less than ten thousand dollars.

Jack Handy was likewise in the full tide of successful experiment. If his sales were not so great, he realized a larger per cent. profit, and his expenses were less than his brother's. He had been absolved from his pledge by the General, who had gone to Europe; and Kate being pleased to remain in Missouri, he resolved to continue in the line of business to which he had become habituated.

Ben Handy had a small branch concern; and although his capital was small, he did not despair of increasing it, and ultimately outstripping the whole family in the race for wealth. His system was to get all he could—honestly and honourably—and to spend nothing. The latter rule was not quite practicable; but he approximated it. His annual profits were almost entirely added to his capital, and the young giant was growing apace.

There was still another Handy, the eldest of them all, who abandoned his profession and embarked in trade. This was Richard, who with a moderate capital, settled in the southern portion of the State, and began business on the cash system. He kept no books, and declined selling goods to any one who had not the money to pay for them. He, too, was successful, and was fast making a fortune. His goods were mostly bought for cash, and selected out of season. Hence he paid less for them than any one else in his region of country, and could afford to sell at a less price. The fashions, styles, and patterns were matters of no importance to those who bought their staple prints &c. of him. He sold none but good articles, such as he could recommend; and by the undeviating truth of his representations, he acquired the confidence of his customers, and won the esteem of the Eastern jobbers. The latter were always ready to give him a hearty welcome, and happy to sell him any amount he might choose to name.

CHAPTER XXX.

Nap's wedding—General rejoicing—Nap and Polly and Jack and Kate embark for Kentucky.

AT length the time appointed for the wedding was at hand. And it so happened that Captain Jewett landed his fine steamer at Venice on the morning of the day upon which the nuptials were to be celebrated. Quite a number of Philadelphians and New Yorkers, as well as Mr. D., from Baltimore, were on board. They were descending the river, on their way home, having been out on an electioneering and collecting tour. And as several of the gentlemen, Messrs. T., C., P., and J., in particular, were acquainted with Nap, they besought the polite Captain to prolong the lading of the freight he had to take on board until they returned from the wedding. They declared they would witness the ceremony, whether he waited for them or not.

Jim likewise had a conversation with the Captain. He intimated that both Nap, his principal, and Jack Handy, besides several other country merchants, who would be at the wedding, were in readiness to go Eastward for their new supplies of goods; and if he could delay a little while, he would not only have more passengers, but lay the merchants under obligations to ship their goods on his boat when they arrived at St. Louis. Captain Jewett not only agreed to wait until Nap could be married, but likewise resolved to attend the wedding himself. This was announced in the cabin, and was loudly cheered by Nap's friends. It was, however, objected to by a passenger from Boston, who was anxious to get home.

"I will make it up. You shall not be an hour later getting to St. Louis," said the Captain.

"You'll burst a boiler!"

"No, we never do that here. But we will not stop as long as usual at the other places."

"But the water is all running away. As we went up, I heard you say the boat had to jump the bars."

"And so she did. But there is more water now."

"How can that be, since there has been no rain?"

"There has not only been no rain," said the Captain, "but the river has fallen three feet."

"And yet you say there is more water!"

"I do."

"Why, there were only three feet and six inches on the bars as we went up."

"Granted."

"Then there can be but six inches on them now."

"Four feet."

"Instead of the river being called the 'Mad Missouri,' I think the steamboat captains ought to be called madmen!"

"Not at all. The river is not half so wide as it was before it fell, and there is but one channel now. In it the current runs so strongly that the sand is swept away, and there is actually a greater depth of water than there was before the river fell. The most unfortunate thing that could occur at this time would be a rise"——

"A rise?"

"Yes; that is a moderate one of two or three feet. It would conceal the channel, and we should be getting aground continually."

It was precisely as the Captain stated, as all know who are at all conversant with that strange stream.

Just then Nap made his appearance in the cabin, and was saluted with loud huzzas, for some of the "boys" were quite merry. And when the Captain's purpose was made known to him, he declared he felt so happy that if he were not going to be married that day, he would have a "spree," even if it cost him a headache afterward. But

l the rest should spree to their heart's content, and ha
vited as many to his wedding as could find the means of
»ing thither.

Most of the cabin passengers procured horses and
:companied the bridegroom out to Colonel Hopkins's.
aptain Jewett rode Jim's horse. Jim had not been able
» restrain himself on the joyful occasion, and when the
ime came for him to mount, he was unable to do so. He
»clared there were two horses held for him, and requested
ie Captain to ride one of them away. Then he said the
aptain had both.

"Let 'em rip!" cried he; "I'll walk. Give me your
rm, Sam Marsh. We'll go together!" Sam gave him
is arm and led him into the store, where he succeeded in
utting him to bed. Jim had not been "in that way"
ince the time of Mr. Darling's great temperance lecture.
ind he promised Sam, if he would only excuse him to
Jap, that he would never get "so" again.

The company was too large for Colonel Hopkins's house,
nd so it was proposed by Polly herself that the ceremony
hould take place on the green, and beneath the same
iawthorn bower where Nap had proposed to marry her.
This announcement was received with a shout of appro-
)ation, and acquiesced in by Bishop Hawkes, who was on
iis way up the country to consecrate a church, and had so
irranged his appointment as to be present and officiate on
;he occasion.

While the preliminaries were being adjusted by the
iridesmaids and groomsmen, the Colonel had the pigs,
the fatted calf, and an immense amount of poultry killed
for dinner. He knocked in the head of a cider-barrel,
and had demijohns of wine and brandy placed under the
table.

Poor Nap was in a terrible state of excitement when
ever separated for a single moment from Polly. He tore
off the thumbs of both his gloves in the attempt to pull them
on; and one side of his shirt-collar wouldn't stay up.

He ran down to see if all was right about the thorn-bush, and when passing some cows, he had the misfortune to spoil the lustre of one of his boots.

But when in the presence of Polly, he was calm. She was perfectly deliberate, and when near her, he partook of her composure.

At length the Bishop put on his robes and headed the procession. Nap followed, holding Polly's hand in his. On his right were Jack Handy, "Joe" T., Jno. P., Marshall J., Captain Jewett, and Sam C. Polly was attended by Sally Weighton, Kate Handy, and several other young ladies, married and single, of her acquaintance. A crowd of about two hundred men, women, and children, black and white, followed behind. Even the dogs, which had accompanied their masters, joined the procession. The sheep baaed, the pigs squealed, the geese gabbled, and the cows lowed. Agrippa had been ordered by Polly to fasten up the dun bull in the barn, for fear of accident, and the negro had the good sense to put the muscovy ducks in a pen unbidden. But the old black turkey-cock strutted about with his red snout hanging down, and gobbled incessantly.

It was soon over. But it was an impressive scene. Tears fell from the eyes of several. None doubted that Polly, wild as she had been, would make Nap a good wife; and he inwardly resolved to perform his duty as a husband. The Bishop pronounced the blessing, and then fled from the festive scene that was to follow.

It did follow. Eating, drinking, laughing, joking, toasting, and speech-making; but no quarrelling and fighting. All was hilarity and enjoyment. But some fell into the same condition which had prostrated the good-hearted Jim—and some had to be sent to the river in a wagon, or they might have lost their passage on the boat.

Then followed the leave-taking. Kate was to accompany Jack as far as Kentucky; and Captain Jewett tendered the "bridal-chamber" to Polly, who not only consented to go along with them, but expressed a purpose to accompany Nap all the way to the Eastern cities. She had no friends or relations in Kentucky that she had ever seen, and she intimated that it would not seem altogether right to be separated from her husband so soon after their marriage.

Finally, the bride, after bidding adieu to her parents, sprang up in the buggy beside Nap, and departed from her home. She did not take the reins at once, as she was often requested to do, by the equestrians at her side. Nap was an awkward driver, and she was known to be expert at it. But she forbore; and only grasped Nap's hand occasionally, when he seemed to be guiding the horse badly.

The cavalcade was a noisy one, but merry. Horsemen were seen galloping in every direction over the prairie, and often several might be seen cantering back from front to rear, to ask a simple question, or repeat an amusing anecdote to the ladies. As for Captain Jewett, he had disappeared on Jim's fleet charger. Some preparations doubtless had to be made before the arrival of the party on board.

When the main body of the cortege drew near the woods, which indicated the vicinity of the river, they were startled by the booming of a cannon on board the steamboat, which the Captain caused to be fired every five minutes in celebration of the nuptials. And when they rode through the village, their ears were saluted by deafening cheers; and none huzzaed more lustily than Mr. Jameson, who had been prevented from being present at the wedding by the accidental running away of his horse, which, however, now reappeared in the street, neither the bridle nor saddle being in the least injured.

"Rip! rip! Let her rip, Nap!" cried Jim, somewhat recovered, but with a very red face.

"Good-bye, Jim," said Nap. "But don't forget to put my memorandum-book in the trunk before you send it down to the boat."

"That's right, Nap," said Polly. "Don't forget your business on my account. I intended to ask you if any thing was forgotten."

The cannon still boomed as they approached the boat; and when they stepped on board, they were welcomed by repeated cheers. Soon after the boat was under way, and the sun was sinking low in the West. But, by special request, we must drop the curtain here, and skip over what followed until the arrival of the steamer at St. Louis.

Arrived at St. Louis, Captain Jewett furnished the papers with memoranda of his voyage, which were published the next morning, together with a particular notice of Nap's wedding, and an acknowledgment of the reception of bridal cake. This startled both Nap and Polly, when they perused the Republican at their hotel, the Virginia House. They had brought no cake along with them. All that had not been consumed by the wedding guests, was to be sent to Dr. Blue, at Brunswick, and to the editors at Boonville, Fayette, Columbia, Trenton, Lexington, and to St. Joseph. But Ellen, the chambermaid, furnished a solution of the mystery. The Captain, it appeared, who always kept on board the best pastry-cook that money could command, had ordered the cake to be made during the voyage down, and which he had politely sent to the editors with the compliments of the newly married couple.

Nap had some beeswax, flaxseed, and mink-skins on board, which were sold by the Messrs. D. T. & Co. for him, while he remained in the city, and which brought an unexpectedly high price. The funds were exchanged for a sight draft on Messrs. S. P. & Co., of Philadelphia, and drawn by the Messrs. J. J. A. & Co. Jack Handy procured a check on one of the Eastern banks, signed by Mr. Wm. M. M. & Co., in exchange for his funds.

At the dinner-table, Nap met with Miss D., and had the happiness to be felicitated by her on his recent marriage. Polly was introduced to her. Kate had made her acquaintance during the passage from Kentucky. And our party were complimented with orders for admission to the theatre that night. It was Miss D.'s benefit, being the termination of a brilliant engagement. They attended, of course, and were highly delighted.

The next day they embarked for Kentucky, and had the pleasure of again meeting with Miss D. She was going to perform star engagements at Louisville and Cincinnati.

After a prosperous voyage, during which there was much social enjoyment, our party landed at the usual place, and proceeded by land toward the village of C. When they drew up at Bullock's tavern, where they had arranged to spend the night, they were met by the smiling landlord, who welcomed them heartily, and congratulated Kate on her improved looks. She was in fine health, and in a robust condition.

"But who are *you?*" he asked, taking the hand of Polly, when the travellers were seated in the parlour. "Nap, this ain't the darter of Brook."

"No," said Polly, banteringly, "she is a spawn of the 'Mad Missouri,' which is an 'inland sea.' I am one of the wild girls of the far West. Where's your old *ooman?* I shall play havoc with the chickens."

"The old ooman's down at the bottom of the apple-orchard in a pen."

"In a pen, Mr. Bullock? And with the pigs?" asked Kate.

"No. In the pen with pailings around it. She's dead —but I have another ooman, that I like better. She's young, too. I'm done with old ones, and will never have another"——

"Mr. Bullock, how you talk! Are you not ashamed to allude thus to Mrs. B."

"I'm not ashamed, but I'm a little afraid she'll overhear me. If she war to, I'm durned if she wouldn't bust up the earth and come at me! She was an outrageous scold, and I allers thought it would be the death of her."

"And was it?" asked both the young wives, while their husbands listened with interest.

"It was nothing else! I'll tell you how it happened. We'd hearn tell of capons being worth two dollars apiece in Cincinnati, while common chickens sold for only three dollars a dozen. So the old ooman, as she had a mighty sight of fowls, concluded to have a hundred capons made ready to send to market in the spring. The one she employed to make 'em for her didn't know his business, and nearly all the roosters died the same night. When the old ooman saw 'em laying dead, she doubled up her fists and turned red in the face. But before she could get out the orful words she intended to holler, the blood gushed out of her nose and mouth. We carried her in, but she was gone. So take warning, young wives! It's a dangerous thing to get into a scolding passion!"

Mr. Bullock then called in his "young ooman," and introduced her to the guests. She was indeed very young, perhaps not more than twenty-two years of age, while her husband was upward of sixty. Her parents were very poor, and her mother being a great scold, like the first Mrs. Bullock, she had become disgusted with her home, and yielded to the solicitations of Mr. B., who at once executed a will, leaving her all his fortune, provided she survived him.

The next day our party arrived at C——, where they were affectionately received by the mothers of the young men, and heartily welcomed by all the friends of the families.

Molly, now Mrs. Smart, was the first to call on Polly, and they became intimate at once. As General Frost was still abroad, Kate took up her residence with Mrs. Handy, Jack's mother.

The day after their arrival at C., a letter was received by Nap from his friend and monitor in Philadelphia, congratulating him on his marriage, and urging him to bring Polly with him to the city. Mr. R. had been informed of the good advice that Nap had received from her, and which, indeed, had saved him from destruction; and he expressed a desire to see her. He thought, moreover, if he did not say so, that she might be of valuable service to Nap in the city, in preventing him from yielding to the almost irresistible temptations to buy too many goods.

After spending a few days in C., Nap and Polly and Jack Handy set out for the East. Kate was to remain until a certain very interesting event should occur, which was looked for about the time of Jack's return.

Our party reached the city without accident, and put up at the same hotel where the young men had formerly sojourned. They were waited upon by all their city acquaintances, and made many new ones. The Western men, and particularly those from Missouri, who had heard of Polly Hopkins, which was the case with nearly all of them, for her fame was spread abroad, visited the newly married couple, and cheered them by their many kind attentions. Mr. R. gave them a dinner, to which some half a dozen other Western gentlemen and ladies were invited.

Nap was excessively happy, and at the end of every day his operations were approved by Polly, being mostly in conformity with her judgment previously expressed. Inasmuch as the Jew competitor at Venice had retired, and the rest of the merchants being honest men, who intended to pay their debts, and would of course obtain fair profits, Nap was advised to increase somewhat the amount of merchandise he had intended to purchase when leaving home. This was partly induced by advices from Jim, who informed him that nearly all the planters were busily engaged in improving their lots in Venice, and that an increase of trade might be anticipated.

Nap not only laboured at his business during the day, but he was assiduous in his efforts to entertain his wife every night. He was ever in her company, when not purchasing goods. And having obtained some knowledge of the streets when in the city the year before, he could now conduct his spouse to all the places she was desirous of seeing, without the vexation of being occasionally lost. They visited all the places of amusement, and appreciated the criticisms of each other on the merits of the various performances.

One night, however, there was a performance attempted which was not in the bills. As they were ascending the steps of the Musical Fund Hall, Nap and Polly felt themselves slightly jostled, and, a moment after, Nap grasped the hand of a rogue in the pocket of his overcoat. Nap, as we have already intimated, had a muscular arm, and, like Sir Walter Scott, a tremendous hand. So he held the trembling gentleman fast, and led him toward the gas-light.

"Who's that, Nap?" asked Polly.

"A pickpocket! I'll give him to the policeman."

"For heaven's sake let me go! Have mercy on me!" said the captive, submissively.

"Oh ho!" cried Nap, recognising his old acquaintance De Coy.

"Is it possible! Why, Nap, how do you do?" responded the impudent fellow, making a pretence of having been playing off a practical joke. And his presence of mind was his salvation; for just at that moment, Captain Keyser, the police marshal, who had witnessed the transaction, and had kept his eagle eye on the offender, was on the eve of arresting him. He desisted, in doubt whether the action he had witnessed had been a bona fide attempt to commit a robbery.

"How long have you been engaged in this business, De Coy?" asked Nap.

"Not long. I was driven to it. I could not blow my own brains out, and no one else would do it for me, after they discharged me at the fashionable hell. But, upon my honour, I did not recognise you; else I would not have made the attempt on your pocket. I merely saw your pocket-book."

"My pocket-book? It was my memorandum-book, containing nothing but a list of articles to be purchased for my store in Venice. But still I would not have lost it for fifty dollars."

"We get a great many of them from the country merchants," whispered De Coy; "and they generally offer from ten to twenty dollars reward for their recovery. They always get them back on such terms. Won't you lend me ten dollars?"

"No! You cheated me once out of fifty; but I will give you five dollars. Go, now, and steal no more. Go to work, and make an honest living."

Saying this, Nap led Polly in to the concert. But it was all French and Italian to them, and they resolved to retire early. They did so, and were stared at impertinently through many glasses.

It was well they did retire. For they had hardly reached the pavement before Polly was taken suddenly ill. Nap was in a great perturbation. He did not know what to do. He wanted to ring at the door of the first mansion they came to, place Polly in it, and then run for a doctor. She would not agree to it. Presently they came to an apothecary shop, and he would have conducted her in and called for a remedy, but she resisted this also. When they got to their lodgings, he made a determined motion to go for a physician; but she would not permit him to do so.

"Something must be done, Polly, or you may die!"

"There's no danger, Nap," said she, very pale, but smiling.

"What can be the matter? Perhaps the oysters didn't agree with you?"

"No, it was nothing I ate."

"Then why not have a doctor?"

"Oh, I'll soon be better. I don't want the doctor to

know what ails me. I know what it is very well. It will soon be over."

"What is it Polly? Tell me!"

"No."

She was quite well again before bedtime, it having been merely a passing qualm.

Our party, likewise, visited New York, and made some purchases there. After they had been several days in the great metropolis, Nap was visited by Mr. Pike, who came up to him boldly and tendered his hand, which was taken by Nap. No Western man ever refuses such a courtesy.

"I hope you are not still offended, Mr. Wax, and with me," said Pike. "Throughout the whole transaction, on the occasion of your former visit, I was acting for others. I was in the employ of Messrs. B. & T., and had to obey their instructions. They discharged me, and I had to sue them for my commission on the large sale made to you."

"And did you recover?"

"Oh yes! When the underwriters paid for their goods, B. & T. settled with me. It was a great transaction for them. But it caused their ruin, nevertheless. They were tempted to buy stocks with the money so unexpectedly obtained. At first the speculation was successful. But the Wall-street operators are merely gamblers, and after playing with their victims a while, they destroyed them. Messrs. B. & T. failed hopelessly. Mr. B. is now a clerk in the custom-house, and Mr. T. is a salesman like myself."

"And what house are you in now?"

"In Messrs. ——'s, where you have made a bill. I kept out of your way, for fear you might still dislike me, and become, in consequence, prejudiced against the house."

"Not I. You were not more to blame than myself for the silly purchases I made on the occasion referred to. I was an inexperienced fool, like a great many other young country merchants."

Nap was now fast becoming a sensible man.

CONCLUSION.

As this volume has already grown to the prescribed size, it must be concluded before the career of our hero is ended. He had many other adventures, which might form another book of goodly proportions, and which, no doubt, the publishers would be able to furnish, if there should seem to be a sufficient demand for it.

It may be stated, however, that Nap adhered steadfastly to his business. After his marriage he never embarked in any of the wild speculations which so frequently result in disaster to the country merchant and injury to his creditors. On the contrary, he was content to reap the gains of his legitimate business, and became by degrees a man of wealth, and the happy head of a numerous family. On two occasions, Polly presented him with twins.

Colonel Hopkins moved to Texas, and his son-in-law bought the farm. A mill was built on the fine stream near the hawthorn-tree, (which was sacredly preserved,) and a small village grew up around it, of which Nap remains to this day the sole proprietor. He has measurably retired from business himself, but still keeps a small store in operation at Pollysburg. His property in Venice is leased for $2000 per annum.

The Handys are still selling goods, and making more money than they spend, as capable and economical country merchants in the West, who build up a good credit in the East, may always do.

Mr. Darling is lecturing on the Maine Liquor Law for a dollar a day, having fallen into the clutches of the politicians.

Jackson Farnes is sawing stone in the penitentiary at Jefferson City.

General Frost is still abroad, being disgusted with the democracy of the present day, which makes presidents of men who have no claims upon the people, and who are selected by an irresponsible few, without previously consulting the will of the majority. He declares that the system is an absurdity, and instead of being in accordance with the principles of democracy, is only following the example of the degenerate Romans, who put up the purple to the highest bidder. But he writes to Jack Handy that he derives some comfort from the fact that presidents thus made sometimes prove ungrateful, and decline paying the price of their elevation demanded by those who exalted them. "It is a good thing for the conspirators against the liberties of the people," says he, "to have sometimes a perfidious master."

Sam Marsh, although he stutters as much as ever, is still the main innkeeper at Venice.

The reverend John Smith, the blacksmith, is making a fortune at his bellows, as all the industrious Smiths do in the new States.

Jim Rue, poor fellow, fell a sacrifice to his remedy against the cholera.

Mr. Bullock has at his inn several young children and a baby. His young wife, warned by the fate of her predecessor, is as meek as a lamb, and seems to be very happy. Kate and Polly often think of the fate of the "old ooman," and check themselves when inclined to be angry. If other married ladies would do likewise, this book would be invaluable to the present and future generations. So mote it be.

THE END.

www.ingramcontent.com/pod-product-compliance
Lightning Source LLC
Chambersburg PA
CBHW032022220426
43664CB00006B/331